Developer's Guide

ORACLE®

A Database Developer's Guide

ULKA RODGERS

YOURDON PRESS
Prentice Hall Building
Englewood Cliffs, New Jersey 07632

Library of Congress Cataloging-in-Publication Data

Rodgers, Ulka
    Oracle : a database developer's guide / Ulka Rodgers.
        p.   cm.
    Includes bibliographical references and index.
    ISBN 0-13-488925-8
    1. Data base design. 2. ORACLE (Computer system) I. Title.
QA76.9.D26R64 1991
005.75'6--dc20   90-19623
                                                      CIP

Editorial/production supervision: **Karen Bernhaut**
Cover design: **Wanda Lubelska**
Manufacturing buyer: **Kelly Behr/Susan Brunke**

The publisher offers discounts on this book when ordered
in bulk quantities. For more information, write:

> Special Sales/College Marketing
> Prentice-Hall, Inc.
> College Technical and Reference Division
> Englewood Cliffs, New Jersey 07632

IBM, VM/CMS, DB2, IMS, SQL, SNA, LU6.2, APPC, OS/2 are registered trademarks of
International Business Machines Corporation. JAM, JAM/DBi, and JPL are trademarks of JYACC
Inc. Lotus 1-2-3 is a trademark of Lotus Development Corporation. MS-DOS, Microsoft OS/2 is a
trademark of Microsoft Corporation. ORACLE is a registered trademark of Oracle Corporation.
Easy*SQL, SQL*Forms, SQL*Plus, SQL*QMX, SQL*Report, SQL*Report Writer, PRO*C, SQL*Menu,
SQL*Net, SQL*Connect, SQL*Star, SQL*Calc, SQL*Loader are trademarks of Oracle Corporation.
PROGRESS is a trademark of Progress Software Inc. SQR and Easy SQR are trademarks of SQ
Software Inc. UNIFY is a registered trademark of Unify Corporation. ACCELL/SQL is a trademark
of Unify Corporation. UNIX is a registered trademark of AT&T Bell Laboratories.

Oracle is not responsible for the contents of this book.

Printed in the United States of America

10 9 8 7 6 5 4 3 2 1

ISBN 0-13-488925-8

Prentice-Hall International (UK) Limited, *London*
Prentice-Hall of Australia Pty. Limited, *Sydney*
Prentice-Hall Canada Inc., *Toronto*
Prentice-Hall Hispanoamericana, S.A., *Mexico*
Prentice-Hall of India Private Limited, *New Delhi*
Prentice-Hall of Japan, Inc., *Tokyo*
Simon & Schuster Asia Pte. Ltd., *Singapore*
Editora Prentice-Hall do Brasil, Ltda., *Rio de Janeiro*

Contents

Preface

Do you believe the sales hype that relational technology will solve all of your application problems? If you do, or have learned differently from experience, then, this book is for you. Far too often, development tools have been oversold — not in their functionality, but in the effect they will have on application backlogs. The net effect: frustrated managers, overworked programmers, and disappointed end users. This book is about the right way to implement applications using Oracle.

There are many reasons for disappointment with what database management systems (DBMS) and computer-aided software engineering (CASE) technologies deliver. Product marketing wants you to believe in the high productivity promises of the fourth-generation tools. Although these promises are true in the literal sense, they do not address the problem of defining requirements or managing user expectations. Computer-aided software engineering tools are supposed to help define requirements, but they deal only with diagrams of different types. It is difficult to judge and apply these theoretical techniques in practice. This book is about how to use CASE technology to your advantage.

The pressure to prove the promises forces programmers to dive in and start producing. Naturally, they use the techniques they know: flat file systems and procedural code. DBMS utilities do help: in examining results of processing, testing, and enabling ad hoc access by programmers, but the promise of relational technology remains largely unrecognized. This book provides tips on when and how to use Oracle's fourth-generation tools.

As a consultant, I help many organizations manage implementation of Oracle products: from strategic planning through application requirements definition, development, and implementation. This book discusses many of my experiences — you are likely to face similar challenges. The topics should be of interest to

- Information officers, who are looking for tools and techniques for effective information planning.

- Managers, who need techniques for managing user expectations throughout the development effort.

- Analysts and designers, who face the challenges of enterprisewide systems and require tools and techniques to support their activities.

- Developers, who need tips on using Oracle's fourth-generation tools.

- End users, who need to be involved in the development effort.

Oracle's products support the full life-cycle approach, with CASE products for planning and analysis, a relational database management system (RDBMS) and fourth-generation tools for development, and a methodology for managing the effort. This book covers life-cycle development in four major parts. Each part consists of several chapters expanding a common theme.

Part 1: Managing the Implementation

This part is about strategic information systems planning. Topics of interest include how to implement procedures for data administration and data quality assurance (as opposed to development quality assurance). Oracle's CASE tools are a platform for building and maintaining models of your business. We also examine how to use other, less integrated, CASE tools. The primary focus is how to develop a stable model so changes in the business do not cause a significant impact on the model.

Part 2: Designing Oracle Applications

This part concentrates on design issues specific to Oracle-based applications. The most significant topic is performance. Paying attention to this vital consideration early in design saves uncountable hours of grief later on.

The design decisions follow directly from the earlier analysis phases. We look at how entity-relationship models help in making these decisions. Strategic models and application models are closely connected objects. The right way for building applications means a logical progression through all phases of development.

Part 3: Developing Oracle Applications

This part focuses on the details of using Oracle's fourth-generation tools. Interesting highlights include how Oracle's tools stack up against some of the third-party vendor interfaces. Without forgetting performance requirements, we discuss how to choose the best tool for the work on hand.

Part 4: Distributed Systems with Oracle

Oracle's major strength is the support of multiple hardware platforms. This part is an in-depth discussion of configuring multiple hardware networks, setting up cooperative processing, or implementing distributed databases. We will examine the implications of operating system differences, bit-mapped and text terminal interfaces, and networking issues.

This book includes tips and tricks I gained on a variety of projects. Although not identified specifically, I am grateful to each nameless initiator of those projects for the opportunities for hands-on experience. I am even more grateful to the people who spent many hours in discussing pros and cons of alternative approaches.

Many friends have contributed ideas that I incorporated here. Thanks in particular go to Michael Miller and Peter Schober for discussing many interesting technical twists of the Oracle products. Thanks also go to each of the vendors' staff who helped me in numerous ways: Israel Stern of SQ Software; Paul Mcguckin and Laura Malaspina of Oracle Corporation; John McWillie of JYACC, Inc; and Anu Shukla and Chris Funckhauser of Unify

Corp. My particular thanks go to Paul Becker and all the staff at Prentice Hall who made this book possible. Last but not least, thanks to my mentor and husband Paul for devoting so many hours to reviewing the manuscript and drawing diagrams even while cursing the unfriendliness of my chosen drawing software.

Ulka Rodgers
Annandale, New Jersey

ORACLE®
A Database Developer's Guide

1

Introduction

Oracle was founded in 1978 as a vendor of a relational DBMS product. The company has its headquarters in Redwood Shores, California in the United States of America It has offices worldwide and also distributes its products via value-added resellers. These products run on all major hardware platforms as well some less well-known ones. In fact, portability of the products, and applications developed with them, is one of the main reason for their popularity.

Although its initial product offering was a database management system (DBMS), the company has now a diversified product line including computer-aided software engineering (CASE) tools, packaged applications such as accounting and human resources based on the DBMS; and services such as major systems integration through subsidiaries. Its stated objective is to become a complete solution vendor in the 1990s.

In this introduction, we examine some of the issues faced by the information industry and which of these issues Oracle's products address. Some issues relate to building applications faster, the increasing sophistication of user's demands, and improved understanding of the role of information systems. We also introduce issues of managing application development, the primary focus of this book. This chapter puts the issues of developing applications using Oracle in perspective with the other issues facing the information industry. In particular, this chapter covers the following:

- Buzzwords like "productivity" and "application backlogs" are common. What are the real issues that raise these discussions?

- The relational technology promises to solve many of these difficulties. But can it deliver on its promise?

- What makes an application successful? Does using the latest development technology really suffice?

- Where do Oracle's offerings fit in these myriad promises?

1.1 The Productivity Challenge

Computers have come a long way from their number-crunching predecessors. Today, we use computers to store and manage *information*, not just perform calculations faster. Information may be text, numbers, graphics, voice, and, in fact, any thing that can be transformed into digital storage form. These newer forms of information have become possible recently as technology advances.

Our management information systems (MIS) departments have kept pace with such advances. Information systems today manage not only the company's numerical financial data, but also textual market and technical research data; track prospects and clients; and even send anniversary cards to employees. These systems support national and international exchange of this information — not as printed paper reports, but over networks and phone lines.

Technology advances have changed the expectations of those people who use computers in their daily work. New technology leads these people, the *clients* of MIS departments, to ask for applications to support their functions in new and different ways. These requests come in frequently and fast. Unfortunately, MIS groups have limited resources. These resources may be hardware, software, or development staff. Lead times to acquire new resources are, relatively speaking, long. The hardest to acquire are experienced development staff who can understand and use new technology.

In the meantime, applications already developed do not stand still. Changing business needs require changes to these applications — and, of course, staff to make these changes. The volume of existing applications is directly proportional to this *maintenance* effort. And you cannot ignore it — these applications are the life and blood of your business. They form a large proportion of the predictable, and therefore budgeted, work effort of today's MIS departments.

Just to keep life interesting, technology changes too while all of these other activities are going on. Hardware manufacturers release new products, which means your applications have to be converted to work on the new machines. Software manufacturers, not to be outdone, also release new versions of their products. Of course, your applications must change to take advantage of the new and wonderful features offered by these new versions. This vicious cycle is illustrated in Figure 1-1. All in all, it is difficult to see how MIS departments ever find time to work on new applications.

So requests for new applications pile up — euphemistically called ***application backlogs***. The relative cost of development staff to the cost of hardware and software is far higher than in the early days of data processing. The only way out of this cycle is to get the same number of staff to do more work. MIS departments look for ways to improve the amount of work each staff member can do, that is, to improve their productivity.

There are two areas where we could improve development productivity: by developing new applications faster than is possible with traditional programming tools and by reducing the effort required to incorporate changes in existing applications. These are the two areas addressed by modern development techniques.

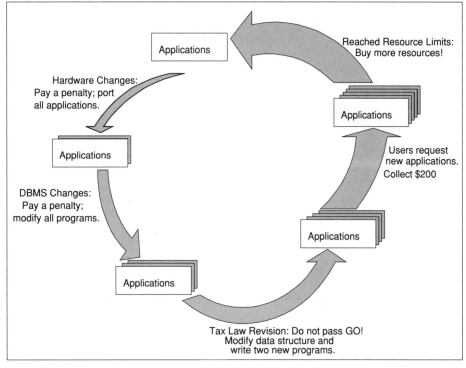

Figure 1-1: The MIS Dilemma

1.2 The Relational Solution?!

Relational database management systems (RDBMS) claim to improve the productivity of your development staff. However, you have no doubt some bitter experiences to relate. You also have had some successes. Let us examine the contexts in which you can expect successes and poor results.

First, you cannot move all of your applications to use a relational database management system overnight. So you typically start some of the new developments in this environment. The fourth-generation tools supplied with the products allow you to prototype user requirements in fairly short order and then turn them into production systems. So you shorten the time from receiving a user request to delivering an application into production. You also require fewer developers to complete this implementation.

Unfortunately, relational database management systems and their fourth generation tools require rather more machine resources than do their finely tuned third-generation counterparts. You run out of resources more quickly and have to upgrade your hardware earlier than anticipated. Thus, the cost of running your applications in production increased significantly. This cost overshadows the success of producing the requested application in a timely manner.

Applications developed in fourth-generation tools require a little less effort when making enhancements than do their third-generation counterparts. Thus, you also shortened the time-frame to modify programs. So changes in business requirements have smaller impact on your ability to change applications. However, you do not perceive this benefit until much later in the life of an application. By that time, the productivity improvement is an accepted part of development. Changes to the data structures, however, are a different story. Fourth-generation tools offer no help in modifying the underlying data structures. Instead, changes to data structures often mean more extensive changes to their code.

When you upgrade hardware, the older applications still require a significant effort to port to the new environment. In addition, you might have to delay installing the new hardware until your DBMS vendor makes their products available on the new hardware. So, if you are already reached the limits of your hardware, you will have to delay upgrades even longer. Figure 1-2 illustrates the proportion of impact and RDBMS may have on the MIS cycle.

If you use a highly portable DBMS product, the changes to your programs due to hardware changes are few. DBMS products usually buffer you from hardware specific dependencies. Thus, the effort required to change hardware is smaller, even if you have to delay installation of the new hardware. The total time-frame is probably shorter than if you were converting third-generation language programs and file structures.

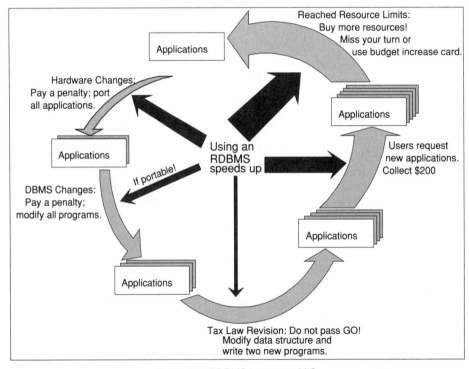

Figure 1-2: RDBMS Impact on MIS

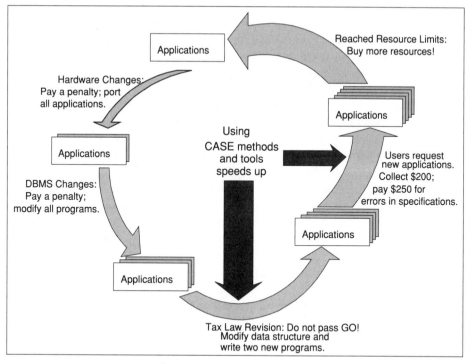

Figure 1-3: CASE Impact on MIS

Relational DBMS and fourth generation tools do not make you immune from poor design of data and applications. They merely shorten the time for implementing an application, whether well designed or not. Thus, an application built in a short time-frame can still fail to meet user expectations — leading to a bitter implementation experience. In the next section, we examine the criteria that make for a successful application.

Handling changes in business requirements can require significant redesign of database structures. These changes have a cascading effect on your programs, whether or not developed in fourth-generation utilities. Although relational DBMS allow you to make changes to data structures more easily, they do not protect your programs from the effects of poor database design. This scenario is where computer-aided software engineering tools claim to improve productivity.

The methodical and rigorous regime imposed by CASE tools and associated methodologies helps you to identify areas prone to changes. However, considerable talent is necessary to identify such areas clearly. Drawing diagrams using CASE tools does not magically highlight them. The correct use of CASE is to help your talented analysts discover potential changes prior to their occurrence.

Thus, CASE tools used by talented and experienced staff are invaluable aids to designing flexible data structures and applications. Relational DBMS provides scant help in this area. Even the models developed with CASE tools will not suffice in handling unexpected mergers and acquisitions, although they will provide some groundwork.

1.3 Successful Information Systems

Experience shows that a well developed application is not sufficient for success. There are many other factors that make your applications successful. One of the primary factors is understanding the role of the application in achieving business objectives. Another factor is gaining users as champions of the application rather than as passive accepters of your offering.

This area has been largely ignored until recent years. Development methodologies and CASE tools help in addressing some of these areas. Realize, though, that these techniques merely aid you in discovering the requirements — their use does not guarantee an understanding of users requirements. The characteristics of successful applications are

- They are driven by end users, not just *accepted* by them. The difference between these two scenarios is one of subtle perception. User-driven does not mean that they dictate the entire design including the technical trade-offs that need to be determined throughout. Instead, they believe that it is their application — not one forced on them by MIS. In other words, they have taken *ownership* of the application. Experienced analysts can subtly direct users to make suitable choices in the design, rather than dictating these choices.

- They are sponsored by managers with responsibility for meeting business objectives, not dictated by MIS staff. This is another facet of users taking ownership of an application. Although, MIS staff may proactively suggest applications which help support a business function, the business managers must be responsible for initiating their development. Typically, this scenario also means funding the application. After all, is there a better way of making managers responsible for its success than to put their money where their mouths are?

- They support the achievement of business plans and objectives. A terrific application which is easy to use, developed with the latest and greatest technology, will not be successful if it does not support a genuine need. For example, a market research database for a company that manufactures only space shuttle parts is useless in the business.

- They are flexible enough to require minimum changes as the business needs change. This is usually due to a good design which implements more than a specific solution to a specific need. The analysts must anticipate the types of changes likely over a period of time and mold the application so that they are adaptable to these changes.

- They are actually used by their target users — not just shelved as an interesting experiment in development. In fact, successful applications are those which clearly meet user's expectations and serve their needs.

Notice that most of the characteristics of successful applications revolve around user perceptions and expectations. This is a hard lesson to learn when developing applications. Whiz-bang features and elegant coding might make a good application, but not necessarily a successful one.

This area is where CASE methodologies and tools help the MIS staff. They provide direction in how to guide user expectations such that they closely match the application direction. In addition, they provide techniques which help analysts understand what the user needs, as opposed to what they ask for. The effect of clear communication with users and clear expectations helps make the application successful. A good understanding of actual user needs improves productivity in application development by eliminating false starts and misunderstanding.

1.4 Where Does Oracle Fit?

Oracle, as a company, seems to have recognized that a database management system is not sufficient. Although, a relational DBMS is Oracle's core product, the product line has diversified into related fourth generation tools, CASE tools, and off-the-shelf application packages. These products all require the RDBMS as the base. Figure 1-4 illustrates the product breakdown.

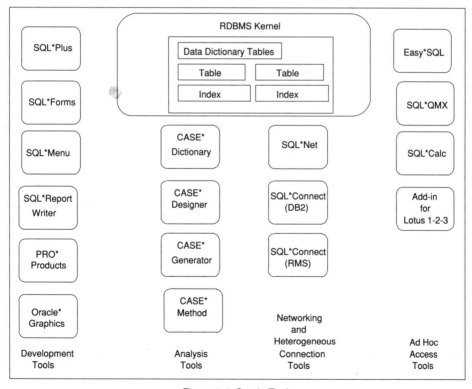

Figure 1-4: Oracle Tools

This set consists of fourth-generation utilities such as SQL*Forms, for building forms-based applications; SQL*Report, for procedural report writing; SQL*Report Writer for nonprocedural report generation; SQL*Plus, for querying the database; PRO*Oracle, for interfaces to the database using a third generation language; and PL/SQL, for procedural batch processing. Most of these tools are separate purchases. Third-party products substitute for SQL*Forms and SQL*Report Writer. SQL*Plus is almost essential if you plan to access data without going through some program.

This set consists of the CASE*Designer, the diagramming utility; CASE*Dictionary, the repository of analysis and design knowledge; CASE*Method, a methodology based on Information Engineering, Yourdon, and others; and CASE*Generator, the tool for generating forms applications. All of these tools use the Oracle DBMS for storing and managing data. CASE*Designer requires CASE*Dictionary. CASE*Dictionary and CASE*Generator are built using SQL*Forms, SQL*Plus, and SQL*Report. Thus, purchasing any one of these tools requires the purchase of each of the underlying tools.

This set consists of tools that are so-called end user tools: Easy*SQL, in my opinion is a tool for computer-literate novices; SQL*QMX, which is Oracle's attempt at imitating DB2's Query Management Facility; and Oracle for Lotus 1-2-3, a set of macros which allow you to bring into your 1-2-3 spreadsheet data from an Oracle database. Anyone familiar with Lotus 1-2-3 likes this interface to Oracle, since they can chart or graph the data, or perform their own manipulations without learning a lot about SQL. I still do not believe that SQL is suitable language for end users who have little technical background, and even less knowledge of data structures of their database.

This set is based on SQL*Net, which comes in many flavors, each appropriate to the underlying network protocol. For example, there is SQL*Net TCP/IP suitable for use on networks running this protocol, SQL*Net DECnet, SQL*Net 3270, and so on. You must already have the appropriate network protocol installed to use these products. They allow cooperative processing, with the front-end tools running on a machine different from the Oracle DBMS kernel. They also allow distributed databases in a limited sense. Oracle supports queries on data distributed across multiple machines connected with a network. There is a flavor of SQL*Net which works on dial-up phone lines as well, albeit the data transfer rate depends on the speed of your modem.

These tools are collectively called SQL*Connect with different flavors for each of the other products supported. They allow you to share data and run Oracle applications against non-Oracle products. For example, there is SQL*Connect for DB2 and SQL*Connect for DEC's RMS. There are usually limitations based on the capabilities of the other product.

Using Oracle tools does not mean you automatically develop successful applications. Only your methods for analyzing requirements and managing user expectations can achieve that success. The user interface presented by most Oracle tools requires a lot of user training. Even the developer's interface lack links to convenient tools like text editors. So be ready to persuade developers and users that faster delivery of applications is worth a little extra training time.

This book focuses primarily on the tools useful for application development, from strategic planning of information systems through implementation of finished applications. I add tips from my own experience on related issues like management. Oracle's methodology addresses only a few of these at present.

This book also covers issues relating to developing distributed systems. This topic is of emerging interest as many smaller organizations discover the power of small machines relative to their cost. We examine the differences between cooperative processing and distributed databases with pros and cons of each. In addition, we examine the types of information analysts must gather in order to develop cooperative or distributed applications. In this context, we discuss what facilities Oracle offers today and some of the promises in the future.

Part 1

Managing the Implementation

"We don't have time for a methodology! It takes too long and our backlogs are growing too fast."

"Since 4GL's allow us to build applications very quickly, why do we need CASE tools? We can change the database and the programs as the users require."

Is this your reaction too? Try answering the following questions before you dismiss this part of the book.

1. *Do you find that users change their requirements frequently, sometimes even before you finish their first request?*

2. *Do you spend a lot of time gathering more detail from users on each of their requirements?*

3. *You have a user representative who knows the business to help with requirements definition. But when you implement the application, do many users complain that it does not do what they need?*

If you answered "Yes" to any of these questions, you really ought to read the chapters in this part. You may discover some of the root causes of your difficulties. If you have tried, unsuccessfully, to use methodologies, look again — development using 4GL tools is different from traditional programming projects.

2

Management Strategies

Information is power in a business: information about your competition, your company's financial well-being, the demographics of your markets, the list goes on. The business can be wildly successful if information systems adequately support the business strategies, regardless of the nature of the business. The information systems group organizes such information and makes it accessible to the company. Successful information systems support business strategies.

Managing information systems development is much more than managing a group of programmers. You have to provide systems that support business strategies. A relational database management system and fourth-generation development tools are some of the tools you might use. But the tools are only as good as the use they are put to. Success requires a few more tools in your kit. A methodology defines some of these other tools and puts them at your disposal.

In this chapter, we discuss some of the key tools. We also examine some of the key features of Oracle's CASE*Method offering and how they might help your endeavors. Here are some highlights of this chapter:

- How to tie information systems to business strategies to help make the business successful.

- The benefits of modeling your business and how it can help you proactively suggest applications needed by the business.

- Roles and responsibilities which help you to gain management and user commitment and manage the quality of your information system products.

- Budgetary issues, including some methods for justifying the cost of information systems.

- A review of CASE*Method and a few other life-cycle management methodologies.

- Approaches for moving information systems from the current environment to a new environment which uses Oracle's technology.

2.1 The Preparation

As we mentioned, information systems are successful only if they help the business become successful. So we need to know what will make our business successful. These criteria are the realm of company managers: the chief executive officer, the chief operating officers or the president. Of course, I am not suggesting that you take the company officers' chair. Only maintain open channels of communication with them. They should communicate to you the directions of their business plan short and long term. In turn, you should provide input to them on how information systems present (or planned) make one strategy more feasible than another. One of your primary goals, as a manager of information systems, is to establish an organization so that such communication becomes possible. Section 2.3 addresses organizational issues in more depth.

As an example, suppose your company plans to grow sales by 25% this year. To achieve this growth, management plans to penetrate a new market which was identified by the marketing department. A system to maintain a database of prospects in this new market and to track its purchasing history would be an invaluable aid to achieving the business goal. Even better if this database is a subset of the data used by the marketing department to conduct their study!

Can you just ask about the company's business plan? Unless the company's officers also read this chapter, the answer is probably no — you will raise red flags in their minds about your understanding of your role. First, you need to educate them. You need to describe your plan to implement information systems most suitable for the company. By the way, this education process is the first step in winning their commitment to your plans!

What should you include in your discussions with company officers? Here is a checklist:

1.   A definition of business mission, that is, a statement of what service your company provides.

2.   A list of short-term and long-term business objectives. Examples of short-term business objectives are "To increase sales by 25% over the previous year" or "To reduce costs by 10% over previous year's costs." A long term objective is "To become the largest supplier of widgets."

3.   Critical success factors for the business to achieve these objectives. Critical success factors are conditions, events, or equipment without which an objective cannot be achieved. For example, a critical success factor to increase sales might be skilled sales staff.

4.   Priorities of these objectives from the view of the business. For example, increasing sales might have a higher priority than reducing costs for a start-up business.

5.   Projected value to the business of achieving these objectives, that is, the benefits expected whether in revenue increase, reputation enhancement, or some other improvement.

6.   A statement of information systems mission.

7.   A list of short-term and long-term information systems (IS) objectives and how they correspond to the business objectives.

8.   An assessment of which of these objectives are satisfied by current systems.

9.   A road map of how you plan to convert, enhance, or build new systems to meet your objectives.

Seems like a chicken and egg situation, right? You need to know the business plan before formulating your information systems plan. Yet you cannot quiz company officers about it. Here is one way around this dilemma. Build a draft plan based on your understanding of your company. Use the draft as the basis of a meeting with the company officers to verify and correct it. Your plan is not cast in concrete, however! You will need to revise it frequently, at least as often as the company revises its business plan.

If it is all so easy, why doesn't every IS manager do such planning? There are a few practical difficulties. In small companies, a well-defined business plan is a rarity. So you need to help company management refine it. Such refinement can be difficult if your company managers do not like to pin down specific objectives with hard numbers. Your efforts at planning information systems are key to revealing the need for them. Services of a management consultant specializing in your particular industry help in developing such a plan.

Large corporations suffer from a different issue. The business plan, developed by high level executives, is common in large corporations. However, the plan is diluted over many departments and divisions, each of which is responsible for one or two of the objectives only. In many such corporations, information systems executives are closely involved in the business planning process. If your company is one of these, you have a head start. In other companies, you may work with only one division or department of the corporation. In such a case, start at the highest executives at the department or division level. Typically, such executives report directly to the CEO or COO or are one level removed from them. Your success at this level may change the company's view of how information systems contribute to the business.

Here are a few more notes for your benefit. The last three items in the preceding list are easier said than done. Listing information systems objectives is easy, but describing how they mesh with business objectives is hard! Refine this list through a lot of interaction with company officers. Remember to use a draft plan in your meetings with them. It keeps your meetings focused. Corrections to the draft are also a satisfying deliverable of your meeting.

How do you assess whether existing systems meet any of your information systems objectives? This is a tough problem. Vague statements of objectives will result in a vague assessment. You really need to know how the business works and what its needs are before making a precise assessment. One of the techniques for understanding the business operations is to build a model of your business. The assessment, then, is comparing each existing system to the model. We discuss some techniques for building a model in the next chapter.

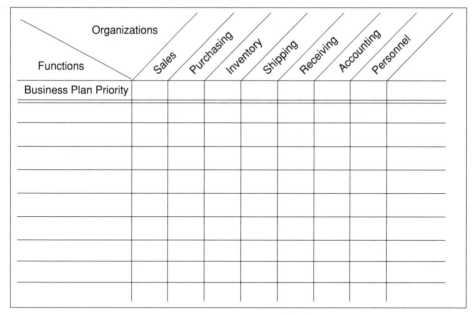

Figure 2-1: Application Priority Matrix

Once you know what needs to be done to bring your information systems up to snuff, you need to prioritize these tasks. Your priorities should match business plan priorities while accounting for dependencies between applications. For example, sales reporting functions require a sales order entry system first. Get input from your company officers for prioritizing your task list. Figure 2-1 illustrates a matrix for recording priorities. The relative priority of the different organizations, such as sales, human resources, and so on; is decided by the ultimate decision-maker, the management committee or the COO. Relative priorities of different functions defines the current focus of the company's business plan. Don't be surprised, therefore, if it changes as frequently as once or twice a year.

Notice how we interact frequently with the decision makers. The key is to get them involved throughout the process. Ask for their input often, even if you shelve it sometimes. They need to take *ownership* of the applications if your requests for budgets are to be successful. Frequent interaction and a sense of ownership are necessary paving stones for a successful information system.

2.2 Why Model Your Business?

Modeling your business means defining the functions and data essential to running the business. Both management consultants and information systems consultants use business models to understand what the business needs to do for its livelihood. The actual techniques for documenting the model vary depending on the methodology used and the results intended. For example, a management consultant may use a function model to help you streamline your organization structure. An information systems consultant, on the other hand, may use it to identify the areas where automation is helpful. The next chapter will examine the techniques used in CASE*Method and supported by CASE*Designer, CASE*Dictionary, and CASE*Generator.

There are three basic components in a business model:

- Organization structure
- Business functions description
- Business data model

These basic components are cross-referenced with each other to define who uses what information to perform which function.

Are you wondering if you already know these components for your company? True, you know what they are overall, and possibly you have some detail on them. Unfortunately, they have probably changed somewhat since you were involved in them. Forms that were used a year ago may be replaced, or new pieces of information added to them. Unless information systems staff are constantly interacting with business staff, you may not be aware of what these changes are or why they have happened. Such changes are often why applications requirement definitions should not depend on one or two users representing several dozens. Other reasons include differences in needs at each geographic location or department which is managed locally.

Ideally, every conscious change in the business should involve information systems staff, so that you identify very early on corresponding changes to information systems. Use the model to identify whether you already accommodate the changes in an existing application which that group of users is not aware of. If you need to enhance an application, use the model to assess the impact on other applications. Such assessment of existing applications is sometimes called *portfolio analysis*.

You need to position the information systems group to get involved in the decision making process which precedes changes. Early involvement means you can detect and implement systems enhancements in a timely manner. You can, thus, control the extent of the application backlog and prevent user complaints about *too little, too late*!

Business models serve many purposes other than information systems impact. During the process of building these models, inefficiencies in business procedures become apparent. By involving departmental managers in detecting inefficiencies, you become part of their planning process. The trick is to get the departmental managers to detect and correct inefficiencies so that it is their idea. You have to facilitate the process. Thus, you can build credibility of your modeling process to help the company in ways other than information systems.

The model cannot, of course, determine how to achieve business objectives. The company's officers will develop creative solutions to do so. What you could offer, with the aid of the model and information systems, is a test bed for their ideas. For example, if the company is considering a new product offering, use the model to determine the impact on each part of the company.

The model is not merely a representation of what information is available today and how it is used. Although many methodologies stop developing it at this point, use it to represent what could be available tomorrow and how new information could prove useful for company growth objectives. Don't wait until the company decides to enter a new market to determine you need a new information system. Start your investigation as soon as someone suggests the idea. You can then play a more participative role in business planning than a passive role by waiting until users request a new system. With some experience in being participative, get ready to try a more proactive role of suggesting new systems. Of course, by getting your users involved in developing the model, they probably will start coming up with their own ideas.

2.3 Roles and Responsibilities

The previous discussions probably implied that you have to build the model yourself. Relax! That is the purpose of the organization structure you put together. In this section, we will discuss the roles and responsibilities of your staff to support your endeavors effectively. Read this carefully if a database management system environment is new to your organization. The roles and responsibilities are significantly different from those in a non-DBMS environment.

Let us examine the functions that your organization needs to perform before we detail roles and responsibilities.

2.3.1 Building and Maintaining the Business Model

For your interactions with the company officers, you need capabilities to define and refine business models. These are typically provided by senior analysts trained in the techniques used for model definition. These analysts should also be able to compare existing systems with the model to pinpoint gaps and opportunities for new applications.

The initial development of a model often requires skills which are of little use afterward. Unless you have sufficient similar work for these analysts, you should not hire specifically for the initial development. Consider using consultants over the short term. Involve your staff analysts throughout the initial model development so they gain intimate familiarity with the techniques. Maintenance of the model then becomes their job.

Analysts skilled in modeling a business are sometimes called **data administrators**. This title can be misleading, however, since their responsibility involves much more than data definition. The model also involves business functions and organization structures. This position is a very senior one, since it crosses all boundaries of functional areas, applications, products, and software. Key talents needed for this position include excellent communication capabilities, ability to abstract from specifics, and the ability to see the *big picture* without getting bogged down in detail. These analysts will frequently interview high-level company executives and must be able to extract maximum information in short conversations.

As the manager in charge of information systems, you need in-depth understanding of the business model. In most cases, you will need sufficient technical training to read diagrammatic models and express its descriptions in terms that company executives understand.

2.3.2 Defining and Maintaining Application Databases

The business data model is closely related to physical database structures. However, further design to meet performance requirements and geographical distribution require special skills. In addition, knowledge of the specific product of choice, in our case Oracle, is a prerequisite to performing this function. These functions are essential throughout the design and development of an application.

After implementing applications, you will need to monitor database activities to improve performance further. Other maintenance functions include planning and executing upgrades to DBMS software, data conversion from old software to new versions, and, in multiple product organizations, downloading data from one product's database to another. Ask these personnel for their input in capacity planning for hardware.

These technical tasks are typically performed by a database administrator. If your organization uses multiple DBMS products, you will need at least one database administrator per product. This role is new in a DBMS environment. In traditional environments, files were designed by programmers with no further monitoring required. Key skills for database administrators include the ability to understand the abstract business models and convert them into physical database definitions with appropriate performance trade-off decisions.

As a manager of information systems, you need only a passing familiarity with the deliverables of this function. You will need an awareness of the trade-off decisions and their expected and actual impact. When multiple DBMS products are involved, consult them when you analyze the impact of a change in the business.

2.3.3 Designing Application Programs

This function equates more closely to the traditional program specification function, although the tools and techniques used differ. This function derives module definitions from the business functions portion of the model. Interactive modules may be prototyped using appropriate fourth-generation tools. The purpose of prototyping is typically to obtain detailed screen and report layouts and user interaction dialogs. Finalizing validation criteria which could not be derived from the data model is also part of this function. These specifications are passed on to programmers for actual coding and testing of programs.

This function is typically performed by analyst/programmers. They need the ability to understand the business model and interpret it into its implementation equivalent. Knowledge of the specific programming tools, fourth-generation languages, and the like is essential.

As a manager of information systems, you will find these personnel invaluable in assessing the specific impact of change. They can also support you in estimating the effort of building new applications.

2.3.4 Building Application Programs

This function involves coding programs from prototypes and specifications using fourth-generation tools. It includes testing of the code together with other programs and making corrections or modifications based on user input. Code optimized for performance is essential. These programmers must be well versed in the specific tools which are to be used.

As a manager of information systems, you need only superficial knowledge of these tools. Accept advice from programmers on the limitations of tools so that you do not promise anything that you cannot deliver.

2.3.5 Assuring the Quality of Application Development

Many information systems organizations ignore this function with detrimental effects. Others expect designers and programmers to monitor quality in an ad hoc fashion. However, this function is more than reviewing programs after they are developed.

Initially, you will need standards for a number of developmental items. Key items include conventions for naming tables, columns, and other database items; standards for screen and report layouts; and conventions for program names. You will need environments set up for individual development, team development, testing, and production. If you use multiple hardware platforms, these environments should enforce portability standards. You will also need source code control for tracking modifications to programs. Regression testing on modifications is almost as important as new development testing to maintain the credibility of your group.

All documentation, from the business model through to individual programs, and user guide is subject to quality assurance checks. Consistency and clear communication are a must for maintaining a harmonious application development environment.

As the manager of information systems, you must be fully aware of quality assurance procedures. Pay close attention to the findings of quality assurance reviews to discover your top performers. Reward good work, and you will encourage others to improve their work.

2.3.6 Assuring the Quality of Data

Everyone knows that computer systems work on the *garbage-in-garbage-out* principle. Yet few organizations make an effort to administer the quality of data. We depend entirely on the validation capabilities of programs to maintain quality of data. Unfortunately, automated validation is only part of the story.

There are many quality judgments that a program cannot possibly make. Consider, for example, a skill matrix that contains Joe's proficiency in the French language. Programs can validate only that Joe is a known employee and French is a valid language. But can they verify that Joe speaks French fluently? Such a judgment must be made by a human. When building applications, we often ignore issues of this type with detrimental effects. Poor-quality data renders an application useless.

What is really needed is a set of procedures which *users* follow prior to entering data requiring value judgments. Ideally, they should be designed by concerned company line managers in parallel with application design. If they take ownership of the application, they will be interested in designing such procedures and of course ensuring that they are executed. For example, language proficiency could be verified by Joe's supervisor initially during an interview or later during periodic performance appraisals.

You will need to lay the groundwork in encouraging company management to develop new procedures as new information systems are designed. The key to the success of this difficult task is users who feel: *It is their system!*

2.3.7 Managing the Development of an Application

This function is really rather different from managing a group of people. An application development manager develops schedules for a project, monitors costs and expenditures related to the project, monitors progress of projects, and works with users to coordinate schedules for implementation. In addition, this manager plans appropriate training schedules for staff, assigns tasks based on the project schedule, and monitors their work. Typically, project management software is of great benefit in this function, especially if it speeds the frequent task of reporting status.

Development managers have a technical background which enables them to assess the impact of technical difficulties. They can also assess staff capabilities so that work is apportioned according to capabilities. A day-to-day involvement in the project ensures that they pay close attention to deliverables and time constraints.

These personnel are your right hand when developing your information systems plan. Their status reports will keep you informed on the progress of every current project while you focus on future needs.

2.3.8 Managing and Operating Computer Systems

This function within your organization is necessary for smooth operation of your systems. It includes installation and maintenance of all hardware, communication networks, operating systems, and utility software. Typically performed by computer operations staff whose role does not change significantly in a DBMS environment.

2.3.9 Typical Organization Structures

Notice that we did not define the number of people who might perform the functions just discussed. Obviously, the numbers depend on the size of your company and business. Small companies may have one person perform data administration as well as managing projects. Many combinations are possible depending on the skills of your staff, their career goals, and training. I leave the possibilities up to your creative imagination.

Figures 2-2 and 2-3 show typical hierarchies of organizations for small and large information systems groups, respectively. Small groups typically mean that one person performs more than one function. Hence, small groups support fewer applications or use outside resources for new development. Larger groups need to be aware of communication

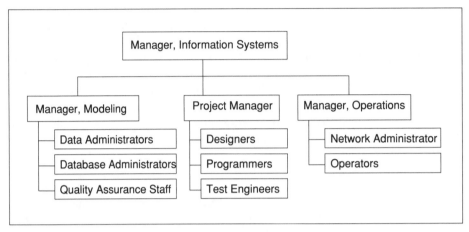

Figure 2-2: Hierarchy for Small Organizations

difficulties within the group attributable to the large number of staff. Formal methodologies and recording tools foster better communication and offset the potential detrimental effects on productivity.

2.4 Obtaining Budgets

Once you have convinced company management that information systems are an integral part of the business, getting budget approval becomes a lot easier. They will not longer view information systems as a luxury, to be indulged in with spare cash. However, you still need to justify expenditure on systems. For example, a company with $10 million revenue is not likely to spend $1 million on its information systems, unless information systems are its business. Here are some tips on how to justify your expenses for a new system.

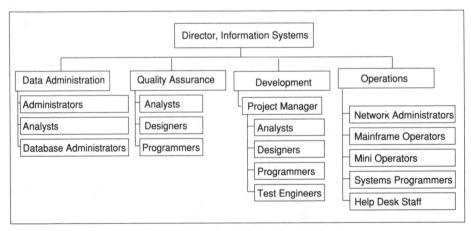

Figure 2-3: Hierarchy for Large Organizations

Get the company into the habit of using annual budgets. This budget will cover your usual expenses of staff, current computer systems, maintenance on current software, and packages.

The next step is to get your company sold on your information systems plan. This step is a little more difficult because first you need to invest some effort in doing a strategy study. If you plan to use outside consultants to help, you will need to obtain approval to spend the money. Even if you have the necessary skills among your staff, you have to dedicate their time it. So your best approach is to sell the company officers on the idea of a strategy study. We have already discussed why an information systems strategy is important in earlier sections. Here is a summary of the arguments for your toolkit:

- Information is an asset to the business, but it is useful only if there are adequate systems to access it.
- Good information systems support business functions and are an integral part of business planning.
- The priorities for information systems development should match the business priorities for most effect.
- A strategy study focuses on outlining the business functions and data in order to determine potential areas of automation.
- The information systems strategy then prioritizes potential areas of automation to match the business priorities.
- The strategy deliverables are essential for you to assess where existing systems leave gaps in the support of the business.

Remember that a strategy study is only the first step in your plan. Armed with the strategy, you can attack the budgetary needs of further work.

The method for obtaining budgets is different for each company. In small companies, you need approval from only a few senior executives. In larger companies, user departments have to fund information systems development. In such cases, try to develop as many of your objectives as possible before you broach the subject. Typically, one or two examples of inadequate support of business functions is sufficient to spark their interest. Don't forget to emphasize how a structured strategic analysis uncovers more such areas and allows you to estimate their impact on the business.

In very large corporations, you will probably need to convince a committee about the viability of your approach. However, getting budget approval for a strategy development is easier in the case of committees, because you can get them excited about the potential. The deliverables of a strategy study are valuable to them, whether or not they like your implementation plan. You will, however, need to educate individual committee members and get their input for your plan prior to presenting the final version.

Regardless of the size of your company, you have to present cost justification analysis before getting approval. Approach cost justification one phase at a time, starting with the strategic analysis phase. Go one step farther: get the target user community excited about the approach so they volunteer cost justification information. Here are some of the items used in a cost-benefit analysis.

2.5 Typical Benefit Items

2.5.1 Cost Reduction — Labor

A new system might reduce labor costs in either the information systems or the user organization. A system built with fourth-generation tools requires fewer programming staff to maintain and enhance programs than does one built with traditional third-generation technology. A system that has been enhanced repeatedly over several years gets harder to maintain as the cumulative changes affect its original design.

A new system might help eliminate inefficiencies in the operation of a department. For example, if fewer paper forms are necessary than in the old system, staff can be more productive. Less time is needed if the new system reduces rekeying of data from one system to another. For example, consider a new human resources system which shares employee salary data with the payroll portion of an accounting system. Human resources staff no longer need to print salary change reports from their system to pass to payroll staff for rekeying into their system.

2.5.2 Cost Reduction — Timely Information

If a new system reduces the time delay between a user's request for information and its delivery, the information is more valuable. Suppose, for example, you plan to replace an aging batch reporting system by an online query system. The shipping department can be more responsive to customers on the phone with online queries than with outdated batch reports produced once a day. If, as a result of this new system, the order entry department can predict more accurately whether an item is back-ordered, your company's service is greatly improved.

Such improvements can be quantified, although not easily. This is where aid from your users is invaluable. Try to determine the amount of time wasted in rekeying, or callback to customers. Then, calculate the dollar value of the delays. For example, if each customer phone call requires 10 minutes of research and a couple of callbacks, an order entry person can service one customer every 15 minutes. If this time were reduced to 5 minutes, the gain is two extra customers for each order entry person!

2.5.3 New Opportunities

The flexibility of the new system might provide new opportunities which the company does not consider today. Try, with help from your users, to quantify the benefit of such improvements. Ideally, such improvements are the result of a considered business plan.

2.5.4 Informed Control

A new system which includes flexible management reporting might provide better control. The benefit of this improvement is intangible, but obvious, to most management.

2.5.5 Quicker Response to User Requests

If you are reducing the bureaucracy necessary in a centralized system, by providing more local control, your users can list many benefits. Some of these benefits might be quantifiable as opportunities lost currently.

2.5.6 Presenting Your Analysis

There is a knack of presenting your cost benefit analysis most effectively. For years, we simply presented the numbers in boring columns, page after page. Today, there are many presentation tools available to us. From small companies, where you present to only a couple of people, to large company committee presentations, a picture really is worth a thousand numbers.

Take the time to use graphing tools to prepare your presentation. A line graph showing the break-even point for cost recovery is more effective than the same figures presented in columns. A pie chart showing the cost of opportunities lost through an inadequate system is an excellent way to bring home the cost justification of the new system.

Once you win the company's trust for your approach, shelling out the dollars should be an easy decision!

2.6 Life-cycle Development Methodologies

A life-cycle development methodology is simply a system for building information systems. There are many books written on this subject by industry experts such as James Martin, Edward Yourdon, and so on. On a superficial level, all methodologies follow a similar structured approach with similar techniques. An application is viewed by all as going through several phases in its lifetime, hence, the name *life-cycle development*. There are separate phases for analysis, design, programming, testing, conversion, and implementation (or production). Each phase uses a certain set of techniques and tools. The techniques vary in flavor and depth based on the methodology and the founder of the technique.

The driving principle underlying methodologies is to change information system development from an art to an engineering discipline. In the days gone by, engineers like Telford designed bridges on the back of an envelope. Today, there are methods for building short-span and long-span bridges that engineers all over the world follow. They can communicate with each other easily since they all follow the same standards. In the information systems industry, we still design systems on the back of an envelope. The information systems industry has recognized the benefits of a common language and standards. However, the frequent changes in our development tools keep our methodologies from the regularity found in engineering.

The principle in the engineered systems approach is *divide and conquer*. You probably have firsthand experience in getting overwhelmed with enterprisewide systems. Relax. Only the strategy phase need consider the entire company. Each subsequent phase divides the scope into manageable chunks such as just one functional area. The strategy deliverables help keep all of the latter separate portions linked. Without the big picture, you would have too many peripheral functions to cover each time you tackle an application area.

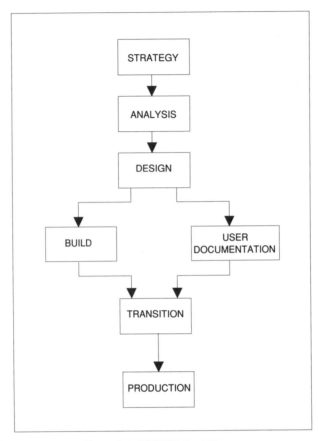

Figure 2-4: CASE*Method Phases

Methodologies are rarely a recipe for system development. You rarely follow one straight out of the box except at first. After gaining some experience, you can adapt it to your environment by adding or ignoring specific portions. The idea is to always maintain a structured approach — primarily to perform tasks methodically and to facilitate clear communication between all parties. Realize that it is very difficult to learn a methodology from a book. Instructors at training classes add real-world knowledge which is difficult to gain from books. Books are useful as reference material. You might find useful additions to your practice of techniques from books.

Oracle's CASE*Method is a proprietary methodology developed by Oracle Corporation. Although this is proprietary product, you are not restricted to using it only for

Oracle DBMS based development. Its principles apply to any DBMS environment and fourth-generation tools. Figure 2-4 illustrates the phases of life-cycle in this methodology. There are three basic components of the CASE*Method product as offered by Oracle:

- Training classes organized by phases
- Books on methods and techniques
- CASE software tools to support techniques

CASE*Method deals with all stages of system development. It advocates a user-interactive approach to software development. In fact, feedback sessions are an integral part of every phase. We discuss its strategy and analysis phases in detail in the next chapter.

In addition to outlining the tasks and activities of each phase, CASE*Method also provides guidelines on estimating. These guidelines can be invaluable for the beginner. Temper them, however, with your own judgment of staff skills. Some people come up to speed on these techniques much faster than others.

CASE software tools supporting CASE*Method include

- CASE*Designer, a graphical interface to the diagramming techniques used in the methodology.
- CASE*Dictionary, a repository of data about business systems. This database is the heart of the CASE software tools.
- CASE*Generator, a tool for generating SQL*Forms programs from an application design stored in CASE*Dictionary. Future versions of this product will probably generate SQL*ReportWriter programs for reports, and some third-generation language code.

There will be undoubtedly many more products added to this array over time. Throughout this book we will refer to these products where appropriate.

2.7 Approaches to Implementing New Technology

Is *dive in the deep end* the only way to adopt a new technology in your organization? There are actually two aspects you need to consider: skill base and disruption to operations. Let us examine each of these aspects in the context of two approaches discussed here. The new technology might be either a relational database management system or methodologies and CASE tools.

I call the two approaches macro and micro. The ***macro approach*** is to start using the new technology for everything, no more use of older technology. Consider the example of adopting a methodology and CASE tools. You would start with a strategy phase, follow up with analysis for the highest-priority application as soon as you have staff available, and so on. No enhancements to older existing systems undertaken, only emergency fixes!

The *micro approach* is to try the new technology on a pilot project to gain experience first, then start applying it to other projects a little at a time. In our methodology example, you would start by using the methodology on just one small-sized project. Then, the veterans of this project would start one or two more projects with several other inexperienced staff, and so on.

Some of the pros and cons should be immediately obvious in each approach. It boils down to two questions: Can you train the majority of your staff together? And can the company survive with only emergency attention to existing systems while new systems are being built? Small companies gain significant benefits from using the macro approach. A consistent software development environment is achieved much more quickly than waiting to complete one project at a time. The macro approach is acceptable if company management already has the right attitude toward information systems: they are an essential asset.

Large corporations, on the other hand, find the training requirements of the macro approach prohibitively expensive. Besides, getting approval for a complete revamp of all systems would be next to impossible. Building all their systems using one technology would be considered much too risky by their commonly used risk assessment programs.

There are technical reasons also for using one approach over the other. If you are less than confident of your chosen tools and techniques, use the micro approach to test them out. For example, if you are not sure if the Oracle fourth-generation tools are the best choice in your environment, use the micro approach. The macro approach is suitable for spreading the knowledge gained in a pilot to the remainder of the company.

2.8 A CASE Study: Widgets Inc.

Throughout this book, we will use examples based on a mythical company. The idea is for you to have a complete worked example from beginning to end. Where applicable, we will use CASE*Method terminology and techniques. In some cases, such as the priority matrix, I use my own conventions. Such facilities were not easily available in Oracle's CASE tools at the time of writing.

Widgets, Inc. is a mail-order company based in Timbuctoo, United States. Timbuctoo was chosen because of tax breaks offered by the township. Cheap labor is plentiful to staff their warehouse operations. It has also made special agreements for quick shipping anywhere in North America with a number of services including Airbourne Express, United Parcel Service, and Federal Express.

Widgets' buyers purchase goods from many different manufacturers. The inventory boasts between 150 and 200 different products at any time. Every month, Widgets, Inc. publishes a catalog and mails it to consumers throughout the United States. Customers can order items using the order form included in the catalog or by phone. Widgets, Inc., staff pride themselves on shipping the orders within 36 hours. Customers can pay either with a major credit card or by enclosing a check with their order. Alternatively, Widgets, Inc. will send an invoice when shipping the order.

Two years ago, Widgets, Inc., bought an accounting package that runs on a small multiuser UNIX system. It includes accounts payable, accounts receivable, payroll, and general ledger. Widgets, Inc. also has an order entry system which was custom built by its programmers in C. Unfortunately, the accounts receivable module cannot import data from the order entry system. The firm also has a PC-based mailing list which consists of 5 million names. This list is used to print labels for mailing catalogs. This list is something of a problem — Widgets, Inc. would like to add many more names, referred by existing customers, to this list. But printing the current list of names already takes several days.

Management would like to increase sales by offering more targeted catalogs, for example, a tools catalog for customers who bought do-it-yourself products in the past. However, their only source of information on customer buying history is the order entry system. This system will require significant modifications to add customer history to the files. Reporting programs will take even longer. Besides, the firm has names of customers on the mailing list who purchased products more than a year ago. Order entry data is typically purged every month when the account books are closed.

Long term, Widgets, Inc. would like to open a similar operation in Europe. This is planned for opening in about four years. Any systems built today should be usable in the European operations as well.

To perform a strategic business analysis, we collected some preliminary information from the company executives.

Widgets, Inc. Objectives

- To provide products to consumers by mail order
  - To the largest number of consumers
  - At the lowest possible cost
  - With fastest delivery
  - For a profit to the company

Business Priorities

- 100% growth in revenue within two years
  - By targeted marketing of catalog items
  - By offering specialist catalogs
- Reduce warehousing costs within two years
  - By improving order-to-shipping time to 24 hours
  - By reducing warehouse time of products
- Open international markets in Europe within five years
  - By opening or acquiring an operation in Europe

Critical Success Factors

- Easy access to customer data, including
    - Product purchasing profiles and history
    - Hobbies profile
    - Payment history
- Integrated order entry, accounting, and shipping
- Impact of currency exchange rate fluctuations

Constraints

- Maintain current head count in all departments
- Budget limit of $1 million

Key Performance Indicators

- Revenue increase of 50% over previous year by end of this year
- Specialist catalog sales to be 20% of total revenue by year end
- Average order-to-shipping time of 24 hours by year end

3

Strategy Techniques

Having obtained an appreciation of the management issues, you are now ready to perform a strategy study. A strategy study encompasses all functional areas of the company. It culminates in a definition of application boundaries with a clear scope for leading into detailed analysis of individual applications. Which application to tackle first depends on the business priorities communicated by upper management.

Our explanations here are based primarily on Oracle's CASE*Method, CASE*Designer, and CASE*Dictionary. We examine how the CASE tools support the methodology in contrast with some other popular CASE tools. Only a limited comparison is possible in this chapter — just enough to appreciate differences in conventions and capabilities.

We will restrict our discussion to the overall principles of techniques. Discussion of every nitty-gritty detail would require a book all on its own. So bear with a little wand-waving, and "then a miracle happens" style. These techniques are more or less standard in our industry — so for detail choose a text from the bibliography. Oracle publishes a series of books on each of these techniques which are, of course, the ultimate source for Oracle's conventions. The topics discussed in this chapter are:

- How to conduct a strategy study in order to obtain the most information. Emphasis is on planning interviewee lists and conducting feedback sessions.

- Components of a strategy study, which you use and revise throughout the life of your company's information systems. They are a living guide to your plan and require frequent nurturing to remain up to date.

- Techniques used in modeling a business for strategic analysis. These techniques include function hierarchies, entity-relationship diagrams, and business unit definition.

- Oracle's products to support diagramming and repository of model information. We examine the integration of these products as well as some of their limitations.

3.1 Strategic Business Analysis Phase

The approach used in the strategy phase is top-down. The aim is to develop a business model together with the planners of the company. Execution is the subject of the detailed analysis phase. The key to a successful strategy study is planning your work and working your plan. Throughout your study, it is important to maintain a high-level interest in the process from the company management.

At the start, you need to establish the scope of your study. From our discussion in the previous chapter, the scope is the highest level within the company that sponsors your study. In small companies, the scope should be all of the business operations. In very large corporations with division-level sponsorship, your scope is the division functions.

Compose your interview list with help from your sponsor. Try to cover as wide a variety of management as possible within your scope. Remember, though, the time required for the study is directly proportional to the number of interviews—so don't go overboard. Interview at least one manager from each functional area to avoid incomplete information.

The basic work plan of a study is an iteration of interview, trial models, and feedback of your findings for verification. Before starting the interviews, a briefing session for all interviewees helps clarify your methods, their roles, and the goal of the study. After interviews and feedback sessions are completed, you will develop the strategic plan.

Throughout the interviewing tasks, you model specific functions and data from each interview. You might repeat functions and entities found in more than one interview. This is called *divergent modeling*. In *convergent modeling*, you consolidate repetitions and specifics into abstract, but more flexible, structures. You can converge models once you have sufficient information about a functional area, typically after completing all interviews for that area. The next chapter describes these techniques in detail. Convergent models are essential for a stable model on which to base your systems strategy.

3.2 Interviewing Techniques

A common way to conduct interviews is one interviewee at a time. This seems a little long-winded way compared to techniques such as the joint application development (JAD) method. However, your mission in a strategy study is fact-finding. You want to hear gripes from your interviewees. They would not be as free with their comments in the presence of their peers and superiors. JAD works well when you already know *what* needs to be done and you are deciding *how* to do it.

Don't conduct all of your interviews in a hurry. Allow time before each interview to prepare your questions. After each interview, take the time to organize your notes. Prepare a trial model after each interview, or refine previous models with the additional information gained. As you prepare trial models, you will find unexplored areas, or ambiguities. Use a subsequent interview to clarify them. If you do all your interviews before attempting a model, you will have to return many times to your interviewees for further questions. Since interviewees at this strategy stage are busy executives, they will not appreciate such a time-consuming process.

Here is a simple work plan. Try to arrange interviews so that you do no more than one per day. If an interview is in the afternoon, leave the next day free for organizing your notes and trial models. Typically, other people in your team have trouble reading your notes. So rewrite your notes into bulleted lists and organize them into logical groups.

Ideally, you should interview executives in a functional area (or business unit) in a time period. Trying to overlap interviews across functional areas causes confusion. You might get a little overwhelmed with the amount of information supplied to you.

The purpose of an interview, in this phase, is to gather as much information as possible about what the company does. Make your questions as specific as you can to your interviewee's areas of responsibility. Prepare these questions in advance. If you are new to the business of your company, here are some common questions you might ask an executive:

- What are the mission and objectives of your group? How do you plan to achieve to these objectives?
- What are the responsibilities and how are they allocated between members of your group?
- Could you give me an overview of a typical work cycle in your group? How long does it take? How often is the cycle repeated? How do you monitor progress?
- What information do you use to support this work? Where does it come from?
- Which other departments do you communicate with? About what? How often?
- What information does your staff provide you? How often?
- What information, if we could get it for you, could you use? What information would help you that you do not have today?
- How up to date does this information need to be?

These are not questions to be asked parrot fashion! Add questions based on your knowledge of the business. Listen to the answers very closely. Find leads for further questions. Make sure you understand what is being said. Remember, though, you don't need detail — you need understanding! Interviews are very intense — you are trying to understand, in a short time, functions in which these executives have years of experience.

The hardest part of interviewing is to not let your misconceptions interfere, especially if your knowledge base is from another company. It often helps to have at least one other teammate with you on every interview. Then, one of you can conduct the interview and the other takes notes. Some people use cassettes to record interviews. This can inhibit your interviewee from being free and open about concerns. Besides, you still have to take notes —cassettes are a difficult medium when searching for specific information.

3.3 Function Hierarchy

A function hierarchy is a representation of business functions, that is, what a business does or needs to do. For example, Widgets, Inc., might have the following functions:

- Accept customer order.
- Send invoice for customer order.

- Ship ordered products to customer.

Simply listing all functions would make the business very difficult to understand. So we organize functions into logical groups as a hierarchy within the business. In such a hierarchy, higher-level functions describe a broader area than lower-level functions. The highest-level function in a business is the mission statement for the business. CASE*Designer contains a diagrammer to develop function hierarchies. Hierarchical organization of functions is also called *function decomposition* by some methodologies. Don't confuse this with a program structure chart decomposition, however. Here, we work with business functions, not program subroutines or functions.

The key to a good business model is to map everything that a business needs to do, whether or not it relates to a data processing function. This allows us to put data processing functions in perspective with other workings of the business. Don't decide at this point whether some function can be automated. Also, don't leave out of the model functions that you think are not data processing functions. In fact, your model of business functions should not depend on any technology, data processing or otherwise. There is more discussion on this subject later.

Figure 3-1 illustrates a function hierarchy drawn using CASE*Method conventions for the highest level of Widgets, Inc. The case study in Section 3.7 contains a complete function hierarchy for Widgets, Inc. The hierarchical organization of functions originated in James Martin's Information Engineering methodology. For more information, refer to the texts in the bibliography. CASE*Method uses this representation in the strategy phase, along with data flow diagrams in the detailed analysis phase.

How far do you decompose business functions? This is a difficult decision. Ideally, the lowest level in the function hierarchy should contain only business functions which cannot be decomposed further, that is, *elementary business functions*. Stop decomposing when you reach a function which once started must continue to completion, or be aborted. There are no intermediate points. For example, once you start the function to *Send invoice for a customer order*, the invoice is sent or not sent. The invoice cannot be half-sent!

You might argue that sending an invoice involves many functions such as print invoice, stuff envelope, address envelope, stamp envelope, and so on. However, such functions are very specific to a *mechanism*, in this case, envelopes in mail. Avoid describing functions in terms of mechanisms because mechanisms depend on technology which changes frequently. Suppose, for example, the company starts sending invoices by electronic mail — there are no paper invoices to print or envelopes to stuff! A simple change in technology makes your business model out of date.

A mechanism is a means by which a task is done. Mechanisms can be difficult to detect, sometimes, as they are deeply ingrained in our day-to-day life. For example, a check is simply an authorization for the bank to pay a certain amount of money — it is a mechanism for the authorization. Therefore, a function description of *Send a paycheck to employee* depends on a mechanism. Today, electronic funds transfers commonly replace

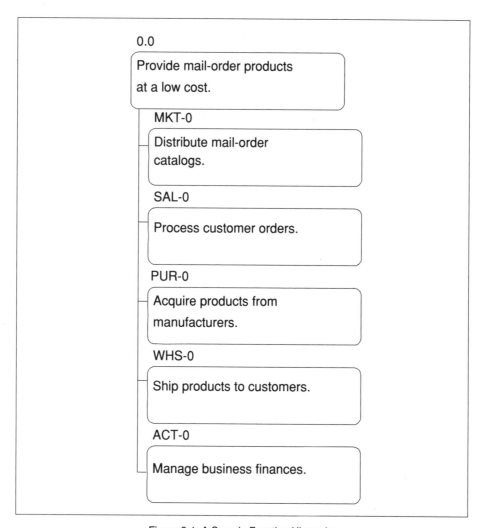

Figure 3-1: A Sample Function Hierarchy

checks. So a better way to describe this function would be *Pay employee*. Then, this function includes payment by cash, checks, electronic fund transfer, or some other means not yet dreamed of.

Notice how removing mechanisms or implied technologies from a function description helps make the wording simple and clear. A clear, unambiguous statement of business functions helps everyone understand the model. Beware also of using grand-sounding long words. If you can use a simple word, do so — you will avoid long explanations to your users. A little classic book about clear writing style, ***The Elements of Style***, by William Strunk, Jr., and E. B. White, is an invaluable aid to any analyst.

There is a drawback to removing mechanisms from your function descriptions. Your descriptions might become too abstract for users. In such cases, add the current method as an example in the function description. Thus, our example description becomes *Pay employee,* that is, send a pay check.

Start function descriptions with an active verb followed by nouns which are the subject and object of the verb. This structure leads to simple wording and clear, concise descriptions. Avoid ambiguous verbs or those that do not specify an action. For example, the verb *process* can mean different actions in each context. The simple rule is: Say what you mean, without any dressing up. There is another benefit to this method — the nouns in a function description are entities, an example of an entity, a state of an entity, or an attribute of an entity. The importance of this benefit will become clearer in Section 3.4.

Occasionally, you might need to add conditional statements to clarify when a function occurs. Use a dotted line for a function requiring a condition to indicate that it is optional. The function description must state the conditions under which the function is performed.

CASE*Designer's function diagrammer lets you rearrange function hierarchies. Use this facility to draw and redraw your hierarchies until the organization makes sense to you. You can also define functions as being common on more than one function hierarchy diagram. Function labels aid you in tracking the sequence within a branch of the hierarchy. Of course, CASE*Dictionary allows you to add a more detailed description of each function using a function definition screen. You can also access this screen from CASE*Designer. The frequency of occurrence, response requirements, and business algorithms are some of the details you can define for a function. This may be a good place to record the current mechanisms used for carrying out a function. In the detailed analysis phase, we will add more information, such as data flows between functions and entities; the attributes represented by each data flow and so on.

One way to prune your list of functions for the model is by using **events**. Events trigger one or more business functions. Any function which is not triggered by an event or another function indicates missing information or a redundant function. Business functions, in turn, can result in an event. For example, the event *End of a pay period* triggers the function *Pay employee*; the event *Resume received* triggers the functions *Maintain applicant information* and *Screen application*. The function *Screen application* might, in turn, result in the event *Candidate found*. Trigger events and other functions triggered are items we define for each function using CASE*Dictionary.

This example illustrates two types of events: time events and change events. Change events may have an external source to the model, as is the case with *Resume received*, or an internal source, as is the case with *Candidate found*. Time events occur usually in an artificial environment, such as cycles of a payroll, or accounting period. Change events indicate an update to some data, an entity, or an attribute. Another type of event is a system event, where the completion of one function triggers the start of one or more other functions. CASE*Dictionary lets us define quite a lot of detail about an event. We can define the condition which causes the event and other details appropriate to the type of event. These details are essential for detailed analysis.

Defining an event and determining which functions it triggers is a good check for completeness. It helps in detecting missing or overlooked functions. It also has other benefits. In fact, I find that grouping functions by an event produces a good logical hierarchy. In the feedback session, you can arrange your presentation by the sequence of events.

A frequently asked question is how to cope with functions which are repeated. Any function in a function hierarchy may be performed in a business multiple times. The conventions do not require indicators of loops, although you might choose to add them for better communication with users. CASE*Method does provide an *arc* notation to indicate an either/or relationship between functions. An arc is placed on the lines between the functions in question as shown in Figure 3-2.

When you are modeling all aspects of a business, you can end up with a large number of functions. For the purposes of a strategy study, you need not decompose every function into its elementary function. You do need to decompose at least three levels deep, however, to ensure a good understanding of how the business works. Three levels may be enough to reach elementary business functions in many cases. Remember the primary reason for building a function hierarchy is understand the business, an essential first step to formulating the information systems strategy.

CASE*Designer and CASE*Dictionary require you to define *applications*, which are typically a single functional area of an organization. This concept helps you to modularize your model. You can, of course, move functions from one application to another, or share functions between multiple applications. Use your own judgment in deciding the boundaries between applications. Be aware, however, that access to information across applications becomes difficult based on your choices. This breakdown also prevents you from getting a view of all functions regardless of which application they belong to.

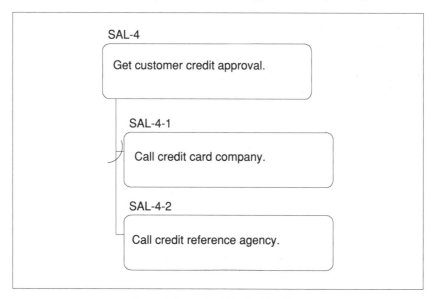

Figure 3-2: Arc for Either/or Condition

3.4 Entity-Relationship Diagram

An entity-relationship diagram models data and how the business views its structure. An *entity* is something about which we want to hold information. For example, at Widgets, Inc., we want to hold information about customers, products, and so on. These are examples of entities. Relationships between entities, represented on the diagram, describe the dependencies between them. Customers each buy at least one, and sometimes more, products. Customers also pay for each product that they buy (well, most of the time!). An entity-relationship diagram (ERD) is a shorthand representation of such relationships. These can be drawn using the CASE*Designer entity diagrammer facility. Figure 3-3 illustrates a simple entity-relationship diagram.

The specific information we want to hold about entities are called *attributes*. For example, we want to hold customer name, address, credit limit, and so on. These are attributes of the entity, Customer. In a strategy study, we need not define all of the attributes of each entity. But a few attributes help in ensuring that we correctly identify an entity. In particular, you should identify all attributes that are unique identifiers for each entity. Unique identifier attributes have values which uniquely identify an instance of an entity. The entity/attribute definition screen of CASE*Dictionary allows us to define entity details as well as attributes of an entity. Entity details include synonyms, volume information, and a description. Attribute details include the format, optionality, domain, unique identifier, and a short note. In addition, a unique identifier screen lets us define unique identifiers which are made up of multiple attributes.

Each relationship, in CASE*Method conventions, is drawn as a line between two entities. Each line actually represents two relationships, one from the first entity to the second, and another in the reverse direction. A solid line near an entity denotes that each occurrence of that entity has a mandatory relationship with the second entity. We read this as *Each <entity 1> **must be**.*. A dotted line indicates an optional relationship, that is, *Each <entity 1> **may be**.*. The type of relationship is written as the relationship name at the end nearest the entity. In our sentence construction, the relationship name follows

*Each <entity 1> **must be** <relationship name 1>..*

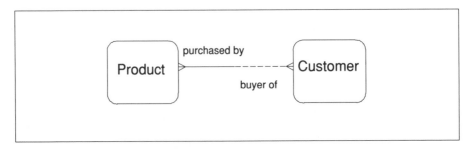

Figure 3-3: A Sample Entity-Relationship Diagram

The other end of a relationship line may be a single line, indicating an association with exactly one occurrence of the second entity. Crow's feet at the end of the relationship line indicate an association with one or more occurrences. Again these conditions appear in our sentence as

*Each <entity 1> **must be** <relationship name 1> **one and only one** <entity 2>.*

or

*Each <entity 1> **must be** <relationship name 1> **one or more** <entity 2>.*

The second relationship is read in a similar manner in the reverse direction, that is, from entity 2 to entity 1. In this case, we use the relationship name closest to the second entity. So the relationship between customer and product entities in Figure 3-3 read as

Each customer may be the buyer of one or more products.

and

Each product must be purchased by one or more customers.

Why do we care about relationships between entities? A relationship defines a business reason for association between two pieces of data. With CASE*Method conventions, we can form structured English statements from the relationship definitions. Thus, we can ask users to verify our understanding by asking them to correct our English statements. For example, we can ask users if it is possible to have products which are not purchased by any customers. If the answer is "Yes," then we can correct the second relationship by changing *must be* to *may be*, that is, change from a solid line to a dotted line nearest the product entity. In such questioning, we improve our understanding of the business.

Relationship names obviously play a very important part in obtaining meaningful responses from your users. Finding the most suitable relationship names requires a lot of effort. Similar to our discussion of function descriptions, avoid using *noise* words such as *process*. Sentences like *Each product may be processed by one or more salesperson* will get user agreement, even though we have not identified the kind of processing a salesperson performs. We may be missing important information by glossing over the kind of processing involved.

Relationships come in several flavors:

- **One-to-one**: This type is rare. It usually indicates misunderstanding of one or both of the entities. Try defining some attributes for each entity. You might find that one of the entities is actually an attribute of the other.

- **One-to-many**: This type is the most common. Typically the crow's feet end is mandatory, and the other optional.

- **Many-to-many**: This type is fairly common. However, you really ought to normalize this further by adding an *intersect* entity in between the two entities. The intersect entity is often something the business recognizes by name. For example, a many to many relationship between customer and product breaks out as shown in Figure 3-4(a). In this case, the intersect entity is an *order*. In this entity, we have a place to

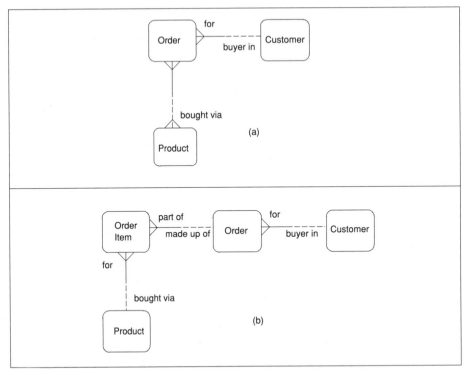

Figure 3-4: Intersect Entities

hold, as an attribute, a shipping address if it is different from the customer's address. The shipping address might even be different for each order, such as when a customer buys Christmas presents!

Unfortunately, there is still a many-to-many relationship between order and product entities. Further breakdown leads to *order item* as another intersect entity as shown in Figure 3-4(b). Thus, we discover two more entities which we might have missed. Finding the names for intersect entities is not always as easy as this example implies. You often need several discussions with users and investigation of their current paperwork.

In addition to drawing relationships in the CASE*Designer entity diagrammer, we use CASE*Dictionary to define volume information and to make notes on each relationship. This screen displays the English statement constructed from relationship information. Note that relationships, like entities, belong to an application. However, defining entity sharing between applications makes associated relationships shared. No explicit sharing need be defined.

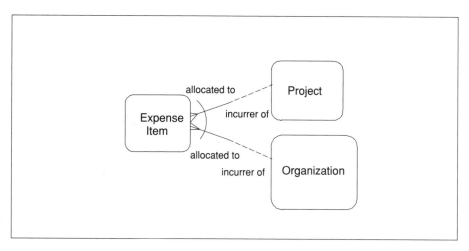

Figure 3-5: Exclusive Relationship

There can be more than one relationship between two entities, although most of the time there is only one. Arcs between two relationships from one entity indicate an *exclusive-or* condition, similar to the use of arcs in functions. The ends of the relationship participating in an arc must be both mandatory or both optional; otherwise the condition does not make sense. As an exercise, try reading such a nonsensical combination using the CASE*Method statement construction. CASE*Designer will report such poor relationship constructions in its quality check reports. The other end of each of the relationships participating in an arc may be different entities or the same entity. Figure 3-5 illustrates an exclusive relationship.

Some entities may be made up of subclasses. For example, suppose Widgets' products might have subclasses: tools, kitchen appliances, and clothing. These subclasses are ***subtypes*** of the entity, Products. The Products entity is called a ***supertype***. Subtypes are mutually exclusive and must cover all occurrences of the entity between them. Subtypes are usually shown on the diagram as entities inside the supertype entity.

Subtypes inherit all attributes and relationships from the supertype. For example, if product has an attribute called catalog number, the subtypes tool, kitchen appliance, and clothing each inherits this attribute. Inheritance rules also apply to relationships. You can view inherited attributes in the implied attributes screen in CASE*Dictionary. Some subtypes may have attributes that are different from other subtypes of one entity. For example, clothing may have an attribute sex indicating whether an item is male, female, or unisex clothing. Such an attribute obviously does not apply to tool and kitchen appliance subtypes. A similar argument hold for relationships which apply to one subtype but not to others. This provides a convenient way to group similar objects. In fact, this technique is the key to convergent modeling as we will see in the next chapter.

If there is a large number of subclasses, say, more than five or six, the diagram gets very cluttered. Create a new entity, in such cases. In our example, we could have the entity product type as shown in Figure 3-6.

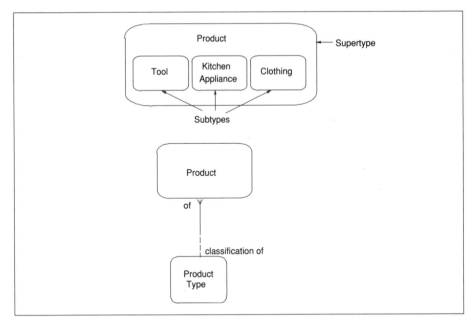

Figure 3-6: Alternative to Subtypes

The CASE*Method convention for an entity-relationship diagram is to arrange entities such that all crow's feet point up or to the left. Diagrams in our case study follow this convention. This convention makes your layout follow a pattern. All base entities, that is, those that have mostly single lines starting from them, filter to either the right or to the bottom of the page. All *transaction* entities, that is, those that intersect between two or more entities, collect in the middle and left. If you then put all person or organization-related entities to the right and product-related entities along the bottom, your diagrams become regular. You can, of course, choose your own convention for layout, say, crow's feet pointing to the bottom or to the right. Such conventions are important for improved communication between members of your team. CASE*Designer does not enforce any restrictions on layout — you may place entities and relationships exactly as you choose.

When modeling several parts of a business, drawing everything in a single diagram is almost impossible. Even if you manage to do so, the diagram is probably useless, as it will be too complex to comprehend. So I suggest a breakdown based on *business views*. A business view is a group of entities which are of interest to a particular group of people in the company. For example, salespeople are interested only in sales-related information, entities like customer, order, order line items, and so on. They have little interest in purchasing information like supplier, purchase order, receipt, and so on. There will be overlaps, of course. Both groups share the entity, product, since they want to know the quantity in stock. CASE*Designer allows you to draw multiple diagrams which contain the same entities. You do not need to re-create entities — simply copy existing entities into a new diagram.

To check completeness of your diagrams, use the CASE*Designer matrix diagrammer. With this tool, you can define which business function uses which entities and how as a cross-reference matrix. For each business function, you can specify whether the function creates, retrieves, updates, or deletes an entity. You can also comment on the usage, for example, a comment might be *retrieve sorted by customer name*. There is more on the subject of cross-reference matrices in Section 1.2.4 and a later chapter.

Diagrams are communication aids. So their layout is almost as important as their content. The CASE*Designer facilities can help you make your diagram easy to understand and memorable, but you have to put in quite a lot of hard work. Here are some hints to make your diagram easily readable

- Do not bend relationship lines—following relationship lines around entities is difficult. Instead, try rearranging entities in the diagram or alter the size of the entity box.

- Use larger size boxes to draw attention to important entities. Less important entities, such as product type, can have small boxes.

- In a feedback session, build up entities and relationships over many overhead foils or pages. Showing the entire diagram at once overwhelms users and distracts their attention from the point you are trying to make.

There are many useful reports and quality checks in the CASE*Designer and CASE*Dictionary products. Explore these reports when you need to find some specific information. One of the most useful reports, I find, is the system glossary. This glossary includes all of the entity descriptions as well as definitions of terms. Thus, you can document your understanding of any specialized terms of the business.

3.5 Business Units

This part of the strategy study is probably the simplest to understand. Define each organization group that is a subject of the study. A business unit can be any division, department, or organization within the company. If your company has more than one geographic location, each location should be treated as a different unit. This way, you record volume and frequency information in the detailed analysis phase essential for analysis of distributed environments.

CASE*Dictionary is the primary tool for recording the name and description of each business unit. I suggest that you record the following in the text description

- **Responsibilities of the unit**: For example, *The sales department calls customers and takes orders*. Be as concise as you can, you don't need to repeat all of the functions from the function hierarchy.

- **Current head of department**: Don't forget list the date of this entry as the information gets out of date quickly.

- **Size**: The number of people within this group. For example, the sales group consists of two supervisors each supervising five salespeople.

- **Planned growth**: The plan for growth in staff, revenue, or some other appropriate measure, over some period of time. For example, *the sales department expects to hire two more salespersons this year and targets a revenue of $20 million by the end of the next year. Last year's revenue was $10 million.*

Use the CASE*Designer matrix facility to define function and entity usages by business units. You can fill in volume and frequency information in the detailed analysis phase.

3.6 Formulating Your Strategy

Having defined the components of the strategy study, we are ready to formulate a strategy. You need to exercise your judgment extensively in this task. There are no recipes.

Compare your function hierarchy and entity-relationship diagrams to your existing systems. Outline the parts that these systems cover. Undoubtedly there are gaps and over-laps. Here are some of the areas you need to pinpoint

- Is there duplicate data between two or more systems? What is the cost of this duplication? For example, duplicate customer data between sales and accounting systems means double data entry.

- How is this duplicate data kept synchronized? If it is not synchronized, what kinds of extra work results? There are probably customers in the accounting system which do not appear in the sales system, or even worse, vice versa!

- Examine the gripes you heard during interviews. Why don't the current systems address these issues? Would it take too long to change?

- How often are requests for change or enhancements received for existing systems? A good clue to an inadequate system is a large volume of requests for change.

- How long does servicing a request for change take, on average? Would using Oracle's or third-party fourth-generation tools speed up this process in the future?

Combine the answers to these questions with the company priorities outlined in the previous chapter. With this combination, try to divide the models into possible system boundaries. Keep in mind current skills and strengths of your group. Use the cross-reference matrices to determine who benefits from each of the identified systems and who provides data in each. The group providing data must benefit in return; otherwise, they are reluctant to participate.

Consider the potential effects of the draft system boundaries. Will you need to change hardware architectures as well as software? How will the user organizations react? Are organizational changes needed for effective implementation? Consult the high-level executives for their input and opinions. You should know whether they will be receptive to your strategy before you finalize it.

3.7 CASE Study: WI Strategy Study

In this section, I present the key components of the Widgets, Inc. model, as a function hierarchy and a set of entity-relationship diagrams. In a strategy study, I typically use only three levels in the function hierarchy. This keeps it simple enough so that most high-level executives can comprehend it quickly. The intent, in this phase, is to focus their attention on parts that are of strategic importance to the business. Those are the candidates for detailed analysis phase, especially if the company executives can prioritize them.

Similarly, the entity-relationship diagrams also represent only the important entities. So, you will see numerous many-to-many relationships. Details such as developing the intersection entities, I defer until the detailed analysis phase. Remember that you are under pressure to show results quickly at this phase, so don't spend much time worrying about the accuracy of details. This way you can keep the strategy study phase short and useful. CASE*Method allows you to partition the phases in this way. It can be customized to suit the needs of the company.

During the strategy phase, we interviewed only the high-level executives of Widgets, Inc.: the president, who decided on sales strategies; the vice president of marketing, who chose product line strategies; and the chief financial officer. Keeping the number of interviews small is *very* important. I have seen many strategy studies which fell into the trap of too many interviews. They took too long to complete, leading to heavy pressure to deliver quickly in later phases. In one to two cases, the developers decided to skip the design phase completely to make up the time. You can guess the quality of the end result! Typically, a strategy study should take less than one quarter of the time estimated for the entire project.

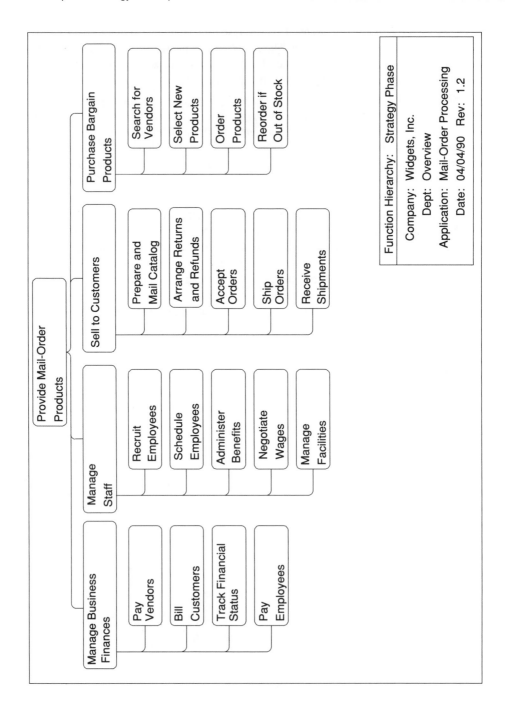

3.7.1 Notes on Function Hierarchy

1. Start the strategic analysis with a top-level function hierarchy. The president provided us with the company's mission statement in the first meeting.

2. Aim to keep the function hierarchy to only three levels. The fourth-level typically means too much detail. Check to see if your grouping of function is incorrect and if regrouping brings you back on track.

3. We also sketched out the departments to give us a tentative second level of the hierarchy. This gave us five functions: the four shown in the function hierarchy and Warehousing as a fifth.

4. During interviews, we followed each second-level function into more depth. We asked our three interviewees to contribute their understanding in each of the departments. If we had a lot more interviewees, we would have restricted discussions with each to departments they were responsible for. We did get a lot of repeated information, but an occasional pearl made it worth the tedious wait. These interviews also helped increase our credibility with these executives, since our questions quickly homed in on the business issues that were important to them.

    This sounds like interviews took days of discussions. They did not! Each interview was less than two hours — but two hours of intense discussions. Organizing notes after each interview took more than a whole day.

5. When we sketched in the detailed third level of the function hierarchy, we realized that sales and warehousing departments are very closely knit operations. So, we merged the warehousing function into sales in the hierarchy. Expect to rearrange your function hierarchy frequently throughout the strategy phase. This is the reason why you should build trial models after each interview — it helps assimilate the information and clarifies interdependencies.

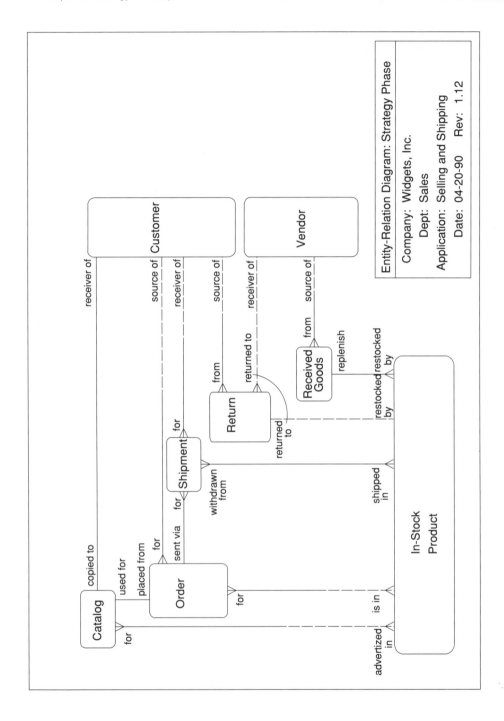

Entity-Relation Diagram: Strategy Phase

Company: Widgets, Inc.
    Dept: Sales
Application: Selling and Shipping
    Date: 04-20-90   Rev: 1.12

3.7.2 Notes on Entity-Relationship Diagrams

1. We developed these diagrams in parallel with the function hierarchy. They help us check that we have identified functions which refer to these entities. In our example, we developed one diagram for each of the level 2 functions, a total of four entity-relationship diagrams.

2. You need to call each of these top-level functions, and associated entity-relationship diagrams, an *application* in CASE*Dictionary. This way, you can get reports for all entities in one application with the DETAILED ENTITY DEFINITION report. I show one page of this report here.

3. Notice how CASE*Dictionary makes sentences from our relationships. This is a good way to check if we named them correctly.

```
Date : 12-MAY-90     ORACLE: CASE*Dictionary      Page :  1
                     DETAILED ENTITY DEFINITION
Entity Name : RETURN              Application :  Sales and
                                                Warehousing
                                 Version      :    1

Subtype of :                     Reference    :  RETURN

Synonyms    :                    Initial Volume :   500
                                 Average Volume :   500
                                 Maximum Volume : 5000
                                 Annual Growth% :     5

--- DESCRIPTION - HAS SIGNIFICANCE AS -----------------
A previously ordered item which the customer is shipping back. It
may be defective, in which case, we return it to the vendor, or
in good condition, in which case we return it stock. Customers
must get a Return Authorization Number from Support prior to
shipping the item.
--- ATTRIBUTES ------------------------------------------
Name : RETURN AUTHORIZATION NUMBER        Domain :
       Opt : N        Format : NUMBER      Length : 9 *
Name : PRODUCT NUMBER                      Domain :
       Opt : N        Format : NUMBER      Length : 9
                 * - Attribute in primary unique identifier
--- RELATIONSHIPS ------------------------------------
EACH OCCURRENCE OF THIS ENTITY :
MUST BE from          ONE AND ONLY ONE    CUSTOMER
EITHER
MAY BE  returned to   ONE AND ONLY ONE    VENDOR
OR
MAY BE  returned to   ONE AND ONLY ONE    IN-STOCK PRODUCT
          * - Relationships in primary unique identifier
--- NOTES AND REMARKS --------------------------------
Is this really a subtype of an order item? Resolve in detailed
analysis.
------------------------------------------------------
```

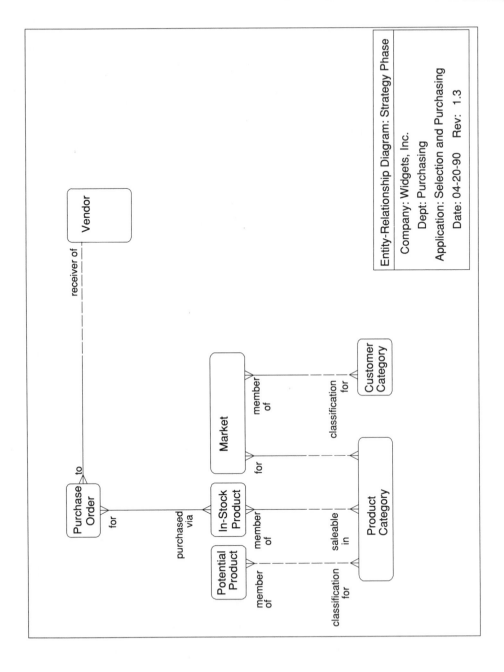

Entity-Relationship Diagram: Strategy Phase

Company: Widgets, Inc.
Dept: Purchasing
Application: Selection and Purchasing
Date: 04-20-90   Rev: 1.3

3.7.3 Notes on Purchasing E-R Diagram

1. Entities like Product Category, Customer Category, and Market exist only in the executive's minds. There is no data on these in current operations. This means that when tackling the purchasing application, we have to find ways of obtaining such information.

2. Notice there are several many-to-many relationships. Purists will argue that we ought to resolve them now, before proceeding further. However, these are red herrings which cause you to get sidetracked from your objective.

3. Keep the strategy project *short*! I really cannot stress this enough. Remember your focus is to gain an understanding of the entire company. Broad strokes are sufficient to set the scope for later detailed analysis. Correctness of relationships and detail are topics for detailed analysis, not strategy.

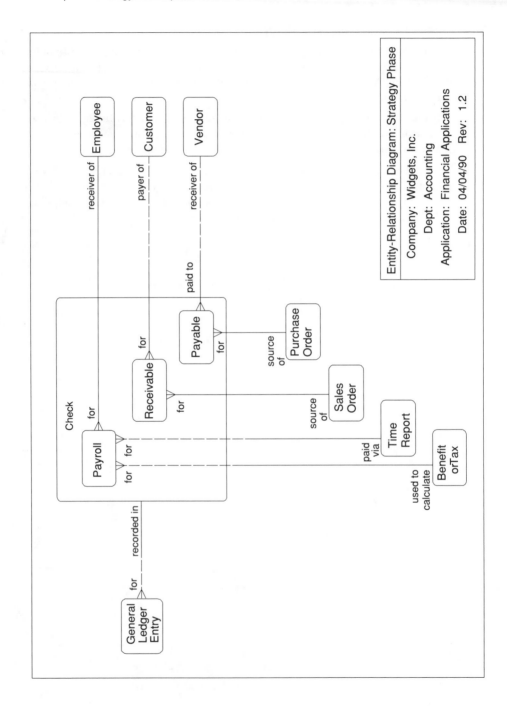

Entity-Relationship Diagram: Strategy Phase

Company: Widgets, Inc.
    Dept: Accounting
Application: Financial Applications
    Date: 04/04/90   Rev: 1.2

3.7.4 Notes on Accounting E-R Diagram

1. Notice the supertype Check and its subtypes. This is a correct abstract representation which simplifies the understanding the functions of the accounting department. Detailed analysis may choose to discard it later, if there is little similarity between the attributes of subtypes.

2. Entities like Sales Order and Purchase Order are shared with other applications. These shared entities are likely to become shared tables when we design the database later.

3. By realizing the relationships of shared entities to entities in each aspect of the business, we hope to avoid applications which have to upload and download data.

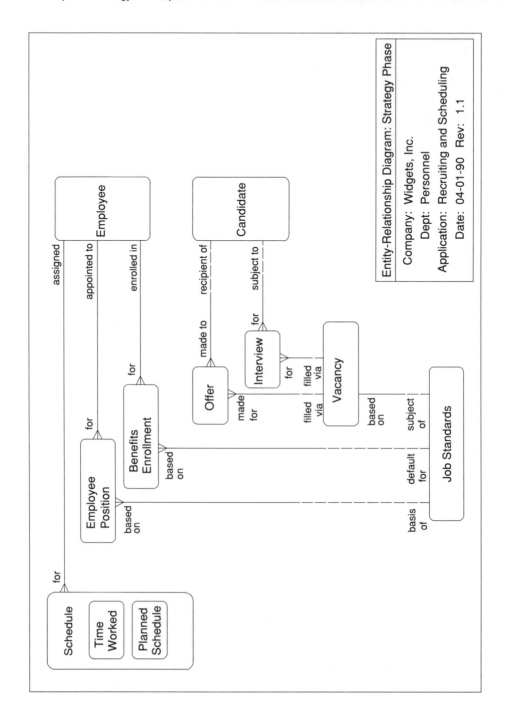

Entity-Relationship Diagram: Strategy Phase

Company: Widgets, Inc.
Dept: Personnel
Application: Recruiting and Scheduling
Date: 04-01-90   Rev: 1.1

3.7.5 Notes on Personnel E-R Diagram

1. The Job Standards entity actually specifies a job grade and each benefit that goes along with the grade. So it may actually be two entities. We simply note this idea in the entity comment field in CASE*Dictionary for later review. The plural entity name also gives us this hint, since entity names must be singular nouns.

2. Notice the mandatory relationship (solid line) between Employee and Schedule entities. This implies that we have no employees that are not scheduled for work time. Apparently, vacation time is also scheduled at Widgets, Inc. Sick time, again, is a category on the schedule.

3. We were given a similar argument for the relationship between Employee Position and Employee. Widgets, Inc. does not hire unless there is a defined position open.

4

Analysis Techniques

The detailed analysis phase addresses a much smaller portion of the company than the strategic business analysis phase. It uses the outputs of the strategy study to make sure other, future projects mesh properly. The shared entities and common functions are of particular value in ensuring easy connections between applications.

This chapter discusses the techniques used for fact-finding during detailed analysis. Remember that we are now concerned with how business objectives are actually achieved, if at all, rather than what those objectives are. We base our explanations on Oracle's CASE*Method, CASE*Designer, and CASE*Dictionary. We will briefly contrast these techniques with some other popular CASE tools — to appreciate the differences in conventions.

Similar to the previous chapter, we will restrict our discussion to the overall principles of techniques. For further detail refer to the texts in the bibliography or books published by Oracle. The topics discussed in this chapter are

- Techniques used in detailed analysis including data flow diagrams, normalization, and cross-checks for completeness.

- Techniques for deriving the essential model which is free of the limitations of the technology currently in use.

- How to develop models for stable systems. This is one of the techniques that requires experience but yields a flexible model. Such models require little change even though business needs change over time.

- How to start developing plans, together with your users, to ease their transition from current methods to procedures necessary for the new system. Remember that organizational and cultural changes take time to implement.

4.1 Detailed Analysis Phase

The detailed analysis phase usually addresses one application at a time. The order in which you address them depends on your information systems strategy and available resources. If you need a sales system for company growth and only have two analysts available to do so, you cannot address sales and warehousing systems at the same time.

The approach taken in a detailed analysis phase is bottom up. We aim to analyze an area of operation together with the key *doers* in that area. Typically, we interview line managers, supervisors, or their right-hand people in our investigations. These people have direct responsibility for the day-to-day work, although they may not perform it themselves.

We take a bottom-up approach to ensure that we do not miss any detail as is possible in a top-down approach. However, the bottom-up approach cannot take into account company objectives, plans, and goals. The top-down approach provides this information without going too much into the actual workings of the company.

We usually start by developing data flow diagrams representing the current operations and based on current mechanisms. Then, we derive an essential or logical model from the physical model. The essential model is free of technology and mechanisms. It should be very close to the elementary business functions we developed in the strategy phase. Unlike the intuitive methods we used in the strategy phase, here we used a more rigorous approach. Such rigor is necessary for analyzing the details. We also tackle a much smaller portion of the company so that attention to detail is possible.

Many methodologies use data flow diagrams, or a similar technique, popularized by Chris Gane and Trish Sarson in the late 1970s and early 1980s. The Yourdon methodology specifies data flow diagrams as a primary analysis technique, although this methodology requires more rigor than the one proposed by Gane and Sarson. Until the mid-1980s, this method was used together with normalization techniques, without the support of entity-relationship diagrams. ERDs have added method to the data analysis in the same way that data flow diagrams helped process analysis.

The work plan in this phase is similar in structure to the strategy phase. We interview selected company staff in the chosen area. We model based on notes from these interviews using data flow diagrams as techniques. We then feedback our models to verify their correctness. Once we understand the current physical system, we derive the essential or logical system model. We also normalize the data details from the data flow diagrams. The normalized data model should be close to the entity-relationship model from the strategy phase, albeit more detailed. There are checks for completeness involving a comparison of what we found in the strategy phase and the detailed analysis phase.

Detailed analysis phase interviews are with people who perform the work. In these interviews, we find how the company actually works, as opposed to strategy phase interviews when we found how the company is supposed to work. These interviews take more time since we need all the details of each function. We collect, for example, all forms and reports currently used and make sure we understand their contents in the interviews. We obtain algorithms for any processing needed as well as frequency and volumes for all data and processing. Realize that users at this level have in-depth knowledge but little breadth. So you will discover additional interviewees through earlier interviews. Schedule sufficient time in your project plan to cover such extra interviews.

There are a lot more interviews to conduct in the detailed analysis phase than in the strategy phase, even though we tackle a smaller functional area. Each interview also takes much longer. In this phase, we are not only gathering information about how work is done, we also look for performance expectations, cost justification, and acceptance criteria. For example, suppose the users expect to increase their productivity because the system is supposed to provide data much faster. Ask them for the worth of hourly availability of data currently available overnight, or within minutes for data which they get once an hour today. Answers to such questions not only provides ideas for cost justification but also describes their expectations. Use an interview as an opportunity to set realistic expectations.

4.2 Data Flow Diagram

A data flow diagram is a model which shows how data flows through functions and how each function manipulates the data. These functions may be manual, automated, or some combination of the two. It is also a tool for communicating our understanding to users who actually do the work. A sample data flow diagram is shown in Figure 4-1. A data flow diagram is made up of

- Processes which are analogous to functions in a hierarchy. We describe how to manipulate incoming data into the outgoing data in a process.

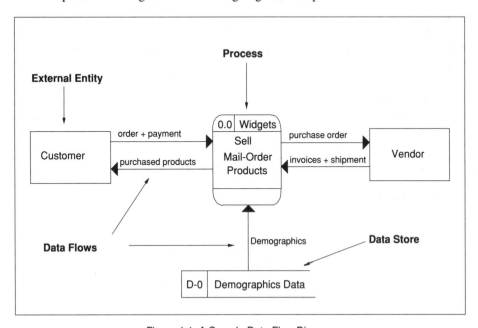

Figure 4-1: A Sample Data Flow Diagram

- External entities which supply all of the input and receive output of the system. Typical examples of external entities include customer, supplier, and so on. Do not confuse them with the entity-relationship diagram — these are terminators of all information rather than a definition of what information we wish to hold. Sometimes they are also called *sources* and *sinks*.

- Data flows which indicate movement of data between processes and data stores. They are drawn as lines between two processes, with arrows indicating the direction of flow. Data in the data flows may be elementary, that is, not processed, or derived, that is, processed in some way.

- Data stores which are repositories of information over time or for later use. Information stored in a data store is the basis of our entity-relationship diagram.

Describing an entire system in a single diagram makes the diagram very complex and almost impossible to understand. So we develop it in several *levels*. Higher levels establish the context of the system, and each subsequent lower-level shows more detail. Thus, the highest-level, the context level, consists of a single process with all external incoming and outgoing data flows. The next lower-level *explodes* this process into a few major component processes, and another level lower, each of these processes explodes into more detailed processes, and so on. Figure 4-2 illustrates an exploded process. Process explosion in data flow diagrams is similar to function decomposition in our function hierarchies used in the strategy phase.

Each explosion of a process should result in no more than seven or eight processes. Restricting each level of explosion to this number makes each explosion easy to understand as well as manageable. Of course, every data flow to or from the exploded process must be shown on the lower-level diagram. Figure 4-2 shows an explosion of the example process from Figure 4-1. Checking that a lower-level explosion accounts for every data flow from the higher level is called *level balancing*.

This description implies that we develop data flow diagrams in a top-down fashion. Not always true — developing lower-levels first and then leveling upward is quite common for initial diagrams. One way to start may be to break down the context-level process by the physical organization of the area being analyzed. Remember that we start with a model of the way work is done today, so partitioning based on current structure is okay. This may not be the best partitioning for the new system, but worry about that later when we derive the essential model.

CASE*Designer provides a facility to draw data flow diagrams in a top-down fashion, that is, by exploding higher-level processes. In this facility, each explosion is a new diagram. Level balancing is easy in this tool since each explosion shows the higher-level process and all of its data flow connection to other entities, data stores, or processes. It also prevents mistakes such as drawing a data flow directly from an external entity to a data store. There must always be a process to receive and manipulate data from an external entity before storing it in a data store.

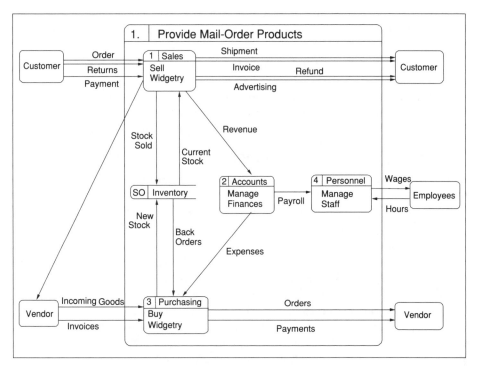

Figure 4-2: Process Explosion

Process details, data flow, and data store definitions are facilities of CASE*Dictionary. As you draw items on a data flow diagram, they automatically get stored in CASE*Dictionary database. You can then add detail using forms accessible from either the diagrammer or CASE*Dictionary. Data flow and data store details in CASE*Dictionary are in terms of entities and attributes. Thus, you can create them in the data flow diagrammer with just names. But before defining their contents, you must complete the entity-relationship diagram details. The entity-relationship diagrams from the strategy phase should make this task easy.

Process details explain the data manipulations performed. There are no restrictions on the format of this explanation in CASE*Dictionary. Other products include structured English, action diagrams, or state transition diagrams as techniques for detailed process descriptions. CASE*Dictionary may include some of these techniques in the future.

How many levels do you need? A rule of thumb is until you can completely describe a process in about half a page. In many cases this means at least three levels, and typically no more than five. In our case, slightly longer process descriptions are acceptable since we plan to use Oracle's fourth-generation tools for development. Remember the power of the SQL query language. Some of my consulting clients could dispense with the lowest-level data flow diagrams because of the complex processing a single SQL statement performs. They needed even less decomposition with SQL*Forms. If you understand how these tools work, you can judge when you have sufficient detail. Concentrate on getting accurate details on your data entities and attributes. Most of these tools are data driven. Attention to detail on data pays off in the long run, especially if you plan to use CASE*Generator for screen application generation.

The CASE*Designer data flow diagramming facility serves for drawing both physical and logical data flow diagrams. Developing a physical data flow diagram from interviews is straightforward. The case study in Section 4.7 shows the physical data flow diagrams for Widgets' sales system. After completing the diagrams, conduct a feedback session to verify its correctness. These diagrams illustrate how the company works at present.

4.3 Deriving the Essential Model

In the strategy phase, we derived essential functions mostly by intuition. In this phase, we use much more rigorous methods. The end result is an essential model which is verified with users for its correctness. Don't try to derive the essential model before completing and verifying the physical model, however. Without a verified physical model, you cannot be sure of its completeness.

An essential model is the way our system would work if it used perfect internal technology. With perfect internal technology, there are no resource limitations. There is no need for communication — once some piece of data is known to one part of the system, it is available to all of it. Perfect technology does not require translation from one medium to another, or storage merely for processing as a batch. An essential model consists only of essential activities, or functions, and data flows between them. After we derive an essential model, we design the new system by adding the proposed technological and procedural changes to it.

Once we have a set of leveled diagrams for the current physical model, we start by joining together all of the lowest-level diagrams. Discard the higher-level diagrams. Connect the data flows of the lowest-level diagrams and consolidate common data stores and external entities. By the way, our method described here is the reason why the actual partitioning of the higher-level diagrams in the physical model is of small importance. After determining the essential processes, we level upward to derive new higher-level diagrams.

To derive essential processes, we discard any physical aspects or technology from our connected data flow diagram. For example, suppose one of our processes sorts orders received in the mail from all other mail. Discard this process as it implies the physical arrival of mail as a batch of letters. After discarding this process, connect the data flows incoming to that process to its outgoing flows as if the process never existed. Here is a summary of other types of processes to discard

- **Transporter processes:** These processes merely move data from one location to another without transforming it in any way. For example, processes to send mail, receive faxes, and so on. In most cases, they imply a technology or a mechanism and are easy to detect.

- **Translator processes:** Some processes translate data from one medium to another. For example, the process *Enter customer order* translates data from paper to a computer system. Discard these processes as they do not transform data.

- **Batching processes:** We often find processes which collect a number of transactions as a batch before processing them. Such processes are particularly common in manual systems. Discard these processes, again, because they do not transform data.

- **Edit processes:** Processes for editing that are internal to the system verify the correctness of information and possibly correct errors. In perfect technology, no errors occur and format conversions are unnecessary. Since we plan to change such methods in the new system, we discard such processes. Instead, the editing criteria are part of the definition of the data.

- **Audit or approval processes:** These processes represent the current methods for reviewing or approving data. Discard them. In perfect internal technology, there are no errors. In the new system, we design new procedures for them.

There are other items we discard also from the data flow diagram. We discard data flows that carry no information, data stores that merely exist to collect batches of data, historical storage, or duplicate copies of data for backup. Here is a summary of some of these:

- **Data flows for physical movement:** These flows represent some physical item moving from one location to another but carry no information. For example, a data flow representing an assembly moving from one test station to another is a physical movement data flow. In perfect internal technology, we do not need to move physical items.

- **Batch or buffer data stores:** These stores are merely repositories for collecting data into batches. In perfect internal technology, we process data instantaneously as soon as we receive it — there are no time limitations or restrictions on the number of processors available. Discard these data stores. Connect any incoming data flows directly to outgoing data flows.

- **Magic hat data stores:** Data stores which only have outgoing data flows are suspect. Where does the data come from? They may be disguised batch data stores where you forgot a data flow coming from an external entity.

- **Black hole data stores:** Data stores which only have incoming data flows simply collect information which no one needs. Be careful, you may be missing a process which does use it. If no such processes exist, eliminate these data stores and the associated data flows. They are redundant.

As you eliminate each item from the data flow, make sure you do not lose any data. When you eliminate a process or a data store, connect incoming data flows to outgoing data flows. Draw and redraw your diagram and compare it with the original physical model until you are sure you have captured everything without any implied technology. Typically, the majority of processes should either retrieve data from a data store and pass processed data to an external entity, or vice versa.

Group the remaining processes, data stores, and data flows by events. Events in detailed analysis are probably more numerous than in the strategy phase. Start by drawing a separate diagram for each event. All responses to that event must be on the diagram. Then, level upward using sequences of events to obtain a logical group. In a functionally organized company, the logical grouping is likely to be quite close to the organization structure.

The essential processes derived in this process ought to match very closely with the elementary business functions defined in the strategy phase. In fact, CASE*Dictionary treats the two as synonymous. This is a good check to make sure your model is complete. Another check is to define the cross-reference matrices between functions, entities, and business units. Now that we have a lot more detail, we should be able to define all usage completely. Each entity must be created, updated, and retrieved by some function. You may need to add processes to purge entities. The logic described in the process descriptions should match the usage described in the cross-reference matrix.

This process of developing a current physical model and then reducing it to an essential model seems a little long winded. However, the methodical approach produces better results than with a intuitive approach even if you have very talented, experienced analysts. Even good people make mistakes some times. We all know the cost of discovering a mistake or misunderstanding later in the life-cycle.

4.4 Normalization

In the bottom-up approach, we end up with a lot of data elements. They appear in data stores and data flows. Of course this list is much more complete than the attributes we identified in the strategy phase. Now, we normalize the list, plug in attributes into appropriate entities, and perhaps create a few more entities. Realize that entity-relationship diagrams naturally lead to normalized model, although that is largely dependent on the analyst's skills. The normalization process is more rigorous.

There are many introductory texts on how to normalize data using the two methods, decomposition and synthesis. So we skip the details of the process. Instead here are some informal tests for the normal forms.

There are five normal forms formally defined at present, although only the first three are most commonly applicable in database design. These normal forms, called first normal form, second normal form, and so on, form a layered onion. The first normal form is the outermost layer of the onion, and the fifth normal form is the innermost. The inner layers of the onion automatically pass the test of any layer outside it. Thus a relation in the second normal form is automatically in the first normal form. The converse does not, however, apply; that is, a first normal form is only in the second normal form if it passes the test for the second normal form. The normalization process aims to decompose data up to the most sensible inner layer.

4.4.1 First Normal Form (1NF)

The test for first normal form is whether each attribute in the relation takes only *atomic values*. By atomic values, we mean individual values such as taken by attributes like customer number and customer name. A first normal form relation cannot have any attribute which takes multiple values packed into a single attribute. Note that a date could be treated as an atomic value whether as a combination of day, month, year or as three separate attributes of day, month, and year. Whether to separate or not depends on your business needs.

4.4.2 Second Normal Form (2NF)

The test for whether a first normal form relation is also in the second normal form depends on identifying the key attribute of the relation. Each value of the key must uniquely identify a row in the table. For example, in a ***customer order*** relation, the key is obviously ***ord_no***. The test for second normal form is whether every nonkey attribute depends on the key.

4.4.3 Third Normal Form (3NF)

The test for whether a second normal form relation is also in third normal form checks for any dependencies between nonkey attributes. The end result is attributes that depend on the key (unique identifier) and nothing else.

The Boyce/Codd normal form is actually a stricter definition of a third normal form, but applies rather rarely in a business application. For details on the difference between this form and the third normal form, please refer to the book, *An Introduction to Database Systems,* by C. J. Date.

4.4.4 Fourth Normal Form (4NF)

In most everyday databases, third normal form is a sufficient level of decomposition. Occasionally you might notice update problems even in third normal form, when there is a multivalued dependency. In this case, some nonkey attribute has multiple values for each key value, independent of other attribute. For example, each seminar uses more than one textbook but has one title only. We decompose, in such cases, into two separate relations, seminars and seminar-texts.

4.5 Models for Flexibility

So far we only looked at entity-relationship models for specific things encountered in our analysis. We could base our design on such models. However, a relatively small change in business practices can alter our model. In traditional methodologies, we relegate such changes to the maintenance phase. What if we could make our models more flexible so that we can accommodate changes in the business? This exercise is called convergent modeling.

4.5.1 Convergent Modeling

The main principle in this approach is to look for patterns in our entity-relationship model. We then try to merge similar patterns. Our convention of diagram layout really helps in making patterns noticeable. The end result is usually a simpler overall model which actually accommodates those unforeseen changes without restructuring our model or our design.

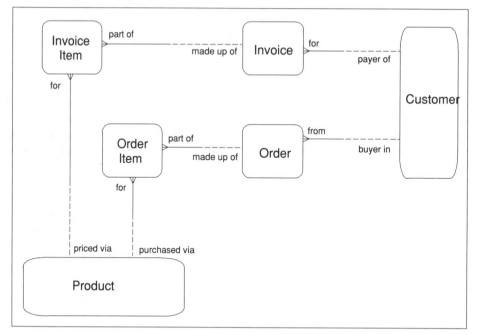

Figure 4-3: Orders and Invoices Patterns

Consider the example in Figure 4-3 which illustrates the entity-relationship diagram of orders and invoices. Don't the patterns look similar? The question to ask is: Can we represent both patterns with one set of entities? Before doing so, we need to make sure that we can account for all of the attributes in each entity by a common set. In this case, we can. So the merged entities are shown in Figure 4-4.

Let's take this one step further. Compare our example in Figure 3-4(b) and Figure 4-4. Similar patterns again, except that customer is a separate entity. What happens now if one of our vendors becomes a customer? We really would need to keep that information once as the vendor entity and again as the customer entity. Suppose, we invent a supertype called *party* with *customer* and *vendor* as subtypes. Our generalized *transaction* entity can cover our dealings with customers as well as vendors. Actually the relationships clearly define in which transaction someone is a vendor as opposed to a customer, so we don't really need the subtypes customer and vendor. Instead, we might differentiate between individuals and organizations, so that we can deal with both types of vendors and customers. This pattern is shown in Figure 4-5.

As we generalize our models, we abstract data in our entity-relationship model. This abstraction makes our models more difficult to understand. They are further removed from our users' perception. However, these models are much more flexible and powerful. In our transaction example, we can represent any transaction involving parties pertaining to a product. In fact, we could easily extend the product entity in the future to include services not supplied today without changing the model.

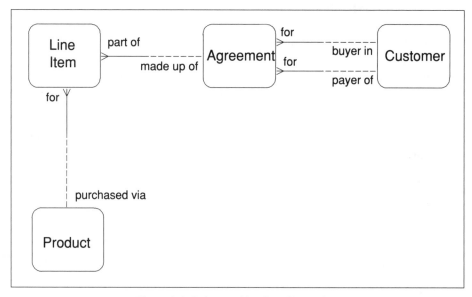

Figure 4-4: Orders and Invoices Abstraction

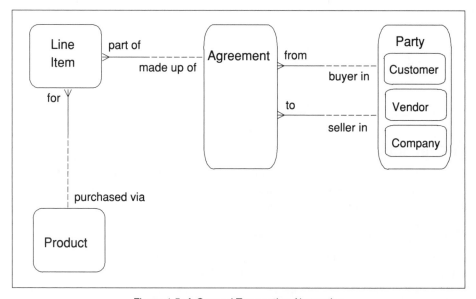

Figure 4-5: A General Transaction Abstraction

There is of course a price to pay if we implement these abstract patterns in our physical database — more difficult access and lower performance. These issues are topics for a later chapter. Don't dismiss the power of these abstraction out of hand. Oracle tools provide some extensions which might relieve some of our worries. We need a methodical assessment of what our performance needs are before we design databases.

4.5.2 Abstraction to the *n*th Degree

The process of abstraction can get extreme if we are not careful. We can actually model anything in the world with the general model illustrated in Figure 4-6. In some cases this may make sense, as it does for the model underlying the CASE*Dictionary database. There are even real-world cases when some parts of this model reduce development significantly. However, exercise extreme caution before adopting it!

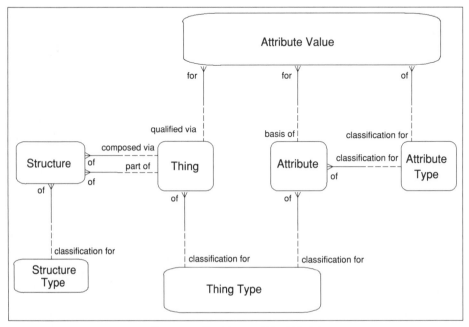

Figure 4-6: The Abstract World Model

4.6 Transition Plan for the New System

From our essential model, we can design the new system together with user management. We choose the new mechanisms for the new system and user management devises procedures for performing functions with these mechanisms. Remember, however, that the new functions should not be overly dependent on the mechanisms if our stable model is to survive changes in the business.

You will need to draw data flow diagrams which illustrate the new flows. In this activity, the relationship built with users really helps. Remember, they know the business. So they are probably the best equipped to design new procedures which are acceptable to them. Besides, it is another step toward them taking ownership of the system. Our task is to guide them through this process.

During the detailed analysis phase, we lay out the plan for transition into the new system. From here on, the design of the new procedures proceeds concurrently with our system design. Obviously, we will continue frequent interaction with the procedures designers to ensure a good match between technical and manual systems.

The transition plan should define how we will test the system, once developed. Users should be closely involved in all of the testing for best results. You should define the test environment, including how detected errors are reported, corrected, and released back for testing. A similar plan is necessary for transitions into the production environment.

User training is probably the next most important task in a transition plan. Define carefully the types of training users will require. For example, the majority of users will require training in using the menus and programs. Some users might need training in ad hoc query tools such as SQL*QMX and Oracle for Lotus 1-2-3. Plan training classes to be just before the system goes into production, so users will remember it. One way to gain acceptance is to designate *champions* from each group of your user community. These champions are closely involved in design and receive extra training, possibly during system testing and verification. They will spread the word on the features of the new system.

Another task is to plan how the system will be put into production. Will you need to run the existing system in parallel with the new one? Consider the consequences of a potential failure of the new system on the business. Can you really throw out the old system before the new system is verified? What extra personnel will be needed? Should all users be brought online at once, or one group at time, in some meaningful sequence?

What types of final verification of outputs is necessary? For example, accounting systems might be verified by using one-month-old data which is run through the system from beginning to period end closing. If the outputs match the old systems outputs, we have a good system. Does a similar approach satisfy the needs of other systems?

You have to resolve most of these questions with user management. They should take the lead in determining and defining your answers.

4.7 CASE Study: WI Sales System

As we presented the findings of the strategy study to the Widgets, Inc. executives, we started getting a lot of questions. *It seems that you understand how we work*, they said, *but how will this help us meet our business goals?* Then, we outlined the next phase of the project — aims to analyze the sales and warehousing application. We explained why warehousing could not be left out of the picture and how we could judge this from the strategy study.

The highest-priority business objectives were to offer specialist catalogs and more targeted marketing. To address these, we needed structure for tracking customer buying patterns. So we have to tackle the way Widgets handles their customer information. In addition, this project lets us seek ways to reduce order-to-shipping time down to 24 hours. There are notes with the data flow diagrams and ERDs which explain how we came to the conclusion that sales and warehousing must be treated as a single project.

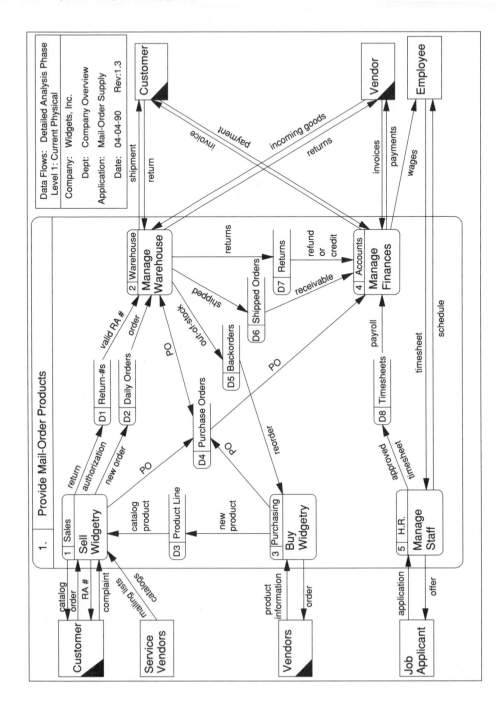

4.7.1 Notes on Data Flow Diagrams

The initial three diagrams show the detailed workings of Widgets' sales and warehousing operations at present. We gathered this information after another set of interviews — this time with lower echelons of the company. The second and third diagrams are explosions of the first, shown on the facing page.

1. Don't be surprised at the *clutter* on these diagrams. Paper-based systems, or even poorly partitioned applications, are always messy. If yours is neat, you have probably missed something, such as exceptions, or you have made assumptions which simplified it. Beware of making unwarranted assumptions — they will bite you in some later phase.

2. Processes in these diagrams are synonymous with the functions in the function hierarchy. Data flows are associated with them by CASE*Designer or directly in CASE*Dictionary.

3. Draw data flows with just names, initially. Then, after you complete the detailed entity relationship diagram, fill in the detail. Data flow detail consists of which entities and their attributes make up the data flow. You cannot define a data flow with any other components.

4. Use the CASE*Dictionary function detail report together with these diagrams. Remember that detail diagrams are insufficient, you need the narrative associated with it to get user verification.

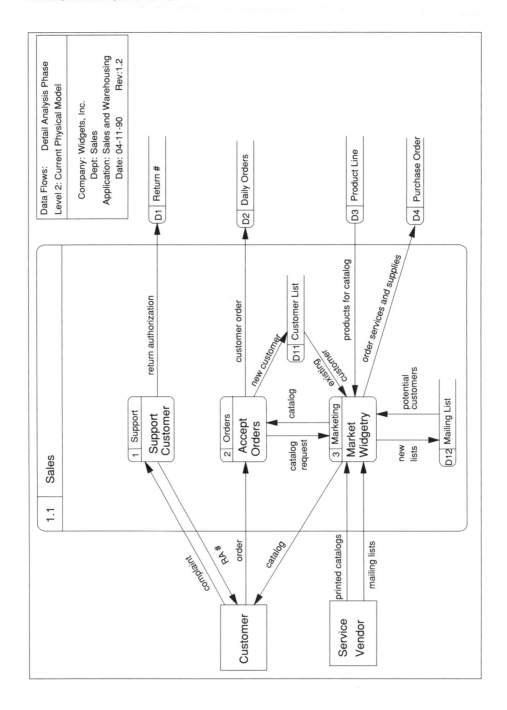

4.7.2 Notes on Sales Process Explosion

1. By this time, we are down to interviewing people on the shop floor, usually the foreman or supervisor level. This is so we can find out what really happens, as opposed to what company management would like to believe.

2. We identified two new internal data stores: customer list and mailing list. They are not used by other departments. There are many similarities between them.

3. This was our first chance to get real users involved in the analysis. Marketing staff came up with a whole bunch of ideas on improving their work. These ideas will affect the way we build the proposed functions and database.

4. Remember to give credit to users who supplied ideas. This gets them enthusiastic about what the new system will be able to do.

5. Throughout this process, sell the concept of the new system — not for money, but for the successful implementation later! Enthusiastic users are essential to the success.

6. Sales had no idea of the current inventory position.

7. Currently, there is no way to differentiate between *real* customers, that is those who purchased something, and mailing list customers. Mailing list is internal to the marketing department.

8. Note that within one group, the diagram is much less chaotic. This shows a well run group — only its interfaces to other groups are numerous and complex.

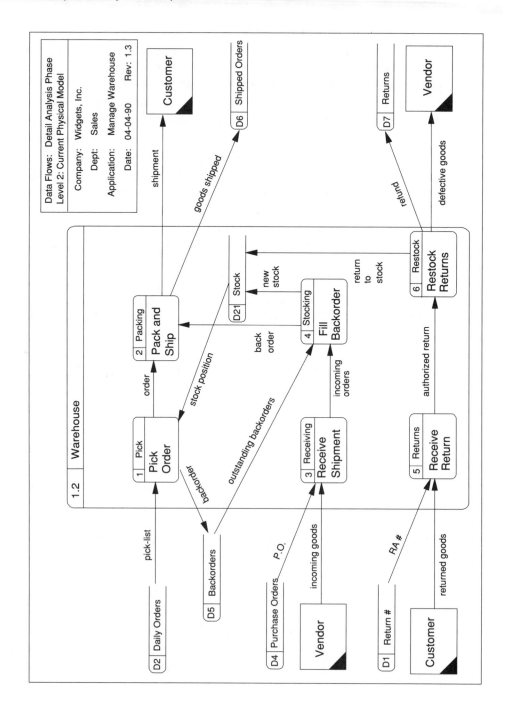

Data Flows: Detail Analysis Phase
Level 2: Current Physical Model

Company:	Widgets, Inc.	
Dept:	Sales	
Application:	Manage Warehouse	
Date:	04-04-90	Rev: 1.3

4.7.3 Notes on Warehousing Process Explosion

1. When we completed the sales data flow, there were a lot of data stores shared with warehousing. We suspected this during the strategy phase by looking at the mandatory relationships in the sales and warehousing entity-relationship diagram. We already had management approval to consider warehousing as part of this project, so we set out to investigate this department in depth.

2. Unfortunately, the warehouse manager was not very cooperative. He was miffed at being the target of a *productivity improvement* project, as our project objective was described within the company. *I run a very tight shop*, he said, *There is no room for improvement here*. This was the dragon on this project. There is always at least one on every project.

3. After much flattery, we got a tour of the warehouse and were introduced to the foreman. This person was our work around. We had to get the actual detailed working somehow. The high pile of paperwork on his desk was a good sign that our project could help the foreman.

4. Follow the tips mentioned earlier on drawing these data flows initially. Fill in the detail later. The reports you get are the same regardless of the level of the data flow diagram.

5. The warehousing group has no means of anticipating sales until they get the actual order forms. Then, it is too difficult to analyze them. They are under too much pressure to get the shipments out to worry about how many of each product there are orders for. They are too busy to optimize their picking and packing operations.

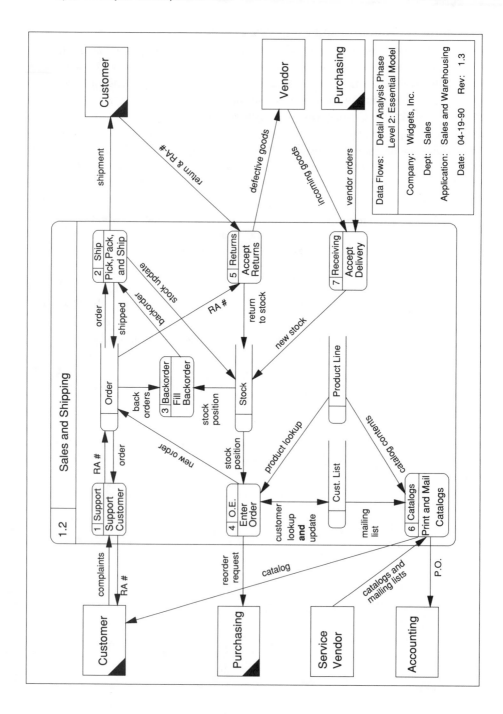

4.7.4 Notes on Combined Essential Model

1. This is where the fun starts. We pasted together the level 2 data flow diagrams on a large piece of paper; then we started eliminating processes and data stores.

2. We eliminated *batch* data stores to start with: Daily Orders (these are just unshipped orders) and Shipped Orders (these are just marked as shipped by warehousing). Shipped Order is simply an attribute of the Order Items entity. Accounting will be able to query them online when payments are being reconciled. So we eliminated a lot of paper shuffling and multipart order forms.

3. Picking and Packing processes are one logical function. The data flow between them is a physical transport of products. So we eliminate this data flow.

We added a few facilities to improve the working conditions of sales and warehousing staff. These were some of the suggestions made by them during interviews.

4. The current physical system has no means for the customer support staff to verify an order and date shipped before issuing a return authorization number. We could not estimate the losses to Widgets due to this oversight. However, in the essential model we added the facility for verification. Note that the RA # is just an attribute of the order items entity.

5. Order entry now has direct access to the current stock position to verify that an ordered item is in stock. The product entity provides online descriptions of products, so they no longer need a paper copy of a catalog.

6. Customer support did not have a catalog, at least officially. So they could not even be sure that a return was for a product that Widgets sold. In practice, they sneaked a copy of catalog from someone's desk every so often. In the new system, they can look up the item online.

7. We combined the mailing list and customer data stores so they are shared by order entry and catalog mailing personnel.

8. Order entry can request a catalog for a customer by simply updating the customer list. Since this list is shared, the customer automatically gets the next catalog.

9. Warehousing can query and get a summary of products and shipping quantities for a set of orders (pick, pack, and ship process). This process will help optimize their picking function. It allows them to carry a larger number of each product from the shelves to the packing area. They also get a better handle on the day's shipping volume and will be able to arrange warehouse staff schedules better.

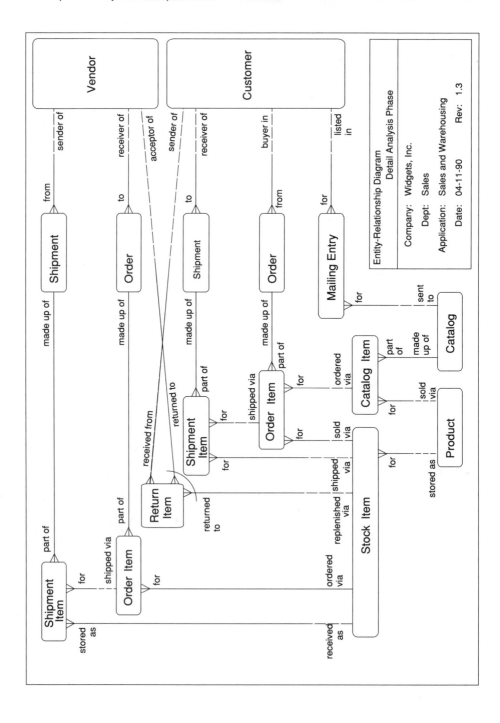

4.7.5 Notes on Detailed Entity-Relationship Diagram

1. We drew this diagram as we conducted interviews. Once we completed it, we could see a lot of similar patterns. This diagram is shown only to help you appreciate how we derived the convergent model. Notice the disparity in the number of entities in this diagram and the convergent model shown next.

2. Notice the complicated handling of return items. Return Items might be shipped back to the vendor or, if there is nothing wrong with it, returned to stock. Watch out for arcs, indicating an exclusive or relationship. These lead to complex database design.

3. We differentiated between orders from customers to Widgets and orders from Widgets to vendors. This is the easy way initially. However, the diagram becomes quite complex as a result of being so specific. But it helps us notice the patterns.

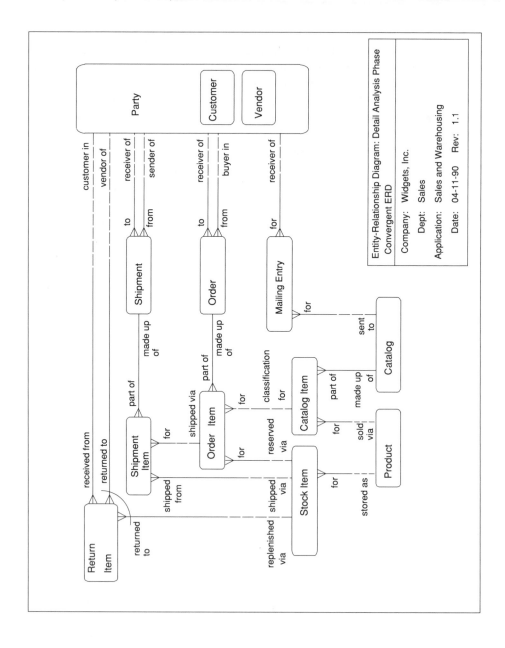

Entity-Relationship Diagram: Detail Analysis Phase
Convergent ERD

Company: Widgets, Inc.

Dept: Sales

Application: Sales and Warehousing

Date: 04-11-90   Rev: 1.1

4.7.6 Notes on Convergent Entity-Relationship Diagram

1. From the previous diagram, we noted similar patterns in the interaction with customers and vendors. In both cases, we have orders, order items, shipments, and shipment items. So we merged these entities.

2. We also merged the customer and vendor entities using a supertype, *party*. With this new entity, we can use relationships to define the *from* and *to* parties.

3. These two steps simplified the diagram a lot. We have fewer entities overall.

4. One side effect of this abstraction, we discovered that some of the items received at the dock are actually for office use at Widgets. For example, the file cabinet ordered for a manager's office is received by warehousing. With our convergent model could deal with these with two minor changes: the relationship between Order Item and Stock Item must become optional, that is a dotted line rather than the solid line shown here. Also Stock Item becomes a subtype of a new supertype entity called Asset Item. A new subtype called Office Item is part of this supertype. Office Item has information about items ordered for internal use. This entity will eventually form a part of the asset control system for office equipment. Of course, no such system exists at present — but our analysis uncovered the need for it. The asset control application was deferred as a topic for another project.

5

Analysis for Distributed Systems

So far we assumed that the database and the programs supporting business functions run on the same machine. Oracle is capable of running in a networked environment with the database running on one or more independent machines also. For potential scenarios consisting of networked environments, we need to do a little more analysis. The purpose of this analysis is to explore the impact of networked configurations. It provides the basis for choosing one configuration over another, although our judgment (and our users'!) is the final selector.

Some applications lend themselves to distributed processing or distributed databases. Distributed processing allows us to use the mips at the user's desk. Distributed databases give us flexibility for better local customization while retaining central consolidation. In our analysis, we have to collect information which will allow us to weigh these options. Just because distributed is the latest buzzword does not mean that your application is suited to it. In this chapter, we discuss analysis which you can do up front to decide whether a distributed solution is feasible. In particular, we address the following topics:

- We review the advantages and disadvantages of distributed processing and distributed databases. In particular, I suggest scenarios when distributed processing versus distributed database makes sense.

- We identify important areas for investigation, including geographic locations and business units. We examine techniques for determining whether your data is suitable for partitioning into distributed databases.

- We examine the performance costs of distributed processing and distributed databases. We discuss ways of estimating network traffic volume and throughput to determine the feasibility of distributing. The type of networks in existence between locations may make your decision easier; otherwise, you may incur significant costs to set up networking.

5.1 To Distribute or Not to Distribute

The advantages of running in a networked environment are obvious. All users have their own machines over which they have complete control. Any work on an individual's machine does not affect anyone else. For data sharing, we could install Oracle on a server machine shared by users on the network. Forms, reports, and other programs run on individual machines with the database server processes on the server machine. This scenario still uses a single shared database. However, networks have a limit on their transmission capacity. So we analyze the transaction which cause data transmission over the network.

The single database server scenario works well when all users are local to the server. The network is a local area network. We cover more details on potential networking configurations in a later chapter. What if the department is actually spread over long distances? Some users will be remote. We could connect their individual machines to the departmental server machine. But the speed of transmission of data goes down as distance increases. For better performance, these remote users may need their own local database server. So we need to partition the database such that each remote location gets its own server, and all servers communicate with each other for data sharing.

Let's consider another scenario. Suppose that more than one department wants to share data while retaining their departmental databases. Traditionally, this scenario was an argument for a single large machine located centrally. Oracle's networking capabilities offer nontraditional solutions. We need to consider a database that is logically a single database but is distributed over several physical machines. We need to analyze the natural partitions of our data for feasibility of such an installation.

There are many other reasons for partitioning data over several physical machines. For example, we might implement applications with local variations if we distribute the database. We could use cheaper, smaller hardware for such configurations than the traditional large central mainframe. We reduce perceived bureaucracy of the information systems group if we work in smaller groups that closer to the users and their machines — like mini information systems groups.

The basic analysis components we need are geographic information, traffic analysis for networks, and database partitioning. Note that Oracle's CASE tools support us in recording most of this information, even though, the methodology merely skims the surface upon the issues of such analysis. The information industry has only recently begun to acquire experience in distributing data.

5.2 Business Units and Locations

We recorded each of the company business units in the strategy phase. These units were not only logical groups, such as accounting, but also geographic locations, such as manufacturing plants. Noting the geographic distribution of company personnel is necessary for our analysis of distributed systems.

It is easy to identify geographic locations as business units. But how should we handle a location where multiple logical groups exist? For example, consider a printing company. Each printing plant in this company has its own accounting group, sales group, and so on. There are companywide policies on how the sales group functions, but, there are local variations. Should we treat each such group as a separate business unit? Yes! The main reason is that each sales group in a remote location is potentially a system. Another reason is that with local systems and information systems group, we can be responsive to local needs. Each location could have its own local system while sharing customer data with sales groups in other locations.

With local systems, we could implement minor variations in applications to satisfy their localized needs without affecting the rest of the company. Before we can do so, however, we need to define what data is strictly local and what data is a companywide resource. Here is one way of determining this.

You need a definition of each local group as a business unit. You also need a complete definition of functions or processes, and the data entities used by those functions. Then, we construct matrices, using the CASE*Designer matrix diagrammer for business unit against each of the functions and data entities.

One matrix shows not only that a unit performs a given function, but also how often. For example, if there is a local order entry group in each location, a business unit, we show the number of orders entered per hour (or per day, whichever is meaningful) for that unit. In addition, we note how many people do the function in each location. Thus, we can determine the average transaction rate per person per hour in each location. From our function to entity matrix, we can derive the size of that function, as a transaction. Then, we can calculate the amount of data that has to travel over the network.

5.3 Volume and Traffic Analysis

We record entity volume information in CASE*Dictionary. Unfortunately, this information is on an annual basis. For distributed database analysis we need volumes by location. The CASE*Designer lets us record it using the matrix diagrammer facility. A key to making the matrix diagram useful is to select a unit of time consistently. If you choose volumes per hour, stick to this unit of time throughout your analysis. Figure 5-1 shows a sample matrix of function versus business unit.

The business unit versus function matrix shows the frequencies of each function at that location. This together with the number of users at the location helps us determine the traffic. We use a function versus entity matrix to determine how many rows of an entity the function uses. We also record the specific attributes used by the function, not just entity.

The network traffic can be estimated for each function using the following formula:

```
Transmission size = sum (frequency of function
        * ( number of rows of each entity used
           * sum ( size of attributes used ) )
        + message overhead )
```

The overhead for a message depends on the type of networking software used.

Business Function \ Business Unit	Sales, Timbuctoo	Puchasing, Timbuctoo	Accounting, Timbuctoo	Warehousing, Timbuctoo	Sales, Europe	Purchasing, Europe
Support Customer	15 / Hour				20 / Hour	
Enter Order	40 / Hour				35 / Hour	
Accept Returns			15 / Hour	15 / Hour		
Accept Delivery		1 / Hour	1 / Hour	1 / Hour		1 / Hour
Fill Backorders				35 / Hour		
Pick, Pack and Ship				40 / Hour		
Print and Mail Catalogs		100 / Hour				80 / Hour

Figure 5-1: Volume-Frequency Analysis Matrix

5.4 Database Partitioning

We could divide the database in many ways. Relational theory says that we can partition any relation by columns or by rows. Assuming that each of our entity becomes a table, what types of relational operations will we need? The concern here is for distributed database operations. Each time we access a physically remote database, we suffer from the speed restrictions of a network. This restriction is almost acceptable on local area networks, but on wide area networks it is significantly slower. We also should be wary of loading the network to its capacity which will further degrade response times. Remember, users are not aware that they make a remote access when they perform a certain function.

The types of operations we need to avoid are those that cause a lot of data transmitted over the network. For example, joins of two or more tables where some of these are remote will cause the data from remote tables (yes, all of it!) transmitted over the network. So partitioning a tables by columns where columns on separate machines are accessed together, is not very good. Figure 5-2 illustrates a vertical partition. We can identify the best partitioning by columns from our function- entity matrix. Similarly, a horizontal partition of a table — that is, by rows — where we union the two separate partitions is also a poor choice.

Catalog Items (United States)				Catalog Items (Europe)		
Catalog #	Product #	Unit Price Offer		Catalog #	Product #	Unit Price Offer
1002	123-54	50.99		1002	123-54	35.45
1002	123-56	12.59		1002	123-56	9.99
1002	123-87	34.25		1002	123-87	29.99
1002	154-12	99.00		1002	154-12	58.56

Figure 5-2: A Vertical Partition

Customers (United States)					
Customer #	Customer Name	Company	Address	State	Zip Code

Customers (Europe)					
Customer #	Customer Name	Company	Address	Country	Post Code

Figure 5-3: A Horizontal Partition

Horizontal partitions, on the other hand, allow us to divide the data rather more logically. For example, we could divide customers by geographic area. Each local sales group in a location contains only those customers who are in the designated territory. Figure 5-3 illustrates a horizontal partition. The logical view of the customer table will be the union of all separate tables, but each location primarily uses their local piece only. We can identify such types of access from our function-entity matrix as well as the frequencies defined in our business unit to function matrix.

When we cannot partition data such that most of the access is to the locally stored portions, we need to consider other choices. A potential choice is to replicate data from headquarters' central system to each local system. For example, we might replicate the entire customer table at each location. There are obvious data integrity problems with this approach. How do we update the replicated local copies, and how do we keep them synchronized? Replication is an ideal solution for data that is updated very infrequently. For example, price sheets that are updated a few times per year are a good candidate. Otherwise, we need to warn our designers to build data integrity mechanisms for replication.

Another issue we identify for designers is when the system should update the replicated data. Ideally updates should be done at the same time to all remote systems, so that they are all in sync. However, even with technical support staff in each location, we face potential technical difficulties. For example, what should we do when one of the remote systems is down due to a local power failure?

By the way, individual system outage is a much larger issue. If some of our programs access a remote system for some validation, a system outage makes that program unusable. You need to consider this issue when choosing data for remote access. Consider the business requirements when making a decision. A noncritical function can suffer outages so long as critical business functions carry on. Also, your transition plan needs to define procedures in case of such outages.

Part 2

Designing Oracle Applications

This is where the rubber hits the road. All of those castles in the air that you built while analyzing user requirements need to come down to earth. To accomplish this transformation with the skill of a magician, we need experience in the tool set used for implementation. Theoretical knowledge, while laudable, is no substitute for battle scars.

Ironically, this phase is where many people start when building an application. So we could design an isolated, stand-alone system starting from here. Unfortunately, our applications are rarely stand-alone. They need to exchange data, or share a terminal, or are used by the same person. So we need the earlier phases — to help us avoid kludgy interfaces and associated headaches.

CASE tools help us quite a bit in this phase. Primarily, we use CASE*Dictionary to manage applications boundaries and objects shared across them. Diagramming support for logic specification in CASE tools is still evolving.

6

Database Design for Performance

Bitter experience shows that you have to design an application for performance — retrofitting performance is not only painful but time consuming. And, after all that work, success cannot be guaranteed! Relational DBMSs like Oracle make shuffling tables and columns very easy. Unfortunately, your programs are not immune to the cascading effects of restructuring the database. The time for modifying forms and reports, even with fourth generation tools, is significant.

In this chapter, we examine the variables which control the performance of an application. You must tackle performance issues in the design phase so you can establish appropriate measures for database structure, program specification, and coding. These measures are your primary standards and conventions for development. We examine four major themes in this chapter:

- User requirements analysis, to determine their real needs as opposed to what they say they want. Asking users for performance requirements is rather futile — they always want *instantaneous* response.

- Database design, including analysis of the volume information collected in the detailed analysis phase. We continue the controversy of denormalization as an aid to improved performance.

- Application design, including the types of constructions that lead to slower performance in Oracle. We will discuss the alternatives in the context of Oracle Versions 5 and 6.

- Database administration issues, including the types of utilities you will need as well as how to plan for disaster recovery.

6.1 Real Time, Real Quick, or Human Time

In my inexperienced past, I once asked a supervisor what their performance expectations were. Obviously (although it wasn't obvious then!) the reply was "We need a real time system." This supervisor was thoroughly fed up with waiting several seconds each time the staff ran some program. Knowing the capabilities of the system we were designing, I started back-peddling furiously. Fortunately, my more experienced teammate suggested further analysis. We found that actually 4 or 5 seconds was quite satisfactory for the work done by these users. In one or two functions, anything up to 15 seconds was okay.

Why is there such disparity? The media in our industry frequently misrepresents the technical meaning of the phrase *real time*. I differentiate between these concepts by calling them ***real time***, ***real quick***, and ***human time***. Real time is time at the nanosecond or millisecond level, where only machines dare to tread. This is the stuff of missile guidance, robotics, process-controlled manufacturing, and so on. Real quick, on the other hand, is a range between a fraction of a second to a few seconds. It is the time frame which people think of as very quick. Typically the maximum in this category is 1 or 2 seconds. We need this type of response in telephone order entry, hotel checkout desks, or airline reservations. Human time is any length of time larger than real quick. We use this measurement for any activity that can complete within a reasonable time, but longer times have no direct impact on the user's work. For example, a collections department chasing up receivables have plenty of time to prepare their questions before calling delinquent customers.

So, instead of asking users directly, here is what we can do. For each function or process performed by a user, we should observe how long it takes at present. Then we can question the impact of the current length of time on their work. For example, a data entry clerk whose performance is measured by the number of keystrokes per minute, receives a poor performance record, and hence less pay, due to a slow system. On the other hand, a telephone salesclerk who conducts 10 or 15 calls per hour does not suffer.

Be very careful when justifying a system based on productivity gains. Productivity gains from removing redundant functions do not imply faster system performance. In other cases, you promise faster performance from the new system even if users cannot benefit from it. Make sure users want and can benefit from speed improvement. In certain types of work, improving speed has no impact on productivity.

An important issue is whether users can change their way of working to take advantage of new facilities. If they do not develop work habits which take advantage of faster systems, productivity gains will not occur. Careful transition plans for new procedures are essential in this case, as well as increasing users' enthusiasm in the new methods.

6.2 From E-R Diagram to Database Design

If you used CASE*Designer and CASE*Dictionary for the strategy and analysis phases, database design is easily achieved. Essentially, each entity in the entity-relationship diagram becomes a table in the application database. Of course, if you are concerned about performance in your application, you need to do a little more work.

Let us discuss the simple case first, that is, converting from entities to tables as a one-to-one correspondence. Define the name of each table in the CASE*Dictionary *Table Definition* screen together with its corresponding entity name. Then, use the *Default Database Design* utility to get CASE*Dictionary to generate column definitions from the attributes of the corresponding entity.

CASE*Dictionary uses relationship information to derive *foreign* key columns automatically. The generated column names are long-winded, especially for foreign key columns. So edit them to your liking. You will need to define *tablespaces* (for Version 6 databases) or *partitions* (for Version 5 databases) discussed in Section 6.4. But, your simple database design is essentially complete. In earlier versions of CASE*Dictionary, this simple definition was all you could do.

Version 4.1 and later versions of CASE*Dictionary allow you to specify more than one entity for a table. You need this facility for designing high-performance databases where you choose to denormalize tables.

Note that for simple applications involving small databases, this approach is sufficient. The default database and index design is adequate for these cases. If your application contains large volumes of data, you really ought to look further. Ignore the protests of theorists who insist on pure relational normalized models and at least investigate some of the other avenues before making your decision.

6.2.1 When to Denormalize?

Designing a database for performance involves assessing the trade-offs between faster access and duplicated data. Duplicated data requires more complex data integrity enforcement algorithms and, hence, more complex programs. To speed access, we examine the types of access needed by the performance-critical functions and the impact of using normalized structures.

Concentrate your efforts primarily on the performance-critical functions, that is, functions requiring real quick response times. In most applications, these functions are a small portion of the entire application. For each of these functions, identify the entities accessed or modified by the function. In addition, you need information on the frequency of function execution and entity volumes involved, that is, number of rows affected. You should obtain reports from CASE*Dictionary for these frequencies and volumes, if you recorded them in earlier phases.

The types of operations that potentially slow the execution of a transaction are:

- The number of tables (or entities) to be joined. For a self-join, count the table once for each occurrence in the join. For example, if a table is joined to itself once, count two occurrences.

- Calculation of derived data values, where the base column values do not change. For example, once we complete entering an order, the order items do not change. Thus, our calculation for order total has base columns, the *amount* column in order item, which do not change. Such calculations performed on a large number of rows at runtime slows response time.

- Joining with many reference data entities — such as organization type, customer type, and so on — where we obtain some textual description from reference data entities. Such entities increase the number of tables in a single join.

- Any retrieval which does not use an index. Without an index, Oracle has to read every row in the entire table to select the data requested. We discuss indexes in the Section Access Methods and how SQL statements affect their use in the next chapter.

- Access contention when more than one user tries to update the same set of rows in a table. Oracle controls concurrency by locking rows being updated by one user. All other users must wait until the first user releases these locks. This contention has a significant impact on response time in Oracle Version 5 and Version 6 without the transaction processing option. We discuss locking mechanisms of these versions in Section Concurrency Control Options.

Normalization reduces the complexity of maintaining data integrity by removing duplicate data. However, it typically increases the number of tables accessed by a function. Take, for example, the computer industry's habit of using codes with everything. We use codes for color, category, class, grade — in fact, every item that offers a choice from a pre-defined list. In a normalized database structure, codes require a *reference data* table which includes a description for each code. Our purpose with such normalization is that if a description changes, we need to make the change in only one place.

But do items in such lists actually change? Suppose a car manufacturer chooses cyan as a new color. Is blue, the old color, no longer valid? In practice, we add to such lists rather than replace one description with another. We could store the description in our main table as well as in the reference data table. The reference data table is still useful for validation purposes. By the way, the old argument of preventing typographic errors becomes meaningless when we use *pick-lists* for entering descriptions. The reference data table is useful for presenting pick-lists.

Assess the trade-offs carefully before you choose to denormalize. Putting all of your data into two or three large tables is as bad as using dozens of tables. Denormalization techniques aim to improve performance by

- reducing the number of tables in a join operation, or
- reducing the number of rows in a table, or
- reducing the number of calculations performed at runtime.

Do not get carried away by denormalizing everything, however. Take into account the size of the row in the denormalized table. If this size is large, very few rows may fit into one block on disk. Thus, retrievals will be slow simply because you have to retrieve a large number of disk blocks to get your required rows.

6.3 Oracle Architecture

Oracle uses one or more operating system files for data storage. The size of each of these files is specified when you assign it to Oracle. Once assigned, Oracle treats the storage space in all of these files as a single contiguous space for data storage. Space is then assigned to a table as needed. When Oracle runs out of free space, it does not extend the size of these files. Instead, the DBA must detect this condition before it happens and supply additional space by adding another operating system file to the database.

For best results, a DBA should use contiguous files, that is, files made up of contiguous blocks on the physical disk. Under operating systems like UNIX, contiguous files in its *filesystem* are not possible. Oracle is not aware of the physical mapping of blocks on the disk, and so it assumes contiguity. You can use *raw disks* under UNIX, rather than filesystem files, to ensure contiguous space.

This explanation is, of course, a simplified view of how Oracle manages storage. In practice, Oracle allows you a great deal of control over how it chooses to apportion space to a database objects and where each object resides. The mechanics of this control depend on the version of Oracle and are detailed in these sections.

6.4 Version 5 Architecture

6.4.1 Storage Structures

Consistent with all of its interfaces, Oracle database tables are created, dropped or changed using SQL statements. Query language statements also let you create and drop indexes at any time, provided you have the appropriate access privileges. The software, as distributed, also contains several administration tools at the Shell level, so you can avoid having to type SQL statements.

Oracle implements the many relations per file approach. Each operating system file used in a database can be either a filesystem file or a raw disk. Thus, Oracle allows you to mix the use of raw disks and the UNIX filesystem. It also provides mechanisms that allow you to choose where each table resides.

An Oracle database storage structure actually breaks down into further subdivisions. Figure 6-1 illustrates this breakdown. Note that Version 6 changes some of the terminology associated with the storage structure to match DB2 terminology more closely.

Each *partition* can consist of one or more files or raw disks, in any combination. When you first create a partition, you must add at least one file to it before using it in any manner. Later, you can add more files to the partition as the need arises. Note that each file comprising a partition could reside on any disk. Thus, the size of the partition is not restricted, except by the available total disk space on your machine.

Tables relate to a partition only via a *space*. A space is simply a template for how Oracle should allocate storage for a table. Oracle associates this template with the table when you create the table. Therefore, to change these storage allocation templates for an existing table, you have to create another table with a new space definition, copy the data to it, drop the old table, and rename the new table to the correct name. A partition can consist of one or more spaces, but a space belongs only in one partition. A table must reside in one space. Oracle manages the allocation of *real* resources from the files belonging to a partition into the spaces that a partition contains. Hence, a space can span several files and disks. Since a table is defined within a space, the table can also span disks.

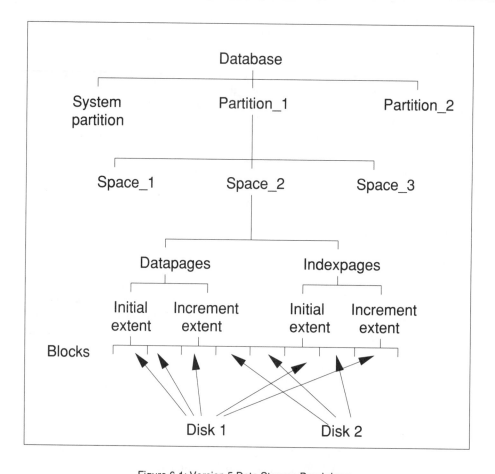

Figure 6-1: Version 5 Data Storage Breakdown

A space is further broken down into *datapages,* which define the space for data in tables, and *indexpages,* which define the space for indexes on the tables. The description of datapages and indexpages each takes parameters for the size of the *initial* and *increment* extents. The initial extent size is space that Oracle reserves when you first create a table. After this extent is full, Oracle will obtain an increment extent to extend the table. The same principle applies to the allocation of space for indexes except that the sizes used are based on the indexpages parameters.

The relationship between a space and a relation table is straightforward: you specify the space for a table when creating the table. The default space definition, in the *system* partition, is used whenever you omit specification of a space for a table. Thus, you can choose where a new table should reside, but once defined you cannot easily relocate it. When you define a space, you are really providing hints to Oracle on how to allocate the space in a partition. The sizes for the extents in datapages and indexpages are in terms of number of blocks which relate directly to Oracle's basic unit of disk I/O. This is why you need to choose carefully the parameters for datapages and indexpages in a space definition. You can, of course, change these parameters at any time, but they do not affect tables already created with the older parameter values. The new parameters only affect tables created after the change.

It should be obvious from this discussion that before you use any partitions, you need an existing empty file. If you use raw disks for your database, you would simply use one of these as the existing file. For UNIX filesystem files, Oracle provides the *ccf* (Create Contiguous File) utility to create empty files of a specified size. The name of this utility might be confusing, since the file it creates might not be physically contiguous at all, under UNIX. It is contiguous if you use raw disks. By the way, using raw disks you may gain significant performance improvements because of the contiguous blocks.

A common blunder is to assume that filesystem files will automatically keep extending as you add more data (provided that you escape the dreaded UNIX *ulimit* problem!). Not so with Oracle: it does not extend a file once it is added to a partition, and nor should you! Attempting to run ccf on an existing database file to increase its size *zaps* all of its contents, bringing down the wrath of users on your head.

In addition to the database files, Oracle also uses a *before-image* file. This file holds data for transactions in progress in order to provide *read consistency*. In this read consistency model, whenever you change a retrieved row, the data prior to the change is held in the before-image file. Thus, a user will see a consistent snapshot of data even if other users have changed some of the rows since the retrieval. Although you do not directly access this file, its size is an important criteria for design. Typically this file must be at least half the size of the database. A larger size is necessary if typical retrievals contain a large number of rows, the number of concurrent users is large, or users perform queries which last a long time. Only those queries which result in updates should be included in your estimate. Don't forget to include background and batch processes when counting concurrent users.

6.4.2 Access Methods

B-Tree Access:

The standard Oracle indexes are B-tree indexes. This type of an index is very versatile. Oracle also supports compressed B-tree indexes.

Oracle stores indexes together with the table data in a space. Remember that the space definition, discussed in Section Storage Structures, included parameters for indexpages. Oracle uses these parameters when you create an index. An index, in Version 5, is in the same partition and space as the table to which it refers. For optimal access, an index should fit mostly into the initial extent. Making the size of the initial extent sufficiently large for an index ensures that the index occupies contiguous blocks. Each increment extent might not be physically close to the initial extent on the disk.

An index can consist of several fields concatenated to form a composite key. The maximum limit on the size of an index key is 240 bytes including 1 byte separators between each field. The fields comprising a composite index need not be in any particular order within the record. Each field can be ordered in either ascending or descending order; by default they will be in ascending order.

There is no limit on the number of indexes you can create on a single table. But assess the performance trade-offs between improved speed of data retrieval versus degradation in speed of insertion and updates. Each time you insert a row or update an indexed column, Oracle has to update all of the corresponding indexes.

Clustered Storage:

Oracle provides intertable clustering, that is, storing data from more than one table close together. Typically, tables which share a column are ideal for clustering. Storing this data close to each other minimizes the amount of disk I/O Oracle needs to perform when accessing the data from both tables together.

Oracle implements clustering by means of a *cluster key*. This key can consist of up to 16 fields corresponding to the appropriate fields in the tables to be clustered. In our customer orders example, we might choose order number as a cluster key to join the order table and the order items table. Oracle can cluster a maximum of 32 tables in a single cluster. The steps in creating and using a cluster are

1. Create a cluster using the SQL *create cluster* statement. Note that you can associate a cluster with a space definition.

2. Create each table to be clustered with the *create table* statement including the cluster clause. Note that you have to specify the table's cluster key in the cluster clause.

3. Load data into the clustered tables.

Given enough spare space in the database, you can cluster an existing table. The basic principle is to create the desired cluster definition, followed by creating each table under a different name. In this case, steps 2 and 3 can be combined into a single SQL statement to load the data from the existing table into the new table during creation. Then, you can drop the old table and rename the new table to the desired table name. You need extra spare space because until you drop the old table, the database actually contains two copies of the data.

It is possible to cluster just one table with this clustering scheme, that is, intrafile clustering. This type of clustering is useful only when the key columns can contain many duplicate values. Thus, clustering one table whose key is always unique is really not worthwhile.

Clustering data really involves rearranging the way data is stored. Thus, changing existing tables to a cluster involves a significant shuffling of data. Clearly, you perform this type of database restructuring while others are using the database at your own peril.

6.4.3 Concurrency Control Options

Oracle implements its own concurrency control mechanisms using the system global area, SGA, under UNIX. It provides explicit and implicit locking mechanisms for a transaction, at table and row levels. The default locking level on SQL*Forms update is row level. Internal Oracle functions, such as the data dictionary cache, also use locking.

Oracle provides three types of locks: ***shared, exclusive***, and ***share update***. By default, Oracle provides committed read level of isolation (called *read consistency* in manuals). It implements a ***before-image*** file which contains a copy of the data at the time of query for each user. Hence, a user always obtains a consistent view of data even though others might have updated the same rows in the database. A dirty read level of isolation is not possible in the Oracle implementation.

The cursor stability level of isolation is rather more complex. You have to use a share update lock which operates at row level. You would obtain this type of a lock using either of these statements:

```
LOCK TABLE table-name IN SHARE UPDATE MODE [NOWAIT]
or
SELECT ....... FOR UPDATE OF column-name
```

This type of a lock prevents someone else from updating the data you are reading and from explicitly locking the entire table in exclusive mode. It does not prevent others from reading the selected data. Other users can obtain share update locks on the same tables.

There are two ways of achieving the repeatable read level of isolation. One way is by using the shared lock which only operates at the table level. In this case, you are preventing other users from performing any updates to the table, although they can read it, until you release the lock. The other way is by using a share update lock which operates as an intention lock at row level. With this lock, other users could still obtain a share update lock on different rows, but their updates will not be applied to the database until you release the shared lock on the table.

You would only use an explicit exclusive lock on a table if you wanted to make extensive changes affecting a lot of rows. Obviously, while a table is locked no one can update any data in it, so you would not do this at peak database usage times. Note that even with an exclusive lock, other users can still read data from the locked table. Implicit exclusive locks occur automatically whenever you change anything in a table; that is, when you use an insert, update, or delete statement. Oracle locks the entire table for the duration of the change. Implicit locks occur whenever you use a SQL statement, whether embedded in a programming language interface, in SQL*Plus, or in SQL*Forms.

If you cannot obtain the lock you want, Oracle normally just waits until the lock becomes available. You can control this default, however, by specifying the ***nowait*** option. There is no way of specifying a ***timeout*** period; that is, wait for the specified time and then, if the lock does not become available during this period, return. You can simulate this yourself with a ***busy-wait*** loop in your program.

Oracle also provides mechanisms for transaction level controls based on the use of locks and the SQL ***commit*** and ***rollback*** statements. Note that Oracle does not supply a specific start of transaction statement. The start of a transaction is implied by the first executable SQL statement. The end of the transaction can be a commit statement, a rollback — that is, abort transaction — any data definition statement such as create or rename, or when you log off from Oracle. Oracle can also automatically unravel transactions in progress when errors such as deadlocks, or abnormal terminations occur.

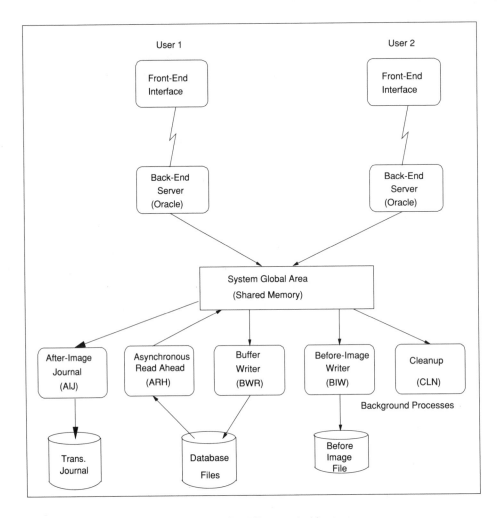

Figure 6-2: Version 5 Process Architecture

An *after-image* journaling facility supplied by Oracle can be used to keep a continuous record of changes to the database. With this facility, you can recover from disastrous situations such as disk head crashes which destroy all database data. Remember, from our discussion in Chapter 3, that such a facility must be used in conjunction with regular backups of the database. After a disastrous loss of your database, you will consider the effort expended in backups and journaling well worth it! Even users who complained of the overhead of using journaling will appreciate not having to manually repeat all transactions since the latest backup.

6.4.4 Process Architecture

Oracle uses a process architecture that is unusual in the UNIX environment. Figure 6-2 illustrates the processes used by Oracle Version 5. Note that the ***background processes*** shown must be running before a user can access the database. One set of these processes exist for each application database. Typically you might start these processes at UNIX boot time by including the start-up procedure in the boot time Shell scripts. Alternatively, you can start them manually at will by running the ***ior*** utility. Version 6, optimized for transaction processing, changes the process architecture to obtain performance improvements.

Oracle uses shared memory to implement the ***system global area***. As shown in Figure 6-2, all user processes access this area indirectly through the back-end server process. In addition, communication between the front-end and the back-end processes can be via another shared memory segment, though you can choose to use either pipes or message queues. Pipes are the recommended method. You make this choice once for the database in Oracle's initialization parameters file, ***init.ora***. There is one init.ora file for each independent database instance which is identified by a system id (ORACLE_SID). Parameters in this file can be changed at any time but take effect only when you start the Oracle background processes.

Multiple databases, one per application, can be set up on one machine. However, you cannot easily use more than one database from one program. When multiple Oracle databases exist on one machine, users choose the one they wish to use by setting the Shell environment variable, ORACLE_SID. Each application database has one system id, SID. For portability, choose an SID which is four alphanumeric characters or less.

Oracle uses the ***system global area*** to buffer data and to share it between users. You can tune the allocation of memory in this area to each of the Oracle buffering and locking functions by changing the ***init.ora*** parameters file. You can determine the effectiveness of the memory allocation using the Oracle performance monitoring utility, ***ods***.

6.5 Version 6 Architecture

Version 6 kernel comes in two different flavors: vanilla and with the transaction processing option. The primary difference between them is the implementation of row-level locking available with the transaction processing option. Version 6 with transaction processing option typically has a higher price than the vanilla Version 6. However, many applications with high transaction volumes or requiring concurrent access to tables benefit greatly from its row-level locking mechanisms.

Oracle has made several architectural changes to the DBMS kernel in Version 6. For example, the background processes which constitute an instance of Oracle are different. Data storage is similar to Version 5, although there are a few terminology changes. There are also a few additional administrative facilities to help DBAs manage storage and partial backup and recovery of the database. The primary changes are in the system global area which are mostly transparent to programmers and users. DBAs need to understand some of these changes since database tuning considerations are quite different. These changes can improve performance significantly in some applications. Before discussing the design issues for this architecture, we need familiarity with its concepts. You also need to be aware of some of the ANSI compatibility options available in this version.

6.5.1 Storage Structure

Version 6 has some architectural changes which improve the database administration process. The storage structure implements the concept of a ***database***. Figure 6-3 illustrates the new storage architecture. In Version 5, there were no formal mechanisms to name a database — an instance implied a database. Version 6 implements SQL statements, such as *create database* and *alter database*, to manipulate parameters associated with a database such as its name. An ***instance*** is a set of processes and shared memory which make a database accessible to users. An instance can open exactly one database. On some operating systems, notably, VMS on clustered VAX machines, more than one instance can open the same database. We discuss the process architecture later in this chapter.

The physical storage of a database consists of one or more operating system files. Each operating system file is part of one ***tablespace***. You can place tables, indexes, and other objects in a specified tablespace. Oracle database dictionary tables and associated indexes always go into a default tablespace called *system*. The system tablespace also holds any objects created without specifying a tablespace. You can create new tablespaces and change their parameters via the SQL statements, create tablespace, alter tablespace, and drop tablespace.

Superficially, a tablespace is similar to the combination of Version 5 partitions and spaces. Here are some important differences. You can associate tablespaces with users by granting them security privileges on tablespaces. You can assign a default tablespace for a user to hold any tables or indexes created by the user. You can define a quota for a user to control potential space hogs. You can also define a tablespace as the default temporary tablespace to hold any temporary tables created by Oracle when executing that user's queries.

A tablespace can be taken offline for backup without affecting users who are accessing data from other tablespaces. Thus, you could perform maintenance functions without ever shutting the entire database. You need not take a tablespace offline prior to backing up the component operating system files. Online backup requires that you use the ***archivelog*** mode, and indicate the start and end of a backup using the *alter database begin backup/end backup* statements. This causes Oracle to mark the backup start and end points in the redo log files. These marks are used during recovery.

A single table cannot span tablespaces. However, a table can span multiple disks due to the operating system files that make up a tablespace. You can place an index on columns in a table in a different tablespace from the one holding the table. Thus, you can balance I/O between separate disks by the placement of tables within tablespaces and the placement of indexes on columns of these tables. Distributing I/O across physical disks in this manner helps improve performance.

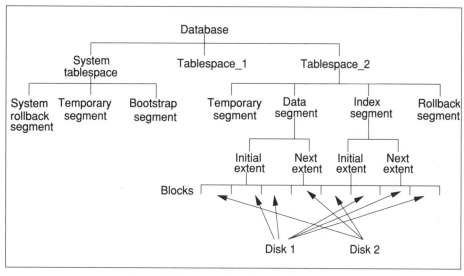

Figure 6-3: Version 6 Data Storage Breakdown

Space within a tablespace is divided into ***segments***. A data segment holds data for a table. Creating a table implies creation of its data segment. Similarly, an index segment holds data for one index. Oracle automatically creates temporary segments during the execution of a query as needed. The bootstrap segment resides in the *system* tablespace. Creating a database implicitly creates this segment. It holds the database dictionary information when an instance opens a database.

A tablespace also holds segments called ***rollback*** segments. Rollback segments hold information about transactions in progress. When you rollback a transaction — that is, undo its effects on the database data — Oracle obtains information on that transaction's effect from the rollback segment in order to undo them. You can create and change rollback segments with the SQL statements *create rollback segment*, *alter rollback segment*, and *drop rollback segment*. Multiple rollback segments may improve performance when you have more than one tablespace, or when many users concurrently use the database.

Oracle also uses rollback segments for implementing ***read consistency***, similar to the way Version 5 uses the ***before-image*** file. You can define multiple rollback segments for an instance. Each instance must have its own set of rollback segments. An instance claims rollback segments at start-up time. Thus, in order to incorporate newly created rollback segments, you need to shut down and restart an instance. Rollback segments can be public or private. Most of your rollback segments should be public. You only need private rollback segments when you use multiple instances sharing a database such as with clustered VAXs.

6.5.2 Access Methods

There are few changes in the access methods implemented in Version 6. B-tree indexes are still the primary means of improving search and retrieval access. Oracle has not changed its SQL optimizer in this Version. So our discussion under this heading for Version

5 still holds for Version 6. The only notable change is that the default index structure in Version 6 uses rear compression only. Version 5 default for indexes causes both front and rear compression.

6.5.3 Concurrency Control Options

Vanilla Version 6 implements a similar locking method to Version 5. Version 6 with transaction processing option has more sophisticated row level locking mechanisms. There are actually two types of locks: latches, which control access to the shared memory structures, and locks, which control access to data. Since locking is intricately tied into the way Oracle background processes work, I defer this discussion until Chapter 11, where we discuss the effect of locking on performance as well as how it works.

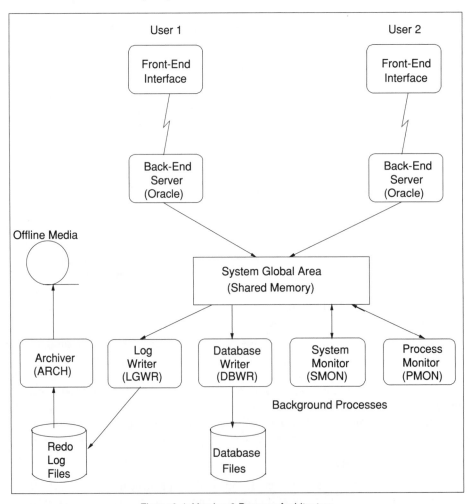

Figure 6-4: Version 6 Process Architecture

6.5.4 Process Architecture

Figure 6-4 illustrates the process architecture of Version 6. Superficially, the processes in Version 6 are similar to those in Version 5. The notable differences are in the timing of writing data from the system global area to the physical disk. Here is how these processes interact.

When you start up the database, the system global area is initialized and the background processes start running. Oracle uses the *init.ora* parameters and the control file to initialize the database. At this time, there will be minimal information in the system global area, for example, which operating system files comprise the database. Oracle uses the control file throughout the time when the database is up and running. The background processes are also up and running throughout.

When a user connects to the database, via some interface utility such as SQL*Forms, the user front-end process and the back-end Oracle process (also called a *shadow* process) start-up. This two process architecture is sometimes called a ***two-task installation***. On some operating systems, you can install the front-end interface and back-end as a single process. This single-user process architecture is called a ***single-task installation***.

As the user retrieves some data, by performing a query, the back-end process retrieves the requested data into the data buffers of the system global area. It also retrieves the related dictionary definitions into the dictionary cache. From the data buffers, it passes the data to the front-end process. If another user also requests the same data, the associated shadow process retrieves it from the system global area, rather than going to the disk files.

Note that under the UNIX operating system, the back-end process must have special privileges to allow it to access protected database files. The back-end process typically runs with the same privileges as the background database processes such as DBWR. Thus, if you use a single task architecture under UNIX, you may risk unintentional damage to the database or the SGA due to errors in your programs.

Oracle writes any updates applied by a user front-end into the system global area. At the same time, it copies the relevant information to the rollback segment, so that Oracle can reconstruct the old data if necessary.

When the user commits the updates, the associated shadow process marks the updates as committed in the SGA and writes the committed data into the redo buffers. Then it triggers the redo log file writer (LGWR) to write all changes pending in its buffers to the redo log file. It may write pending uncommitted transactions from other users as part of this write. Commit processing is complete as soon as redo logs are written, and the user can proceed with other operations. If LGWR needs to switch to another redo log file, it initiates a ***checkpoint***, that is, wakes up the database writer to synchronize SGA buffers with database files.

Throughout this time, the database writer (DBWR) process periodically checks for changed data buffers. The user's shadow process may also awaken DBWR if the shadow process is unable to find free data buffers. DBWR writes the least recently used SGA buffers to the database files, and marks these buffers as free. Notice that there may be time lag between the commit processing and the database writer process writing the change to the physical files. The physical database files may not always be up to date with respect to committed transactions. However, the database recovery processes can always use the redo logs for up-to-the minute transaction recovery. This is one of the major differences between Version 5 and Version 6, resulting in faster transaction commits.

The redo log is written to multiple files in a circular fashion. Thus, when the first log file is full, the log writer switches to the second file. The first file can be backed up anytime after the switch. If you use only two redo files, you must backup the first file before the log writer needs to switch back to it. This time period depends on the number of transactions occurring on your system.

You can automate the backup of redo log files by setting up the archive logger process. You must set this process at the time of starting the database. The archive process copies a redo log file when it is full, so that the log writer can reuse it. Redo log files should be on a fast disk while the archiving destination could be a tape.

You should use a minimum of two redo log files. For applications with a high volume of update, add, or delete transactions, you can either use more log files or larger size log files. Increasing the size of log files increases the length of time between archiving. This may result in losing more transactions if you suffer the disaster of a disk crash. I would recommend that in a high transaction volume environment, the size of your redo log should be approximately equal to one hour's transactions. With this size, you are likely to lose only one hour's worth of work. You will have to guess at the size, since there are no algorithms to estimate it from the number of transactions.

As an additional protection, define a database checkpoint at the appropriate number of transactions. Checkpoints will force the database writer to synchronize the physical files with all changed buffers. But beware of frequent checkpoints that will momentarily degrade system performance.

6.6 Design Considerations

There are two areas of design you should pay particular attention to database design and physical implementation design. Database design considerations are table definitions, indexes on tables, and how well indexes serve the application access needs. Physical implementation considerations are how to place database files on disks, backup and recovery plans, and integrating with the operating system facilities.

Table definitions and indexes have an enormous impact on the performance of the application. The optimum design requires a careful assessment of trade-offs for which database designers and application designers need to work very closely. Unfortunately, most large corporations divide the design functions between two rather independent groups: database administration and application development. Both groups need hands-on experience in both sides of the project. The best design team will have members from both groups dedicated to the particular application at hand, regardless of their separate reporting hierarchies.

One such large corporation that I came across insisted on separating the design tasks. Their application designer was a recent graduate from university and had little practical experience in building applications, even less in building relational database applications. The DBA group consisted of two people who had a lot of data modeling experience. Unfortunately, they had little knowledge of their operating environment or of physical implementation issues and internals of Oracle. Endless number of meetings and status reports later they managed to complete development.

Their first database design was fully normalized (just like the book says!) and had no index definitions at all (physical considerations are not important in relational technology!). Needless to say, they ran into snags when their batch reporting program took 20 hours to run. Just creating appropriate indexes reduced the runtime of this report to 4 hours. Rearrangement of their data distribution on disks reduced another hour. We received many commendations from the operations group who had headaches watching the available resources dwindle on their system monitor.

6.6.1 Database Design Considerations

Determining the best indexing scheme for each table is not quite as simple as CASE*Dictionary leads you to believe. You can use the *default index design* utility as a starting point. However, review the application access needs extensively before finalizing the index design. Here are some tips:

Indexes on Table Columns

As a minimum, you need an index on each unique identifier (primary key) of the table, and on each foreign key. These keys may be made up of more than one column, in which case the indexes are called *concatenated indexes*. The trick to using indexes is in the order of columns in a concatenated index.

Rather than the intuitive sequence of columns in a concatenated index, use the column producing the most reduction first in the sequence. For example, consider an index consisting of the columns company code, account number, and transaction type in a *journal entry* table of an accounting database. If there are only two companies, the account number column reduces resulting rows much more than the company code column. Similarly, transaction type further reduces the resulting rows more than the company code. So the sequence of columns in your index should be account code, transaction type, and company code. Creating optimum indexes can make an order of magnitude difference in the execution time of query.

Storage Parameter Definition

With each table definition, you can specify certain storage parameters. In Version 5, *space* definition include the number of blocks in the initial extents and subsequent allocations. These allocations should optimize the number of contiguous blocks available to each table placed using a space definition. In Version 6, there are *storage* parameters in each table definition to specify initial extents, next extents, and minimum number to allocate at creation time. Aim to store the entire table in contiguous blocks, so that you minimize disk head movement delays. You can use default values for each of these parameters, but to improve speed, define storage parameters appropriate to the volume of table data. There are similar parameters for index definitions also.

Oracle uses minimum space for missing or null data values. In Version 5, there is no overhead for null values. Version 6 uses 1 byte of storage per null value whenever they occur in the middle of a row. When these null values are replaced by data, Oracle must expand the row to include it. Such expansions are called row pieces. Each block contains only one row piece.

Use the *pctfree* parameter when creating a table to reserve space within each block for such row pieces. You will need to understand how the application creates rows and how it updates them to determine the potential growth in the size of a row. If row size grows beyond the available space in a block, Oracle *chains* another blocks to store the extra piece of the row. Chained blocks can cause excessive access delays as they are not contiguous, and Oracle accesses them only through the block at the start of the chain.

The *pctused* parameter determines when a block has space available for inserting new rows. Oracle will insert rows while actual free space is more than pctfree and until the pctused level is reached. Thus it attempts to reserve pctfree amount of space for updates, and uses up to pctused amount of space for inserts. Oracle maintains a list of blocks eligible for inserts and a list of blocks eligible for updates.

Set pctused such that the block is as full as possible without using up reserved free space. An algorithm for calculating pctused might be

$$pctused = (RS * FRS) / BS * 100$$

where

RS	=	number of rows that fit in one Oracle block
FRS	=	size of the fully populated row
BS	=	size of Oracle block
RS	=	(BS - block overhead) / (FRS + row overhead)
FRS	=	row size at creation + row growth size

Although this formula implies that you need an exact calculation, you can use approximate sizes at design time. Err on the side of an overestimate if you use approximate sizes. Realize that there is no defragmentation utility in Oracle, not even a report showing where fragmentation occurred. The only way to defragment your database is to take a complete export, re-create your database with initialized files, and then import the data back. This process may be reasonable on small databases, but for large databases spanning many disks, it is a nightmare. So it is worth spending some time thinking about this issue.

6.6.2 Physical Implementation Considerations

These considerations deal with how to integrate the Oracle database issues with the operating system. We discuss where to place Oracle database files in the operating system, how to plan backup and recovery procedures, and setting up batch and interactive access.

Database Files

In Version 5, you need data files which are associated with each partition in the database. Locate these data files on a separate disk to distribute disk I/O. Remember that a table must fit within one partition. So which files are added to which partition depends on where your table lives. In addition, you need a before-image file. Its size depends on the number of concurrent users and the size of their transactions. Large number of concurrent users conducting small-sized retrievals each will require a large before-image file, approximately half the size of the database. Similarly, a small number of users conducting large-sized retrievals will also need a large before-image file. Don't forget those batch report programs: they also retrieve data. If you choose to use after-image journaling, be sure to place the journal files on a different disk from your database. This way you won't lose your journal file when a disk crash zaps your database disk.

In Version 6, there is no before-image file. Rollback segments serve this purpose. As a result, you will need more space in the database itself than in a Version 5 database. Be sure to allocate sufficient space in rollback segments to meet the needs of concurrent users' retrievals. Version 6 rollback segments contain only changed data as opposed to entire blocks as in Version 5. Thus, the size of rollback segments need not be as large as Version 5 before-image files. It is more important to create a sufficient number of rollback segments than worrying about the segment size.

Keep at least two copies of the control file in Version 6. Losing the control file is hazardous to your database's health. Simply make additional copies while the database is shut down, and modify the init.ora parameters to indicate the location of each copy of the control file. Oracle will keep all copies up to date. At least one copy should be on a separate physical disk. Keep the redo log files on a separate disk also to insure against disk failure. The archiver process should back these up periodically for offline storage, or you may back them up manually.

Distribution of Tables Among Tablespaces (Partitions in Version 5)

In order to balance disk I/O between multiple disks, you need multiple tablespaces. Make administration easier for yourself by using a one for one correspondence between physical disks and tablespaces. For example, each tablespace should contain operating system files from one physical disk. Then, place tables in tablespaces to evenly distribute I/O between disks. Function frequency and transaction size information is very useful in determining your distribution.

Use of Operating System Files

This consideration is closely related to the distribution of tables amongst tablespaces. Ideally, these files should be contiguous on disk. If you have no way of ensuring contiguousness, as on a UNIX filesystem, use UNIX raw disks as files. Contiguous blocks greatly reduces *seek* times when performing disk I/O, thus improving performance. On some UNIX systems, using raw disks has the added advantage: a power failure or system crash does not corrupt your database, since UNIX does not buffer raw disk I/O. Other UNIX systems support synchronous writes which Oracle uses.

Distribution of Data Among Oracle Extents

To maximize the benefits of contiguous files in a tablespace, you need good use of storage parameters on tables. Design these definitions such that the majority of data in a table resides in the initial extent. Use the *storage* clause of the *create table* statement to enforce these parameters.

You can, of course, simply use default settings for all tables. The defaults will always use the system tablespace. You can grow this tablespace by simply adding more files. However, to optimize performance you might wish to distribute database tables selectively over several physical disks. Here is one way to create a database with custom table distribution:

1. Estimate the size of each table and each of its indexes; include Oracle overheads.

2. Using the convention that a tablespace corresponds to one physical disk, create the appropriate number of tablespaces with suitable names in the Oracle database. For example, suppose the filesystems */db1* and */db2* represent two separate disks. You might create two tablespaces called **tabspace_1** and **tabspace_2.**

3. Determine how you wish to distribute the tables on physical disks.

4. In Version 5, use the ccf utility to create at least one file to be used in each partition. If you are using raw disks, just use their node names and change their ownership and access permissions for access by Oracle processes. Add one or more of these files to the partitions. In Version 6, create the tablespaces with the appropriate file names. The *create tablespace* or *alter tablespace* statements will initialize the files.

    In our example, we create the file **data1** in the /db1 filesystem and **data2** in the /db2 filesystem. Then we add data1 to tabspace_1 and data2 to tabspace_2. For optimal space usage, make these initial files somewhat larger than the total size of the tables you intend to store in them.

5. For each partition, if you are using Version 5, create a space definition with parameter settings appropriate to the tables to be placed there. Ideally, most of the table should fit into the initial extent. In Version 6, these parameters are part of the *storage* clause of the *create table* statement.

6. Create each table and its indexes specifying the chosen space definition. In Version 6, specify these storage parameters in the table definition.

Once a table is created and associated with storage parameters, you cannot relocate it easily. For extra space, add more files to the tablespace. If you want to relocate a table from one tablepace to another, you will have to save the data from the table, drop it, re-create it using a different storage definition, and then load the data back.

If you plan to run multiple applications in a single database, I recommend that you define a separate tablespace for each application. You will need to define the tablespace as default for each user of the application and grant them appropriate access privileges. This scheme has the advantage that you can take individual tablespaces offline and back them up individually without affecting users of other applications. You also isolate the effects of contention for rollback segments by allocating them in individual tablespaces.

6.7 Disaster Recovery Planning

Most operating systems buffer data written to their files. The database writer process will not know whether data was actually written to disk or not. If you have a choice of bypassing such operating system buffering, choose to do so for Oracle data files. UNIX offers such a choice if you use raw disks as data files. Under UNIX, this method also bypasses the need for filesystem checks which may recycle corrupted blocks from the file, and thus, unknowingly destroy your database. If you do not have such a choice, consider using an uninterruptible power supply with battery backup to insure against power failures. Such power protection is a good idea in any case, but make sure that you get one that switches really fast. Power conditioners are insufficient guard against power failures.

You should also plan for more mundane backup schedules so that you can recover the database when needed. The SQL*DBA utility in Version 6 provides commands to mark when an online backup was started in the redo log files. Make sure you take a physical backup (also called an image backup) using your operating system utilities of all the data files. An image backup is an image from Oracle's viewpoint.

Under UNIX, use the *dd* utility for physical backups of raw disks. With filesystem files, *cpio* or *tar* utilities are sufficient. This physical backup together with redo log file backups will allow you to recover the database to the last committed transaction.

There are more ways of recovering from corrupted databases in Version 6 than you are likely to use. However, be aware that you can recover from most disasters, with only a minor loss. Some of the more complex recovery methods, such recovering to a specific time, are documented in the release notes.

7

Application Design for Performance

We all know that poor design of a program results in poor performance. So, what makes for a good design? With the fourth-generation tools available with Oracle, the answer is no longer just *structured design*. You need to discard the techniques which were (and still are!) suitable for programming in a third-generation language. Unfortunately, application design for fourth-generation languages has very little theoretical foundation. Even CASE*Method is evolving in this part.

I describe some techniques which I find useful with Oracle tools. Realize that SQL*Forms defines a user interface style which we cannot change. We can only react to user actions. Our specifications, therefore, focus on reactions. The high productivity claims for these tools depend on fitting your requirements to their capabilities. Reports are little more tricky since we do have a choice of report generators. For batch processes, we fall back on industry standard specification techniques. CASE*Method recommends the use of action diagrams for such specification. We cover the following topics:

- Forms specification techniques which focus on defining what data to present to users, and what manipulations to perform based on user actions. We will review the specifications used by CASE*Generator in generating forms.

- Report specification techniques, with an overview of which report generators to use for which types of reports.

- Specification techniques for batch or procedural modules which might be written in a third-generation language or PL/SQL.

- Standards definitions needed prior to starting any coding. These standards will help you control the project. Remember, performance must be designed in; later retrofits are too expensive!

7.1 Performance Considerations

A good design is simple and elegant. However, we occasionally need to make compromises for faster performance. Such compromises must match the development tool used for a particular implementation. Also, we must make a reasoned decision about where to compromise during the design phase. Patchy solutions devised during development — or worse, during testing — can only yield inadequate solutions.

A primary requirement for good design is to know the style and mold of each of the tools you plan to use in development. We introduce the concepts implemented by some of the tools in this section. Later chapters discuss forms management and report writing tools in detail. Successful designers need to be experienced in using these tools in order to be aware of their flexibilities and limitations.

Another requirement is to understand the types of program actions possible and their impact on performance. Fourth-generation tools are very powerful — you can make them do a lot of work with very few statements. Unfortunately, fewer statements do not mean less work when they execute! When performance is critical in your application, you need to understand the amount of work involved in executing each statement. Then, you can judge the best timing for doing that work to offer good response to your users.

SQL*Forms implements data driven screen interaction. It performs best when your screen interaction model closely fits its style of working. For example, a block on the screen roughly corresponds to one table in the database. Insertions, updates, and deletions from this block operate on its corresponding table. Programming in SQL*Forms involves defining reactions to user actions. For example, when the cursor is in *field_a* and the user presses the *next field* key, you might want the cursor to skip *field_b* depending on the value of *field_a*. SQL*Forms calls such reactions **triggers**.

You can, of course, implement multiple tables on one screen. You can make such blocks and their underlying tables transparent to users through program triggers. However, the amount of work in such a screen might defeat your performance objectives. For example, a trigger consisting of several statements is inherently slower than if it consists of a single statement. Triggers causing database access are slower than are those which move the cursor around. My experience shows that increasing complexity of programming in triggers generally leads to slower execution. Thus, implementing a data entry screen which implements complex validation and which will be used by power typists is not a very good idea. Complex validation triggers will probably slow the response sufficiently to frustrate classic data entry clerks, especially if their performance is measured by keystrokes per minute! Remember, you only need a very slight degradation in response to frustrate such users.

Access to an Oracle database is via SQL. All of the application development tools with Oracle use SQL for database access. Even a C program or third party utilities such as JAM from JYACC, Inc., or ACCELL/SQL for Oracle from Unify Corporation must use it. So you must understand the power of SQL as well as its limitations for a good design. Using traditional techniques such as programmatically matching two files one record at a time will not run as fast as a join in SQL.

Some of the other pitfalls occur in unoptimized coding or inadequate database design. A database retrieval which does not take advantage of indexes will be slower. So pay close attention to your retrieval requirements, index design, and volume of rows retrieved. It is rarely a good idea to design your application independent of the database design. The two are very closely related.

When fourth-generation tools are inadequate for the task, you can use a third-generation programming language, such as C, Fortran, or COBOL. SQL is embedded into your program statements in such instances. In addition, Oracle provides an *array processing* feature to improve performance. Using arrays, you can retrieve multiple rows at a time into your program's memory area. Thus, you will reduce the interaction with the database and improve speed of execution.

Oracle allows sharing of the database between multiple users. However, careful design of concurrency control is essential for good performance. Version 5 and vanilla Version 6 reserve rows but lock the entire table momentarily when actually writing to the database. Version 6 with transaction processing subsystem implements row-level locking. Apart from choosing which model you need, your design must specify its best use. For example, you should specify whether locking is necessary for each transaction, and the best sequence of reserving tables.

You need sequencing for transactions which affect the same tables or share more than one to avoid deadlock conditions. Don't forget to release locks quickly, for example, commit changes to minimize the period of locking.

Concurrency control designs depend on understanding how users work through the day. We need to know which of them need concurrent access to the same tables, if any. Remember, even if they do not work on the same rows in the table, they may experience delays under Version 5 and vanilla Version 6.

There are other design decisions that affect performance. Oracle's architecture allows you to execute the programming utilities, such as SQL*Forms, on a workstation while another machine on the same network acts as the database server. We discuss such architectures in depth in later parts of this book. If you choose such an architecture, watch out for database access across the network. Network access is typically much slower than accessing a database on the local machine's disk. In addition, be careful of multi-step processing of data. Try to use PL/SQL for processing all steps on the database server and only transmitting the final result over the network. Otherwise, the intermediate results of each step cause the network traffic to be the performance bottleneck.

7.2 From Business Functions to Programs

The first task in application design is determine boundaries of each program from your logical model. (Note: I use the term program to mean an independently executable unit. Do not confuse it with other common uses of this term such as a source file containing code.) This translation is one of the hardest in a project, and yet methodologies provide little guidance in the task. We use only the lowest level explosions for processes from our DFDs or function hierarchies. Higher levels were necessary for understanding the big picture and for presenting it to our users.

We need to consider two aspects of a business function when deciding program boundaries: processes which are always performed together by one person and the tool used to implement the program. I use a rule of thumb: one program uses one tool, or in process-based architectures such as UNIX, one program is one process. The crux of the problem is: Which business functions should become a program? Let's start by reviewing the information we have that will help us determine program boundaries.

From the DFD logical model, we have a set of business functions which are essential to running the business. A single business function or a group of business functions becomes a single executable program. So start by separating business functions that represent manual activities in the new system. Typically, manual activities involve some physical movement, such as packing a shipment, or some person-to-person contact. They are closely tied to the new mechanisms you plan to implement in the new system. By this stage of the project, your users should be working very closely with you to design such new mechanisms. After all, they will carry out the designed manual procedures. Your role is to make your users aware of which business functions to automate. By the way, this type of design is where joint application development (JAD) techniques work very well.

What to do with the business functions you decided to automate? We need to group them logically. One way of determining a logical group is by using our function-entity cross reference matrices together with the business rules. For each business function, gather the list of entities used. Then, study the relationships between these entities in our entity-relationship diagram. Business functions affecting entities with mandatory relationships (solid line relationship) should be grouped together. Watch out that you don't end up with a single program implementing all of the business functions! Take into account the type of access each business function makes to these entities.

Group together business functions which insert new data: those which insert into several entities that have a mandatory relationship with each other. For example, consider the entity-relationship diagram and associated business functions in Figure 7-1. Business function 1.2.4 adds new occurrences to the *order* entity. There is a mandatory relationship between *order* and *order item* entities. So we group business function 1.2.4.2 with 1.2.4.3. The relationship between *order* and *customer* entities is also mandatory. Thus, we add business function 1.2.4.1 to the group. This grouping is, of course, intuitively obvious to a user: we should be able to add a new customer when taking an order. Our grouping allows us to enforce the business rules defined in the entity-relationship diagram and implements a natural progression of work.

Now, what about the business functions that update these same entities, such as updating order item shipping status? Obviously we group them together as well. But should this update group be different from the add group? The answer depends on what your development tool provides. Some tools, such as SQL*Forms, allow add, update, retrieve,

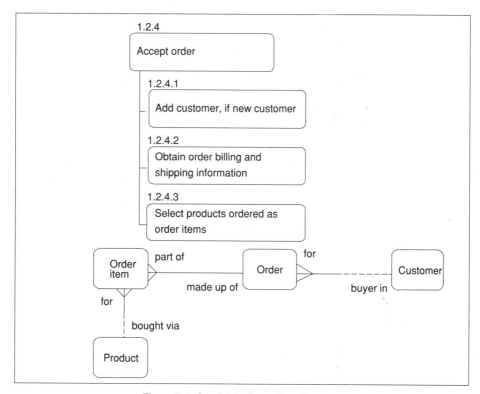

Figure 7-1: Candidate Group for a Program

and delete functions on any screen form you develop. In fact, you have to disable any of these deliberately if you want to offer them as separate menu options to users. So, if you plan to use SQL*Forms, add and update groups should one program.

Consider, as an alternative, JYACC's forms generator JAM. With this tool, you have to write separate code to add and update database tables. So you can choose to use the same screen definition with two separate sets of code: once to add new occurrences and once to allow updates. Each of these sets might appear as a separate option on the user's menu.

There is, of course, a separate business function to maintain *customer* data. This business function has overlapping functions with the foregoing order entry group. Ideally, we should be able to develop the customer entry and update form in a reusable fashion. With SQL*Forms, develop this as an independent form which is called up by the order entry program. If the response time for calling up a separate form is too long, then consider duplicating the code in Version 2.3 or earlier. SQL*Forms Version 3.0 allows you to share screen definitions in multiple programs. To make such design decisions, you need intimate familiarity with your development tools. In fact, a rule of thumb I find effective during design is: *If in doubt, try it out!* Don't wait until the coding phase to discover that you misunderstood a capability of your development tool. Then, *write down your experiment —* and give it to the programmer as hints at coding time.

Report business functions are rather more straightforward. Typically these business functions retrieve entities which are related to each other in some manner, mandatory or optional. If a business function appears to retrieve entities which are only distantly related — that is, with many intervening entities not included — ask your users to clarify the anomaly. You may be missing some relationship, or there is an implicit algorithm for the intervening entities which you do not know about.

Grouping business functions for periodic or batch runs, excluding batch reports, follows a similar logic to the forms business functions. Remember to account for the time factor in your decision process: business functions to be run daily are a separate natural group from weekly or monthly groups. The tools you might consider for implementing these business functions include PL/SQL, if you use Oracle Version 6, a third-generation language interface with PRO* precompilers, or SQL*Report (fondly known as RPT). SQL*Report, although intended as a report generator, does allow database manipulation. Be aware that Oracle may not support this product for long. SQL*ReportWriter is its successor for reports and PL/SQL the successor for procedural database manipulation.

Module design in CASE*Dictionary allows you to define details such as module name, implemented functions, and planned tool for implementation. Think of modules implementing one or more functions in terms of a cross-reference matrix. Similarly, you define the tables and columns used by a module in terms of a matrix. There are utilities which will generate module-column cross-reference matrices available. However in Version 4.1, the details of logic are free-form. You should set your own specification conventions for each tool. In future releases, these tools may implement techniques such as action diagram, and state transition diagram, which CASE*Method recommends. We discuss some of these techniques in this chapter, for completeness.

7.3 Forms Specification

Once you are aware of the capabilities of the tools, you will find writing specifications relatively simple. Functions which you might implement using SQL*Forms characteristically have verbs such as *maintain, add, update, delete, enter* in their descriptions. If you were less rigorous in the analysis phase, the verb *process* used in descriptions might hide some interactive forms based processing.

A forms specification needs to cover the following basics, which are illustrated in Figures 7-2(a)—(c):

- Layout of data on the screen, possibly with multiple pages.

- Relationship of the different blocks such as master/detail and the behavior of detail rows for each operation on the master. Such behavior is frequently called *block-coordination*.

- Data correctness and integrity requirements, including validation of individual data elements, cross-element validation, foreign key constraints, and so on.

- Navigation details, such as which fields have *pick-lists*, which user actions lead to movement between blocks, pages, and forms.

```
                            Order Entry
  ┌─────────────────────────────────────────────────────────────┐
  │  Order No.: _____          Date: _____                 │
  │                                                              │
  │  Customer No.: _____       Ship to: _____              │
  │                                                              │
  │  From Catalog #: _____       Pay with: ___                  │
  └─────────────────────────────────────────────────────────────┘

  Item No.  Product #  Product Name              Qty    Item Total
   _____   _____    _____      ____    _____
   _____   _____    _____      ____    _____
   _____   _____    _____      ____    _____
   _____   _____    _____      ____    _____
   _____   _____    _____      ____    _____
   _____   _____    _____      ____    _____
   _____   _____    _____      ____    _____

                                   Subtotal:      _____
                             Shipping & Tax:      _____
                               Grand Total:       _____
```

Figure 7-2a: Order Entry — Forms Layout

- Operations available from the form and details specific to the operation. These operations may be presented as a ring menu if your use third-party forms tools.

```
                            Order Entry
  ┌─────────────────────────────────────────────────────────────┐
  │  Order No.: _____              Date: _____             │
  │   ┌────────────────────────────────────────────────────┐     │
  │   │             Customer Information                    │     │
  │   │   Customer No.: _____    Name: _____        │     │
  │   │                                                     │     │
  │   │   Company: _____                       │     │
  │   │                                                     │     │
  │   │   Address: _____                         │     │
  │   │   _____                                │     │
  │   │                                                     │     │
  │   │   City: _____    State: ___              │     │
  │   │                                                     │     │
  │   │   Country: _____                         │     │
  │   │                                                     │     │
  │   │   Post Code: _____                         │     │
  │   └────────────────────────────────────────────────────┘     │
  │                                                              │
  └─────────────────────────────────────────────────────────────┘
```

Figure 7-2(b): Order Entry — Customer Window Layout

You could use SQL*Forms itself to design the forms layout. It does have a reasonable screen paint utility. The easiest way is to use the default layout features of SQL*Forms, and then use the screen painter to pretty it up. Unfortunately, you can only do this if your database design is complete and tables created. If application design and database design proceed in parallel, as is common, you do not have tables to base your forms layout definition on. Without tables, your use of SQL*Forms screen painter is less effective. It would be almost as much work to later add table and column names to the form as to re-create it from scratch.

Prog: Order Entry   **Date:** April 1, 1990 **Rev:** 1.0
Dept: Sales
Application: Sales & Marketing
Utility: SQL*Forms (JAM or ACCELL/SQL)
Table Access:
Update   - orders, order_items, customer
Select & Validate   - product, catalog, catalog_items
Block Co-ordination:
Master: Orders. order_number
Detail: Order_items.order_number
Coordinate Operations:
Query, Browse, Insert (at least one order item required), Delete (delete all order_items before the order), Create record, Clear block, Clear record
Column Handling and Validation:

Name	Description
order_number	Generated using sequence ord_seq (Version 6).
order_for_customer	Required. Customer must exist, add a new one using customer information window.
ship_to_customer	Same as order_for_customer
order_from_catalog	Required. List of values on catalog table.
pay_method	M = Mastercard, V = Visa, X = American Express, D = Discover, C = Check, I = Invoice for later payment.
product_number	Required if row exists. List of values on catalog_items: product_number.
product_price	Calculate: product_qty * catalog.items.unit_price_offer
subtotal	Calculate: subtotal + product_price
ship_tax	Calculate: 6% of subtotal
gtot	Calculate: subtotal + ship_tax

Figure 7-2c: Order Entry — Form Specification

Master/detail blocks are more complex than you would imagine. The most obvious coordination is for queries. We discuss an example of coordinated blocks for queries in the next part of the book. However, the design must specify the type of coordination for insert, updates, and deletes. For insert or update operations, specify whether a master row without any detail rows is acceptable. As an example, we accept rows in the customer table without any rows in the orders table. On the other hand, an order without any order items has no meaning (usually!). The business rules in the entity-relationship diagram should be very helpful in determining such design issues.

Delete operations in coordinated blocks should also specify whether to enforce the business rule. Can we allow detail rows which are not attached to any master row, that is, *orphan* rows? So should a deletion of the master row imply deletion of all associated detail rows, that is, cascade the deletions? Alternatively, should we deny deletion of the master if associated detail rows exist? We should derive these answers from the relationships in the entity-relationship diagram.

CASE*Generator requires explicit answers to such questions before generating a form. You enter such details in the CASE*Generator module definition screen. Note that CASE*Generator is a separate product which presents its menus under the CASE*Dictionary Implementation Phase menu.

You need to specify which tables and columns each form uses. The initial specification could use the utilities supplied by CASE*Dictionary. For each column, you need to define validation criteria. If you were thorough in the detailed analysis phase, you already have these criteria. For CASE*Generator, you will need to define range checks, list of valid values, and so on. If you use SQL*Forms for your layout design, use its validation specification facilities for the common validations. For validation against a list of values, you need a database table for lookup or must include it in your free-form specification for hard coding. Remember that a database table lookup at runtime will slow down the form's response.

Foreign key data integrity checks are always lookups into another table. With CASE*Generator, you know which table is the origin for the foreign key since you know the relationships between the source entities. So all you need to specify is whether to enforce referential integrity. You also need to account for the master/detail processing specified. For example, if we allow *orphan* detail rows, should the foreign key value in such rows be null or some default value?

If we plan to force a particular navigation path in the screen, we should include it in our specification. James Martin defines a technique called a ***dialog design diagram*** which illustrates navigation between screens. This technique is suitable if you plan to use a procedural language. With SQL*Forms, you need a field or block identifier and the user action which triggers the navigation to another screen. For example, suppose you want to specify a pick-list on product. You should specify a call to the pick-list screen from the screen field for product number when user presses the *list-of-values* key in SQL*Forms. Figure 7-3 illustrates a diagram which I recommend for specifying such navigations.

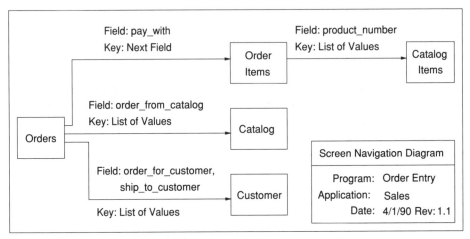

Figure 7-3: Navigation Specification for SQL*Forms

Ideally, you should define shop standards for terminology such as pick-list, and which SQL*Forms key triggers pick-lists, layout standards for screens displayed as pick-lists, and so on. The appendix contains a recommended set of example standards which you may modify for use in your company. This is the only way you will get any real consistency.

Each user interface technique has different performance characteristics. For example, a pick-list lookup in a table is slow compared to a list of values in SQL*Forms Version 2.3 or earlier. It requires a form switch into a pick-list form and back after selection. SQL*Forms 3.0 list-of-values implements a pop-up window for selection. Remember that repainting a screen on a PC or a workstation is quick if the form is on the local hard disk. Repainting a screen in character mode terminals is drastically slower. So avoid operations that require repainting on character mode terminals.

You need specifications for each insert, update, delete, and retrieve operation where you want the program behavior different from the tool's common behavior. For example, the default retrieval in SQL*Forms retrieves rows in random order. If you require the rows to be sorted in some order, your specification should describe it. If you need an audit trail for all changes to a particular table in your form, specify the requirement and the table into which audit trail information goes.

7.4 Report Specification

A report is any function that retrieves information from the database and formats it for presentation. The output medium of the function is irrelevant — it may be to a screen, a printer, a plotter, a microfiche, 35mm slide, and so on. A report only retrieves data, as opposed to a form which retrieves information in order to allow the user to change it. A report may transform the retrieved data before writing its output but does not change the data in the database. You may run a report interactively — that is, initiate its run from a terminal, respond to its prompts, and wait until it completes. You may also run reports in background — for example, submit it to a queue for an overnight run. By this definition, the *invoice customers* function is a report, and so is the *list customers* function. Reporting functions characteristically lie between a data store and an external entity in your data flow diagrams.

A report specification needs to cover the following basics, as detailed in Figure 7-4:

- Layout of data in the report. You might base this specification on some of the standard formats described in this section. Company or project standards for such layouts are essential.

- Runtime selection criteria to obtain from the user. The method to obtain these criteria could be another company standard. Ideally the interface is via a form.

- Tables retrieved, with selection criteria as well as relationships between them. In addition, you need to specify the sort order of the retrieved data.

- Control breaks for the data, if any, with associated layout and processing information.

- Derived data to present together with their derivation algorithms.

There are few utilities for painting a report layout, unlike screen painters. If you have existing tools which you use such as COBOL report layout charts, use them for these report specifications too. You could try using SQL*ReportWriter as a prototyping tool for laying out your reports. However, layout in this tool effectively involves writing almost the entire report. Besides, you need to have your database design complete and the tables implemented before using it. Similar arguments apply to the idea of using SQL*Plus. You may use both effectively for reports required after the application is in production.

You might obtain runtime selection criteria from users either by prompting for them one at a time (ugh! Don't do it!) or by presenting an entry screen which initiates the report. All Oracle tools for report generation, SQL*ReportWriter, SQL*Plus, and SQL*Report (RPT) have facilities for prompting users for one value at a time. There is no limit on the number of selection criteria obtained at run time.

If you prefer the entry screen method, you will need to use a combination of SQL*Forms and a report generator. In this case, the report generator must allow selection criteria values as part of the command line. Note that running such combinations requires a multitasking operating system, such as UNIX or OS/2. You cannot run the SQL*Forms and report generator combination on a single tasking MS-DOS system. You should take these limitations into account when designing a specific application.

Obviously, you need to specify which tables and columns the report uses. You also need to describe how the selection criteria affect retrieval of data from these tables. In addition, you need to specify any calculations or transformations necessary on the retrieved data. The type of calculations and transformations determine which report generation tool you could use. Selection of the most suitable tool also depends on the type of layout requirements.

One of key elements of layout specification should be the report size, based on your standards. You should define a very few sizes for reports, say, 80 columns by 66 lines and 132 columns by 66 lines. Header and footer styles and contents should be part of your standard specifications. Report might fall into the following layout categories

```
Prog: Sales by Product Category      Date: April 1, 1990 Rev: 1.0
Dept: Sales
Application: Sales & Marketing
Utility: SQL*Report Writer (or SQR)
Table Access:
orders, order_items, customer, product, product_category, state
Report Type: Matrix
Matrix Definition:
Product Categories as columns across page, States as rows down the
page, Cell is volume of sales for the state in a product category.
Column Handling:
```

Name	Description
State Total	Total sales over all categories for a state.
Category Total	Total sales over all states for a product category.
Grand Total	Total sales for company over all states and all categories.

Figure 7-4: Report Specification Items for a 4GL

- **Tabular reports:** This category covers the majority of analysis reports in a typical business. It is made up of columns of data items across the page with totals for data grouped over some column value. Figure 7-5 illustrates a tabular report.

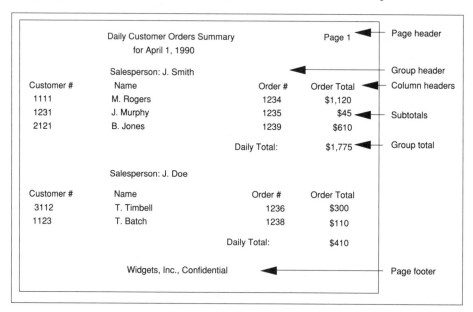

Figure 7-5: A Sample Tabular Report

SQL*Plus is a good tool for these types of reports provided that you can retrieve all required columns in a single SQL statement even if the data comes from several different tables. Computed values should be based on control breaks — that is, whenever the value of a particular column changes. For example, order totals by order and customer columns. Any SQL constructs which prevent sorting of data on control break columns prevent the use of SQL*Plus. Computations should be on individual columns without requiring intercolumn comparisons or comparisons between row values and group totals. For example, you would not use SQL*Plus for a report that requires a column where the order item price is expressed as a percentage of order total. The performance of such processing in SQL*Plus is typically slow. Instead consider using SQL*ReportWriter or SQL*Report for better performance.

- **Form reports:** This category covers most of a business's interaction with the outside world. It includes any report based on a form, preprinted or otherwise, such as invoices, checks, labels, and so on. With preprinted forms, alignment will be necessary and the report generator must provide data for alignment. You may need to print serial numbers, as needed on checks, and may have strict formatting requirements. Using SQL*ReportWriter or SQL*Report is the best choice for such reports. SQL*Plus usually is less flexible in its formatting options and has no alignment facilities. If you use modern laser printers, you may have special templates for use with this report which you must include in the specification.

- **Matrix reports:** This type of report looks similar to a spread sheet. Typically, the column categories and row categories come from tables in the database. When the report consists of a very few column categories which rarely change, you might consider using SQL*Plus reporting facilities. In this case, categories will be hard coded in the report definition, so you compromise flexibility for faster development. Figure 7-6 illustrates a matrix report.

	Appliance	Clothing	Tools	State Total
		Sales by Product Category		
		April 1, 1990		
My State	500	1000	45	1545
State1	100	30	5000	5130
Quebec		500	2000	2500
Category Total	600	1530	7045	9175
		Widgets, Inc., Confidential		

Figure 7-6: A Sample Matrix Report

Your specification for a matrix report should include a definition of which data items make up the column headings and row titles. In addition, specify the data for the cells. In each case, define which tables the data comes from and any calculations necessary before presenting the output.

SQL*ReportWriter has specially designed facilities for developing matrix reports. However, these facilities insist that each cell value come from a single SQL statement. If the cells under each column require different SQL statements, you will have to resort to SQL*Report (RPT). The penalty is longer development time with the rather old-fashioned SQL*Report which does not even implement control breaks and automatic totaling facilities.

- **Embedded data reports:** Typical of this category is a form letter where we embed data from the database within some text. This type of report is common in bulk mailings of *personalized* junk mail such as letters announcing *"You may have already won $50,000."* Page formatting and fancy fonts are of paramount importance in such reports. You will need to specify the type of margin justifications, default fonts, font changes, paragraph characteristics, and so on. These specifications will be similar to those for a desktop publishing package.

Early mailings used preprinted letters with your name inserted with a regular printer — in an obviously computerese type. Today, I relegate such tacky presentation to the garbage file instantly. Fast laser printers make it possible to present a uniform font style and page formatting. The best presentation among my most recent junk mail was one that included my name in the caption of a cartoon! — obviously my name in their database indicated me to be a computer aficionado. SQL*ReportWriter is probably essential for at least the text-oriented reports since it provides better font manipulation capabilities than do any of the other choices. In future releases, it promises to support even more facilities for desktop publishing-style capabilities.

7.5 Procedural Program Specification

If some parts of your application need procedural processing, you can resort to using a procedural fourth-generation language or a third-generation language interface to Oracle. Typically, you might use PL/SQL, or in Version 5 RPT, for batch updates to the database, or a batch integrity checker, and so on. Writing in these languages will be much faster than writing the same code in a third-generation language. You can even write a series of SQL statements in a SQL*Plus script to do some of the simple processing.

Consider using a third-generation language when processing huge volumes of data in a limited-time window. Oracle's PRO* interfaces offer array processing features which improve performance when you access a lot of rows returned from one SQL statement. Use these interfaces for temporary downloading or uploading data between the new application and other databases. There is little difference between writing specifications for these procedural programs and our traditional programs. Do remember, however, that any interaction with the Oracle database will use SQL. So, the amount of code in these programs will be somewhat less than in traditional file-based systems.

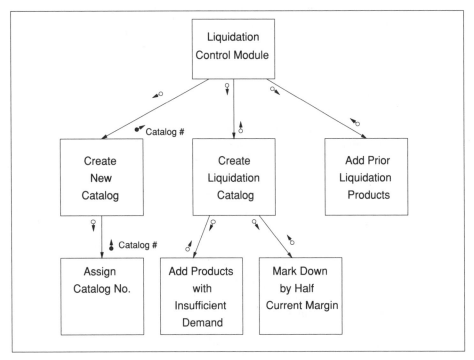

Figure 7-7: A Sample Structure Chart

One of the popular techniques used for specifying procedural code is using a structure chart. Figure 7-7 illustrates a sample structure chart. There are formal techniques for decomposing a problem into such a hierarchical solution. The primary concept underlying this structure is to have clear division of data manipulation between modules. Each module receives as input, shown as data couples, the data it should manipulate. In turn, it returns a status, shown as a control couple, as well as processed data. Typically, all input and output is segregated into separate modules. Ideally, all communication with a module is via passed parameters. Unfortunately, many programming languages, notably COBOL, make it very difficult to implement such segregation.

CASE*Dictionary allows you to define one module to be a submodule of another. Thus, you may define hierarchies of modules. You can also define recursive calls to a module, that is, a module calling itself. Any number of modules may call the same submodule, allowing you to define reusable library components. Thus, CASE*Dictionary acts as a documentation tool. This documentation is particularly valuable in maintenance mode for determining the potential impact of a change. However, keeping the documentation up to date with this tool can be very tedious.

A structure chart is a good way to document an overview of the program structure. However, we also need to specify the detailed logic for each module in the chart. There are many formal methods for this specification, although, CASE*Dictionary Version 4.1 does not enforce any. The most popular ones include pseudocode, structured English, decision trees, decision tables, action diagrams, state transition diagrams, and several others. Several of these techniques are useful in specific contexts only. For example, decision trees and decision tables are useful when program actions depend on a set of conditions.

Action diagrams and state transition diagrams are two of the most commonly automated techniques. You can think of an action diagram as one step up from pseudocode or structured English. They can be used for both high-level definition of modules and low-level logic of each module.

In action diagrams, we draw blocks to identify a module or a block of processing. A block is used in a similar fashion to its meaning in structured programming: a function, subroutine, each clause for a condition, and so on. Figure 7-8 illustrates a simple action diagram. This representation is uncomfortably close to writing actual code — necessary if your function really requires a procedural solution. An example of a suitable function is one introduced due to a design decision to store derived data: an integrity check and recalculation function for running overnight.

We can map higher-level action diagrams to structure charts on a one-to-one basis. Detailed action diagrams are, however, just like pseudocode with blocks delineated. This similarity is probably a reason for their popularity in code generation CASE tools.

State transition diagrams, drawn using Yourdon conventions, may look similar to data flow diagrams. There is a very important distinction: they are really not procedural! Typically, these diagrams are common in designing software where asynchronous processing occurs, that is, events can occur at any moment and our process must react to it promptly. State transition diagrams do have wider application. Figure 7-9 illustrates a state transition diagram of a customer order.

Each box in the diagram shown in Figure 7-9 is a *state*, and each arrow between two states is a *transition* from one state to another. We annotate the arrows to indicate the event, or input which causes the transition to the next state. In addition to changing the state, an input might also cause an output. Inputs and outputs are annotations on the transition arrows.

Procedure Create_Liquidation_Catalog

  For Each Product

    If sold_qty < qty_in_stock / 2
      Call Add_Product_with_insufficient_demand
      Call Markdown_Product_price
    End
  End

Figure 7-8: A Sample Action Diagram

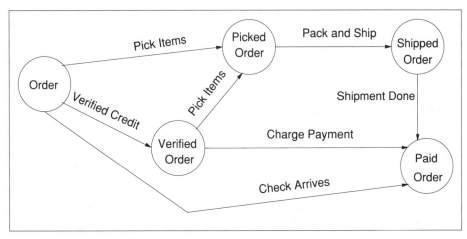

Figure 7-9: A Sample State Transition Diagram

Realize that CASE*Dictionary Version 4.1 or earlier allow only free-form module logic definition. There are no diagramming tools to support action diagrams or state transition diagrams in CASE*Designer Version 1.1. The rapid improvement of these CASE tools by Oracle means that these facilities or similar ones may be added. Remember, however, that the actual choice of tools depends on how CASE*Method evolves in the future.

7.6 Project Controls

There are a few components of a design that we have not dealt with explicitly. We need a definition of the application environment, security, and administrative functions. The strategy phase provided most of the guidelines for our hardware and software architecture. However, we must add detail in the design phase. Similarly, we analyzed the requirements for security and administrative functions during the detailed analysis phase. In this phase, we need to detail how our design fulfills these requirements.

7.6.1 System Architecture

This is a definition of the hardware and software environment for the production application as well as the development and test environments. Since Oracle provides a very portable environment, development, test, and production systems may not necessarily be on the same hardware platform, or the same operating system.

If you plan to develop on one platform and implement on a different one, you should define your programming standards to maintain complete portability. For example, if your production environment uses a block mode terminal interface, all SQL*Forms programming should conform to the requirements for block mode terminals. You can develop forms intended for a block mode environment on an MS-DOS PC, provided that you carefully avoid using certain functions.

Ideally, your test and production environments should be on identical platforms — at least the same operating system and Oracle versions. Thus, you will be able to train users who are part of the test and conversion team. You could trial their transition plans and procedures in an environment that resembles the production environment as closely as possible.

Your architecture should document the types of equipment planned for the project, from computer models through terminals and printers on users' desk. Communications details should be included, that is, the network hardware, software, protocols, provider services, maintenance agreements, and so on. Define also possible disaster scenarios and design your solution to overcome them. Be sure to outline the limits of your design. For example, battery backup for power failure lasts for two hours maximum. Power failures lasting beyond two hours will cause system unavailability. Discuss your design decisions with your user management so that they know the limitations of the architecture. Ask them if the limit, which you consider reasonable, is actually sufficient from the business per-spective. After all, if user activities stop the instant of power failure because all the lights went out, keeping your computer up might be meaningless except where you service remotely located users.

Clearly define the service levels your application will offer, including the hours of availability. These definitions will help set user expectations. Take into account, however, time for regular maintenance, backup of database and transaction logs, and any other administrative duties which will prevent full access to the application. We discuss these administrative duties in a later section.

7.6.2 Access Security

Throughout analysis, you probably emphasized the security requirements of the users. Almost every project I have worked on emphasized the importance of access controls — and in every case, no one wanted to pin down its details. So take the time to pin down your details. Remember that security restrictions at the database level are frequently insufficient. You will require controls at the application level as well.

We discussed database level controls in the previous chapter. Oracle enforces these controls only when a user attempts an operation against the database. For example, users with no access to a particular table will discover this restriction only when they attempt to retrieve data from it. Instead of showing them a screen only to deny them access to the data, I recommend that your application prevent access to the screen itself. You may use SQL*Menu to implement such a control, assuming you can synchronize user names and access controls between SQL*Menu and the database. Alternatively, you might define your own security database and application controls which must be hidden from all users.

7.6.3 Administrative Functions

Typically, we give very little consideration to how to administer the application once it goes into production. We should include in our design definitions of

• Administration of user ids and passwords.

- Integrating these Oracle user names and passwords with the operating system user ids and passwords. After all, making users sign on more than once is a very poor user interface. Why should your users have to appreciate the difference between an operating system and an Oracle database?

- Assignment of access security privileges to new users and reassignment when user roles change.

- Scripts for backing up your application data, programs, and user setups.

- Procedures for recovering data in case of a disaster.

Design of these functions is really operating system specific. Integration of user id creation with Oracle user names under UNIX is considerably different from doing it under IBM VM/CMS. Designing these functions and developing them is a relatively small effort that pays off handsomely in later stages, particularly in impressing user management with your efficiency.

As an application developer in a large data processing shop, you might consider design of these functions beyond your job description. But they are an important part of your project. Recruit staff from the appropriate organization, the database administration group, or systems programming group, to design and build these functions. I have seen too many applications seriously delayed because we overlooked such functions at design time and did not include them as tasks in our project plan.

In a small organization, designing these functions in this phase is even more important. You cannot afford the chaos of putting the application into production without any of them in place. Ignore them at the risk of burning a lot of midnight oil — and losing credibility in the view of your users. Now, you know what I have been through before becoming a good consultant.

I find that including tasks in the project plan for designing and building these functions raises many eyebrows. Management resistance is highest when development time is rather short. However, the smooth transition from development to test and then into production convinces even the worst skeptic. In one of my projects, we smoothly installed turnkey systems at dozens of installations across the United States without any on-site UNIX expertise — or any technical knowledge. I convinced my manager only after we expended several weeks installing the first system and recovering from disasters stemming from trivial user typos!

7.6.4 Standards and Conventions

CASE*Dictionary and CASE*Designer are powerful tools for analysis and database design. However, you need project standards to use them most effectively. CASE*Dictionary allows you to define and manage applications. All dictionary elements, including entities, functions, relationships, and so on, are owned by applications. Other applications can share dictionary elements, although they have severely restricted privileges for modifying these elements.

It is easy to dream up applications and define them in CASE*Dictionary. However, the subsequent administration can become a nightmare, if you do not lay down project standards and conventions. For example, distinguishing between the name of an entity and its corresponding table with some simple convention saves your development team countless hours. I have outlined some sample standards in the appendix which you could use as a starter kit for your company.

Remember to document the exact setup for your project team's working areas. Defining directories or the appropriate equivalent for source, binary, and test files; providing tools for accessing them with minimum effort; and other small utilities will keep your team organized. I usually appoint a chief architect on each project who is my right hand in building such utilities and enforcing their use. Ideally, such tools would be built and maintained by a *project support group*, possibly a subset of systems programming group in large corporations. The support group could then define and maintain corporation wide standard — establishing a corporate programming culture: the technical equivalent of blue pinstripe suits.

Part 3

Developing Oracle Applications

Now we get down to the nitty-gritty — how to build what we set out to do. The Oracle DBMS provides fourth-generation tools for building interactive forms, reports, and batch programs. We will focus on these tools in the following chapters.

You are not stuck with Oracle supplied tools, however. Many third-party vendors make a living supplying forms utilities, report generators, and high-level procedural language interfaces to Oracle. So to add a little spice, we examine some of these tools. I do not intend this to be an exhaustive survey of third-party products. There are too many good products, which are changing too quickly to include in this book. Instead, I provide a flavor of what is available.

These chapters use the example programs we designed in the previous part of the book. So refer to them if you need details on layouts or processing design. I have chosen at least one example of each type of program.

There is little hand-holding, tutorial-style step-by-step description in these chapters. Instead, I show heavily annotated code illustrating typical and nontypical techniques. Replacing Oracle's substantial set of manuals is not my intention. Expand on the techniques illustrated for your own applications. If you grasp the philosophy underlying them, you are well on your way to building successful applications.

8

Interactive Screen Programs

Interactive forms are a major portion of today's applications. They are not, by any means, merely interfaces for entering data, as in more traditional systems. Data entry is still one the major functions served by these tools. However, they allow users to query in a targeted manner — to find just the one row they need. You might also use forms as a means to obtain runtime values for reports.

Building interactive forms using fourth-generation tools such as SQL*Forms is very different from using traditional procedural programming languages. Instead of coding each step of a user's navigation through the form, you let the utility do most of that work. Development, then, consists of defining the characteristics of each field, and the program action when the cursor initially enters a field, or after it exits the field. The form specifications, shown in an earlier chapter, reflect this approach.

A side effect of this approach is that your program cannot direct each of the user's moves in an interactive session. In fact, attempting to build such a program in a fourth-generation language is a big mistake! The resulting form will be slow, and development will take significantly longer. We address such issues of fourth-generation forms development in this chapter. We use Oracle's SQL*Forms as the primary example, although we also examine the way one or two of the third-party vendors' tools perform the same function. In particular, we cover the following topics

- Defining a form and each of the typical components of a form. Components include blocks, fields, and triggers to program specific actions.
- Coordinating blocks for master/detail relationships. We will use the order entry example from the Widgets' sales application for this purpose.
- Common screen-handling concepts, such as pick-lists, and how to develop them in SQL*Forms. We also examine how third-party tools handle these concepts.
- Some of the ways third-party tools connect to Oracle. You might consider these and other vendor's offerings as alternatives to SQL*Forms.

8.1 Oracle Tools

Our primary purpose with screen forms is to allow users access to the data in the database. There is more than one way to kill the cat. SQL*Forms provides a controlled interface to accessing data. It is suitable for well-defined, repetitive tasks, such as order entry or customer lookup. Other Oracle tools allow ad hoc access, where the user does not wish to wait until a program can be developed. They are particularly suited to one-off access. Unfortunately, they all depend on the user understanding the structure of the tables in the database, at least superficially. So, before you give these tools to the user, you must train them in the database structure, and the use of SQL. Teaching nontechnical users to use SQL is not a trivial task.

Easy*SQL is a self-contained tool which allows users to create their own tables, build simple forms and reports to access them, and manage the database with administrative utilities. It is a dangerous tool, if you want to control the contents of the database. However, it may be useful to users who simply want to build simple applications outside of the company's database.

Easy*SQL is menu-driven, for the most part. It uses SQL*Forms as the tool for building forms — with some prompts to simplify building master/detail relationships. It generates a form based on the responses complete with appropriate triggers. In fact, several novice developers use Easy*SQL functions to create block coordination triggers in master/detail forms. Its report generator, however, is unlike any of the other report generator tools provided by Oracle for developers. It can handle most of the typical tabular reports, although it cannot handle preprinted form reports, matrix reports, and so on.

You define field validation criteria, in Easy*SQL, when you create tables. Then, when you generate a form, these validation criteria are automatically included in the form. So developing a form with Easy*SQL is much easier than in vanilla SQL*Forms. If you need more capabilities than available, you can always revert to SQL*Forms. It is a shame that Oracle did not make SQL*Forms always work in this manner.

SQL*QMX is another optional package — Oracle's attempt at imitating the DB2 Query Management Facility (QMF). It is a little better than QMF because it provides templates of SQL statements, almost like a form that you can fill in. It is useful when you are learning SQL for the first time, and accessing one table at a time. This package also has a built-in report generator which takes the results of the SQL statements and allows you to format them with headers, footers, and totals. Formatting requires you to fill out a set of forms. Again, it seems a shame that Oracle did not include such an interface for developers, for most of the simple reports, rather than a tool like SQL*Report (aka RPT).

You might offer SQL*QMX to users who are learning SQL, if you really believe the hype that SQL is an end-user query tool. I would not recommend allowing users to access the database directly via SQL. Expecting them to maintain data integrity across tables, if they even understand it, is not very reasonable. Keep in mind that you will have to help them frequently when they need to do multiple table retrievals. More help is necessary, when they find that the report-generating tool limits them from developing some of the more complex reports they need.

Oracle Add-in for Lotus 1-2-3 is one of the tools which has been very successful with aficionados of Lotus spreadsheets. This optional tool is a set of macros added to the spreadsheet package, to allow access to the database. Typically you use SQL statements to retrieve data directly into the cells of a spreadsheet. Then, you can manipulate this data to your heart's content, create charts, graphs, and so on. The interface to Oracle is transparent from the spreadsheet user's view.

One of the nice features of this product is that it provides help when you compose the SQL statements. It will display a list of table and column names, so you can correct spelling errors. Almost none of the other Oracle utilities offer you such a list. Of course, it still does not display the comments associated with the tables and columns in the database — which would be useful if the names are cryptic. So I would recommend using meaningful names for tables and columns, even if they are long winded.

The SQL statements defined in a spreadsheet live with it. Thus, you can move the spreadsheet to another machine, which also has Oracle for Lotus 1-2-3. They are implemented as another 1-2-3 function, called @SQL. You can use any valid SQL statement in this function, provided that you have access privileges to the tables and columns mentioned in it. Thus, you can not only retrieve data, you can also update it. Though, I would recommend that you revoke users privilege to update data directly — to preserve data integrity.

With this basic understanding of alternatives to SQL*Forms, realize that you need not develop every interactive access as a SQL*Forms application. Tools such as the Add-in for 1-2-3 are very useful for offloading some of the development, allowing users some control over retrieving data on an ad hoc basis. However, if you provide Easy*SQL or SQL*QMX to your users, better set up a help desk to provide full-time support. In fact, I would recommend that you use SQL*Forms for all data entry, update, and repetitive access functions.

8.2 Basic Forms Development

SQL*Forms is a developer's utility. It has a development part, started with the command *sqlforms*, and a runtime part, started with the command *runform*. When you develop a form, it goes through several distinct stages before you can run it. Figure 8-1 illustrates these stages and the associated location of your form definition.

When you start defining the form, its definition is in memory. You can *file* the definition in the database tables used by SQL*Forms. Then, you need to use the *generate* option to, in effect, compile the definition. The compiled definition is stored in an operating system file. This compiled definition is used for running the form. You may copy this file to any other machine that has the same application tables and run it using runform. Of course, developers can run the form without exiting the development environment (except on the Oracle for MS-DOS Version 5.1A).

When you compile the form, it actually goes through two transformations. The definition is first written to a file, popularly known as the *inp* file due to its extension part. This file is a printable file, containing a set of prompts and responses. It's format is a leftover from the days before SQL*Forms became a interactive, screen-based development tool. The second step converts the inp file into the final compiled form definition file, called the

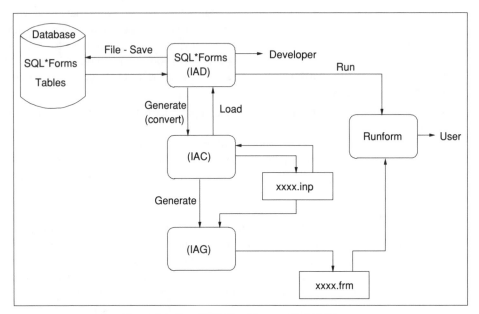

Figure 8-1: Form Definition Stages with SQL*Forms

frm file. Some veterans of SQL*Forms edit the *inp* file directly, although I would recommend that you do not. The file format is very sensitive to the number of spaces, semicolons, commas, and other esoteric characters. Instead, use the screen-based development interface described here. Future versions of SQL*Forms promise to make this file less cryptic with free form commands.

The development environment with SQL*Forms is window based. Each window provides some input fields and some options. You execute an option by placing the cursor on the option and pressing the SELECT key. The actual key you should press varies depending on the terminal or keyboard you use. Realize that SQL*Forms is entirely based on using a keyboard. Don't be fooled by the windows on your screen, especially when using a PC, into thinking that you can point and click with a mouse. You have to use arrow keys to move the cursor around the screen. *Note that it is possible to fool SQL*Forms into letting you use a mouse on a DOS PC, if you define a set of mouse menus. The mouse menu should generate keystrokes for every mouse movement that you make.*

Figure 8-2 illustrates the windows you would invoke when defining a default screen form. Building a default screen form is often the best way to start developing a new form. Default forms can be one row at a time, as indicated by the *Rows Displayed* field in Figure 8-2 or multiple rows if you change the value of this field.

An application in SQL*Forms is made up of **forms**, each of which can be one or more **pages** that is, screens. A form consists of one or more **blocks** each relating to one database table. A block can span multiple pages. You can also have **control blocks** which are not associated with any database table. These blocks might be used for displaying custom menus, help screen, and so on.

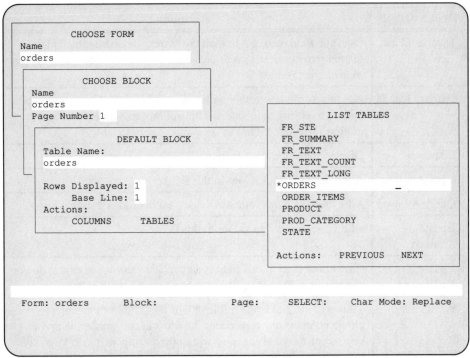

Figure 8-2: SQL*Forms Definition Windows

A block is, in turn, made up of *fields* each of which may relate to a database field or a display-only field, or be a hidden field. A display-only field is commonly used for displaying data when some change occurs in some other field. For example, when a user enters a customer number, you might use a display-only field to display the corresponding customer name. A hidden field is not displayed on the screen at runtime, but might be necessary to perform some calculation. For example, you might use a hidden field to hold the sales tax rate.

You can define the characteristics of a field, for example, if input is required (mandatory), or convert input to all upper case. Table 8-1 lists all of the characteristics possible for a field and their meaning.

In addition, you can specify field validation criteria, for example, a range or look up valid values from a database table. You can specify a list of values table and column in this window. This causes SQL*Forms to display values from the specified column in this field one at a time, allowing the user to select the currently displayed value. You can also define a help message here, typically to indicate whether a list of values is available, or the valid range of values.

The display length of a field can be different from its query length. This feature allows query conditions such as greater than or less than which increases the space needed for a field value at runtime.

Field Attribute	Description
Database Field	Does the field map to a field in the current database table? Fields mapping to other database fields such as product description are not in the current table.
Primary Key	Use this attribute together with *Check for Unique Key* block-level option, to ensure uniqueness. This option can degrade performance of your form since it has to access the database table.
Displayed	Display the values in this field.
Input Allowed	Allow user to input values in this field.
Query Allowed	Allow user to enter values as selection conditions during a query.
Update Allowed	Allow user to change values in this field.
Update if NULL	Only allow entry if this field is empty. If a prior value exists, do not allow user to change it. Useful for one-time entry fields.
Fixed Length	Values in this field take full length of the field, for example, for phone numbers or postal codes. Use this in conjunction with *Autoskip* to get smooth data entry without requiring *next field* key — to reduce key strokes.
Mandatory	Do not allow user to leave this field empty.
Uppercase	Convert input in this field to uppercase as user enters characters.
Autoskip	As soon as this field is full, move cursor to the next field without requiring user action.
Automatic Help	Display help comment (from validation window) as soon as cursor enters this field.
No Echo	Do not display input to this field: useful for hiding passwords.

Table 8-1: SQL*Forms Field Characteristics

For a user-friendly screen, we should display the product name as soon as the user enters a product number. Such a facility helps them to verify the product immediately with the customer. To build such a facility, we can use a *trigger*. Figure 8-3 illustrates the trigger window on the field *product_num*.

A trigger is custom code that we can write to make SQL*Forms perform a particular task. The language used has two parts: slightly modified SQL statements, and macros. The trigger example shown in Figure 8-3 uses the modified SQL language. It retrieves the product name from the *product* table by matching the value in the *product_number* field in the *order_items* screen block against the *product_number* column in the *product* table.

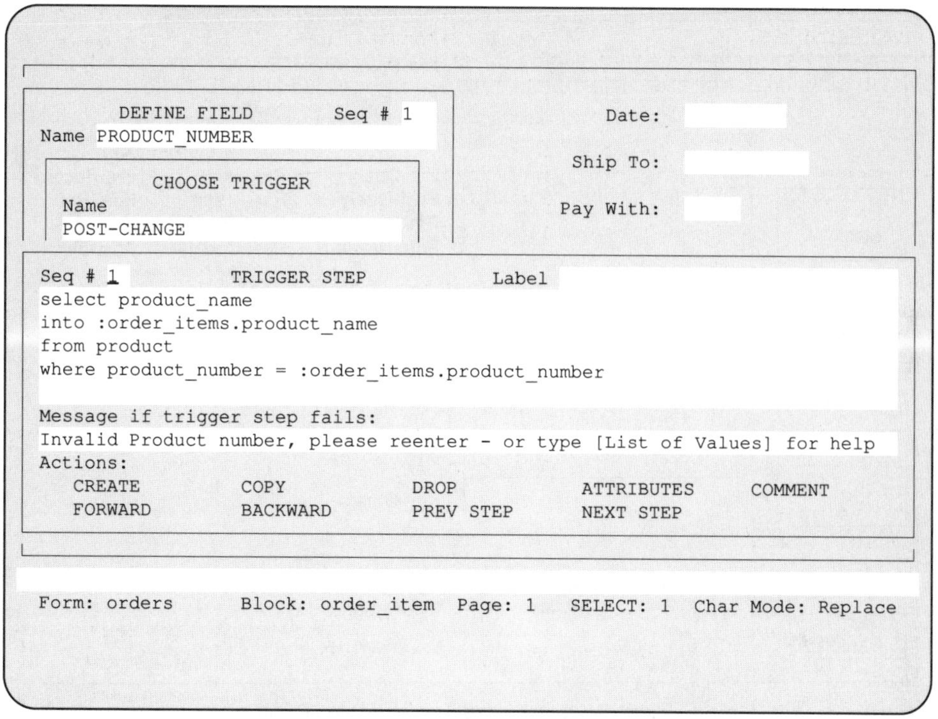

```
         DEFINE FIELD          Seq # 1                    Date:
Name PRODUCT_NUMBER
                                                       Ship To:
            CHOOSE TRIGGER
   Name                                                Pay With:
   POST-CHANGE

Seq # 1              TRIGGER STEP            Label
select product_name
into :order_items.product_name
from product
where product_number = :order_items.product_number

Message if trigger step fails:
Invalid Product number, please reenter - or type [List of Values] for help
Actions:
   CREATE          COPY           DROP          ATTRIBUTES      COMMENT
   FORWARD         BACKWARD       PREV STEP     NEXT STEP


Form: orders        Block: order_item  Page: 1    SELECT: 1  Char Mode: Replace
```

Figure 8-3: Trigger Definition Window on product_num field

Screen field names start with a : (colon). We can use the *product_name* screen field without naming its block, *order_items*, since this field name is unique within the form. For ease of maintenance, I recommend always specifying the block name together with the screen field name.

The *into* clause specifies the destination of the value retrieved from the database table, namely, the *product_name* screen field in the *order_items* block. We can retrieve more than one column in this statement with a list of corresponding destination fields. The order of fields in the into clause must match that of columns in the select clause. The order of columns in the select clause is arbitrary.

Notice that my screen field names match corresponding database fields. Block names correspond to tables. This habit has saved me many hours of work when modifying a form. SQL*Forms is a good tool when you are developing a new form, but very difficult to navigate around when modifying a form. This difficulty is one of the reasons that many experts modify the *inp* file rather than using the screen-based interface. Be warned, however, that you may face difficulties with loading an inp file, after manual modification, back into the SQL*Forms tables, even though it generates a usable compiled form.

The trigger name defines when SQL*Forms will activate it. For example, our product_name retrieval trigger is called a *POST-CHANGE* trigger — it is activated whenever the value in its associated field changes. The change occurs when the user enters a value in it the first time, as well as each time they change it. Since we want the product name to always

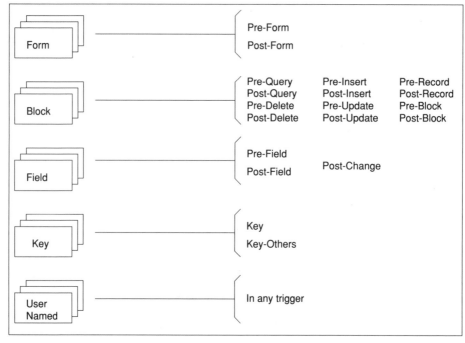

Figure 8-4: SQL*Forms Trigger Control Points

match the product_number entered, we associate this trigger with the product_number screen field. Note that SQL*Forms is sensitive to spelling of trigger names. It will consider POST_CHANGE spelled with an underscore as a user-defined trigger — and will not activate it when the field value changes. The best way to avoid mistakes in naming triggers is to use the TYPES option of the CHOOSE TRIGGER window to select the appropriate name.

You can associate triggers with any one of the objects in the form, such as a field, a block, or the form itself. In addition, you can associate a trigger with a key that a user may press, or a database access by SQL*Forms such as insert, update, delete, or query. Figure 8-4 illustrates each of the form objects that can have a trigger associated with it. Trigger names starting with PRE- are activated just before SQL*Forms executes that action, and similarly names starting with POST- are activated immediately after the action is complete. Thus, SQL*Forms activates a PRE-FIELD trigger just before the cursor enters the associated field. SQL*Forms activates a POST-DELETE trigger immediately after executing the delete access but before executing a database COMMIT. Remember that you can perform a number of updates to the database which Oracle will not actually write to the database until you COMMIT them. You may undo such updates with a ROLLBACK statement at any time prior to the COMMIT.

SQL*Forms has over 35 different keys for users, so Figure 8-4 does not list all of them. Each key has a particular meaning, such as execute query, move cursor to the next block in the form, and so on. These keys are most of the macros available in writing key-based triggers. By associating a trigger with a key, you can change the actions that SQL*Forms performs whenever a user types that key.

Triggers associated with keys are the most frequent types of triggers you will see in a form. There are a few additional macros:

COPY: This macro allows copying of a value from one screen field to another, regardless of the blocks in which the source and destination fields belong. You can also use it to save a value in global variable, which is declared as a result of mentioning it in this macro. The destination variable name, in this case, has the form *GLOBAL.var*. In Section 8.4, we illustrate a novel way of using this macro to fake windows in SQL*Forms 2.3.

ERASE: This macro erases the value of a global variable. SQL*Forms releases the memory used for the global variable as a result of this macro.

EXETRG: This macro executes another trigger — typically your own triggers. The COORD trigger in Section 8.3 is a custom trigger.

CALL, CALLQRY, NEWFRM: These macros allow you to call another form while suspending processing in the current form. The CALL macro allows unrestricted processing in the called form; CALLQRY restricts user actions to those implied by the macro name. With these two macros, each called form definition stacks over the calling form definition in memory. Thus, when the user exits from the other form, control will return to the calling form. The NEWFRM macro replaces the definition of the calling form with the called form definition. Thus, control cannot return to the calling form. This macro allows you to use memory efficiently, important on MS-DOS PCs with a limit of 640K memory.

CALLINPUT: This macro allows you to obtain user input from a trigger.

PAUSE: This macro suspends processing with a message *Press any function key to continue*. It is useful when displaying messages to users — to allow them time to read the message prior to continuing.

CASE — WHEN — END CASE: This macro allows you to test the values of a variable or screen field and conditionally execute macros: call your own triggers, call another form, and so on. This facility is commonly used to build a menu form which calls other forms based on the option number typed by the user. The default case is specified by WHEN OTHERS, that is, when the value does not match any other WHEN clause in the CASE statement.

NOOP, NULL: These macros perform no tasks. The NOOP trigger displays the message *Unrecognized command*; NULL displays nothing. They are useful in CASE macro WHEN clauses to specify no action.

Simple triggers are sufficient for a simple forms application. Consider, however, the behavior of a screen consisting of two blocks — such as our order entry screen which has one block for orders and another for order items. Since there could be many items in each order, we defined the order items block as a multiple row block. In this form, if we perform a query in the order block, say, using the order number, SQL*Forms does not automatically display all of the associated order items in the order items block. We need to coordinate these two blocks.

8.3 Coordinating Screen Blocks

Let us start by defining the way we would like the form to behave if we had the orders and order_items blocks coordinated. We need to examine the required behavior for each type of operation: query, insert, update, and delete.

There are two ways a user can query in the orders block: by pressing the execute query key to retrieve all rows or by pressing the enter query key, entering a search condition in a field such as an order number, and then pressing the execute query key to retrieve specific rows. In either case, we would like the order_items block to show the items corresponding to the order displayed in the orders block. Of course, when we browse through the retrieved rows using the next record and previous record keys, we would like the order_items block automatically to show the rows corresponding to the newly displayed order.

Similarly, inserting a new order should force the entry of order_items as well. In our example, we require that each order must have at least one order item. When the user deletes an order, we must first delete all of the associated order items and clear the order_items block, before deleting the order itself.

Figure 8-5 illustrates the triggers to perform all of these functions. Since SQL*Forms displays only one step of a trigger at a time in the trigger window, illustrating all of these triggers on screen is a difficult proposition requiring dozens of screens. SQL*Forms 3.0 alleviates some of these difficulties by allowing triggers written in PL/SQL in file. You can then import the file into a trigger definition.

Before implementing these block coordination triggers, you have to define the order_number screen field in the order_item block to be copied from the corresponding screen field in the orders block. This definition is part of the field *validation* window. Don't confuse this copy with the copy macro used in trigger language. When the cursor moves into the order_items block, due to a *nxtblk* command in one of our triggers, SQL*Forms copies the current value of the order_number from the orders block into the corresponding field in the order_items block. Thus, subsequent macros in the trigger can assume the existence of this value in the order_items block. As a result, when the trigger executes an *exeqry* macro, only items for the current order_number are retrieved.

You should hide this order_number field in the order_items block from the user — so they do not get confused by seeing the order_number appearing on every order item. One way is simply to define the field as not displayed in the attribute window. A better way is to cut this field from the displayed form page and pasting it into page 0. This method frees

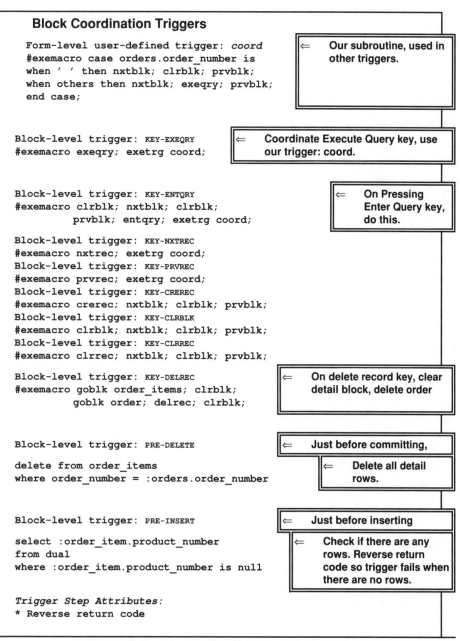

Block Coordination Triggers

Form-level user-defined trigger: *coord* ⇐   **Our subroutine, used in**
#exemacro case orders.order_number is   **other triggers.**
when ' ' then nxtblk; clrblk; prvblk;
when others then nxtblk; exeqry; prvblk;
end case;

Block-level trigger: KEY-EXEQRY   ⇐   **Coordinate Execute Query key, use**
#exemacro exeqry; exetrg coord;   **our trigger: coord.**

Block-level trigger: KEY-ENTQRY   ⇐   **On Pressing**
#exemacro clrblk; nxtblk; clrblk;   **Enter Query key,**
      prvblk; entqry; exetrg coord;   **do this.**

Block-level trigger: KEY-NXTREC
#exemacro nxtrec; exetrg coord;
Block-level trigger: KEY-PRVREC
#exemacro prvrec; exetrg coord;
Block-level trigger: KEY-CREREC
#exemacro crerec; nxtblk; clrblk; prvblk;
Block-level trigger: KEY-CLRBLK
#exemacro clrblk; nxtblk; clrblk; prvblk;
Block-level trigger: KEY-CLRREC
#exemacro clrrec; nxtblk; clrblk; prvblk;

Block-level trigger: KEY-DELREC   ⇐   **On delete record key, clear**
#exemacro goblk order_items; clrblk;   **detail block, delete order**
      goblk order; delrec; clrblk;

Block-level trigger: PRE-DELETE   ⇐   **Just before committing,**

delete from order_items   ⇐   **Delete all detail**
where order_number = :orders.order_number   **rows.**

Block-level trigger: PRE-INSERT   ⇐   **Just before inserting**

select :order_item.product_number   ⇐   **Check if there are any**
from dual   **rows. Reverse return**
where :order_item.product_number is null   **code so trigger fails when**
  there are no rows.

Trigger Step Attributes:
* Reverse return code

Figure 8-5: Block Coordination Triggers in Order Entry Form

up space on your display page. Users do not see page 0, unless it has a field where input is allowed. So, remember to disallow input, update, or query on the order_number field once you place it on page 0.

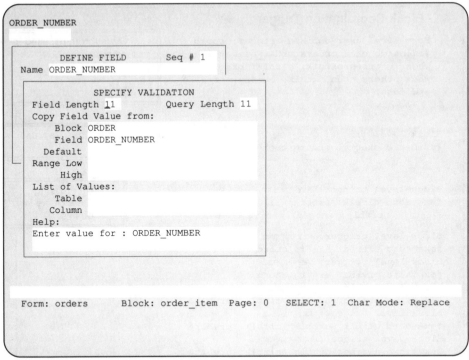

Figure 8-6: Defining Copy on Order_Number in Order_Item Block

You can define similar triggers for any form involving master/detail relationships. Notice that we have to anticipate each key that the user might possibly press at runtime and code an appropriate trigger for it. Our code cannot force the order in which the user works. This peculiarity is common to most fourth-generation forms development tools. It is important that you understand this method of coding for successful development using SQL*Forms.

It is possible to set up loops and branching based on the success or failure of a trigger, by defining labels for trigger steps. The trigger step attributes window allows you to specify the step label for success and failure. I would recommend that you use this method as a last resort. Use the CASE macro wherever you can for conditional execution. It is much more efficient than branching based on the success and failure of a trigger step.

Multiple-step triggers are possible, although I discourage their use. Increasing the number of steps in a trigger slows the user response. Also, use macros wherever possible rather than select statements. Each select statement implies a database access, even if it is to a tiny table like dual. Macros require no database access and hence execute faster. In SQL*Forms Version 3.0, using PL/SQL helps you to avoid unnecessary database accesses.

8.4 Forms Tricks

You are probably wondering, by now, how to decide whether a trigger should be field level, block level, or form level. These levels are a nested set, with field-level triggers the innermost set. Field-level triggers are active only when the cursor is actually in the field on which you defined the trigger. Block-level triggers, similarly are active only when the cursor is in a field within a block. Thus, the *key-exeqry* trigger in our example is not active when the cursor is in the order_item block, only when the cursor is in the order block. Form-level triggers are active anywhere in the form.

If your define a trigger in a field and at the block level, the field-level trigger takes precedence when the cursor is in that field. In all other fields, the block-level trigger takes precedence. So, before you define a trigger, think about where the cursor will be when the trigger is executed. If the cursor will always be in a particular field, define your trigger on that field. This was the case in our trigger which retrieves the product_name given a product number. If you cannot predict which field the cursor will be in, define your trigger at block level. For example, we cannot predict which field the cursor will be in when the user presses the EXECUTE QUERY key. So our query triggers for block coordination are block level triggers. When deciding where to define a trigger, ask yourself the following questions:

- For a derived field value, when should a new value for this field be calculated? For example, we derive the item *total* field value from the *qty* field. Thus, every time this qty value changes, we should recalculate the item total value. So, we define a POST-CHANGE trigger on the qty field.

- To change the action of key under specific circumstances, where will the cursor be when this action is to be performed? What should occur when the user presses this key? For example, after the user fills the order block, we would like the cursor to move to the first line in the order_item block. The cursor, at this point, will be in the last field in the order block, that is, the *pay with* field. So, when the user presses the *next field* key after entering this field, we would like the cursor to move to the *item no* field in the order_item block. The trigger, then, must be called KEY-NXTFLD defined on the *pay with* field. In all other fields, pressing the *next field* key should move the cursor to the next field in the order block.

- To change the meaning of a key, determine the sequence of keys you would have to press manually to achieve the desired result. For example, we want an *execute query* in the order block to

    1. Perform the query on the order block (key: EXECUTE QUERY, macro: exeqry)

    2. Move the cursor to the next block (key: NEXT BLOCK; macro: nxtblk)

    3. SQL*Forms copies the order_number value from the order block into the order_item block.

    4. Perform the query on the order item block (key: EXECUTE QUERY; macro: exeqry)

    5. Move the cursor back to the previous block (key: PREVIOUS BLOCK; macro: prvblk)

The sequence of keys you would press manually is the sequence in which to write the corresponding macros! Thus, this type of a trigger is merely pushing the keys for the user.

Here are some more tricks for developing in SQL*Forms. Notice the totals block on the order entry screen. This block, called a *control block*, is not associated with any database table. It contains display only fields. We define triggers on the item total field to add the current value into the subtotal field. The subtotal field has a trigger which calculates the shipping and tax as a percentage of the current subtotal and then adds it to the subtotal to get the grand total. The trigger on the item total field calculates the new subtotal, which cascades to the trigger on the subtotal field, which in turn cascades to the shipping and tax field. Thus, triggers can cascade causing multiple changes to the display.

This block contains data derived from previous fields. In our database, we do not keep this derived data. However, it is nice to display this information as users enter orders, so that they can quote the final order total to the customer. Control blocks are a very useful technique for such data.

Another way to use control blocks is for fake windows in SQL*Forms 2.3. Remember that Version 3.0 allows you pop-up windows as well as windows for called forms. So this technique is only useful in the older version. Figure 8-7 illustrates the end result of our customer data form. The order entry form calls this page to allow entry of customer data. The orders block seen partially in the back is just a control block. Form-level triggers copy the values into its fields from the order block.

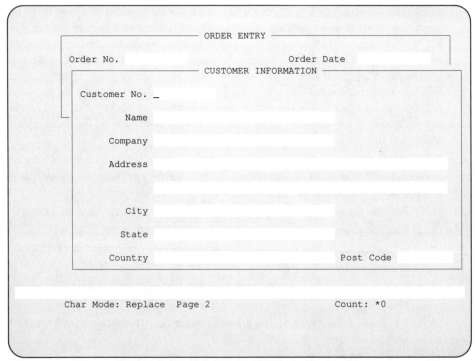

Figure 8-7: Fake Windows in SQL*Forms Version 2.3

We can extend the Widgets order entry example to many other industries. For example, suppose your order entry is more complex than just picking items from a catalog. You have to consider dependencies between products, as when configuring a computer system. The salespeople probably try out many different configurations before proposing one to the customer. You could implement such a scenario by using a *scratch pad* of tables. Then your order entry consists of writing trial configurations using the scratch pad and then copying the final order into the main tables.

In this example, the orders always use the trial scratch pad tables. Designate a SQL*Forms function key, such as the CREATE RECORD key, which the user will press to convert a trial order into a real order. Define a key trigger at the form level which will copy the appropriate rows from the scratch pad tables to the main tables. You can keep the data in the scratch pad tables so that templates for other types of orders are available.

The scratch pad idea has many applications other than in order entry. For example, I have used it in a design for a user id and security administration system. The scratch pad tables were actually for submitting the user id and security access information to a batch utility. The batch utility would run overnight to create the appropriate operating system ids, Oracle user names, security access views on tables, and so on from information stored in the scratch pad tables.

I have mentioned SQL*Forms 3.0 several times in this chapter. This release incorporates many facilities missing in Version 2.3. Its look and feel to the developer is similar to SQL*Report Writer. It displays a list of menu options on the top line with pull-down menus under each option, just like SQL*Report Writer. In addition, you can browse through the definitions of all fields within a block, without going back to the screen painter between each field, as in Version 2.3.

From a user perspective, Version 3.0 is capable of a better interface. It supports the concept of a pick-list, based on the LIST OF VALUES key. You can choose to present the pick list as a pop-up window. In fact, you can define any page as a pop-up window to be called from another screen. So the fake windows we illustrated earlier are not necessary. Another useful feature is the format mask that you can define on a field, especially on dates. Thus, if you prefer a / (slash) between the components of a date, you can define it as a format mask, to override the Oracle default date format.

Trigger definitions are easier in Version 3.0 due to two facilities: the ability to import them from a file and the use of PL/SQL. Version 3.0 supports triggers in the old 2.3 format as well as the new PL/SQL format. As explained in an earlier chapter, Version 3.0 PL/SQL runs local to the forms environment. So you no longer need to write the awkward SELECT ... FROM DUAL statements just to perform a minor calculation. The procedural flow of PL/SQL is much better than writing multistep triggers, as illustrated in a later chapter. Be aware, however, that PL/SQL has no built-in facilities for user interaction, so it may not always be suitable. Realize, also, that the choice of Version 2.3 format triggers and Version 3.0 format triggers is for the entire form. You cannot build one trigger in Version 2.3 format and another with PL/SQL in the same form.

8.5 JAM Alternatives

JAM is a third-party forms development tool by JYACC, Inc. It can connect to several SQL based DBMSs via its JAM/DBi interface. We briefly review its capabilities here, to illustrate the kinds of facilities available, as an alternative to SQL*Forms. JAM is popular because of its easy prototyping facilities. It allows you to switch from development mode to test mode easily, without requiring compilation of the form. You can define screens and windows even without an underlying database definition, unlike SQL*Forms.

JAM consists of three components: the *formmaker*, a screen forms utility; JPL, a procedural language for writing triggers; and DBi, the interface to connect to an Oracle database. The formmaker tool allows you to define screens without regard to which table the underlying database field belongs to. Thus, JAM does not restrict you to using data from one table, nor does it have the concept of a block such as in SQL*Forms.

You define each data window separately. The window need not occupy the entire display on a terminal. You can call a window from another window, with the option to clear the screen prior to displaying the new window. Thus, if you do not clear the screen, the called window display overlaps the calling window. In addition, you can specify the display coordinates for each window. This facility, together with overlapping display capability, is the way to build pop-up windows in JAM.

Figure 8-8 illustrates our sample order entry form. This form is actually made up of several individual window definitions, the order master, the order detail, the summary, and the customer data window. The order detail window is triggered from the order master and the summary window from the order detail. The customer data window pops up as soon as the cursor enters the Customer field. JAM stores the entire form, including all of the window definitions, in a small file which it interprets at runtime.

JAM stores each field definition in a dictionary. Multiple windows can share the basic definition, such as field name, data type, and validation criteria. Field display characteristics, such as color, are specific to each window. You can build the dictionary as you define a window. Figure 8-9 illustrates the types of field characteristics that you define from the formmaker. Simple math calculations are part of the field definition — you do not need to write a trigger for them. You can also hard-code pick-list values in the field without resorting to a database access. For short lists which rarely change, this method avoids database access. For example, the payment method field has a pick-list listing credit cards accepted by Widgets, Inc. Since very few new credit cards become available each year, this list is a good candidate for a hard-coded pick-list. The response for such hard coded pick-lists is impressively fast.

More complex manipulation of fields you need to use JPL to write triggers. JAM supports two types of triggers, *pre-field* and *post-field*. So you can specify actions before the cursor enters a field, and after it leaves the field. There is no *post-change* trigger — you can implement its equivalent by comparing the previous value of a field to the value, determine if the value changed and then performing the necessary action. JAM also allows triggers before and after a window and a form.

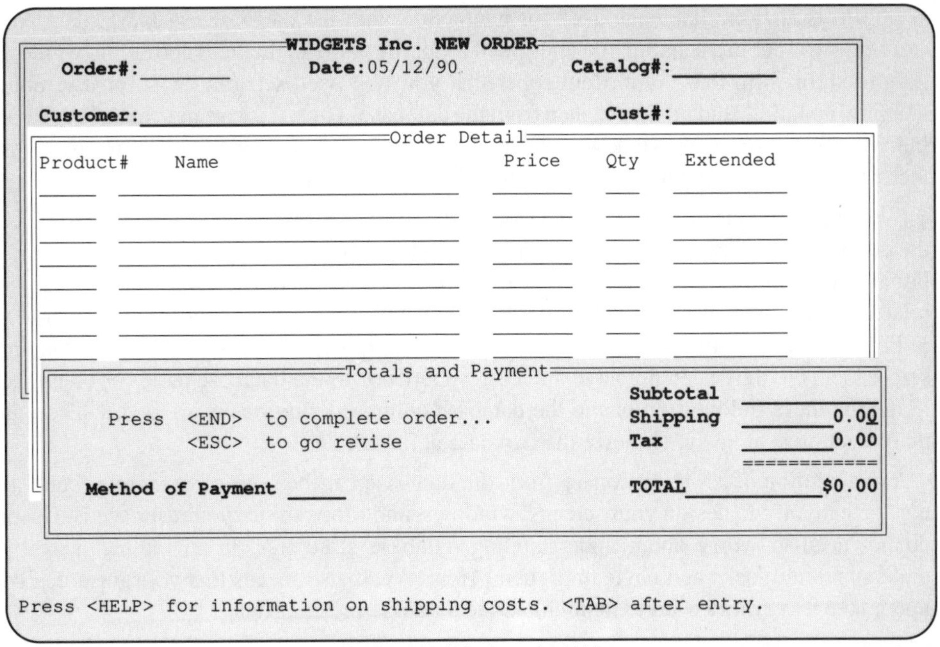

```
                        WIDGETS Inc. NEW ORDER
   Order#:_____       Date:05/12/90.        Catalog#:_____

  Customer:_____        Cust#:_____
                         Order Detail
  Product#    Name                        Price   Qty    Extended
  ____    _____    ____    ___    _____
  ____    _____    ____    ___    _____
  ____    _____    ____    ___    _____
  ____    _____    ____    ___    _____
  ____    _____    ____    ___    _____
  ____    _____    ____    ___    _____
  ____    _____    ____    ___    _____
  ____    _____    ____    ___    _____
                      Totals and Payment
                                           Subtotal  _____
     Press  <END>  to complete order...    Shipping  _____0.00
            <ESC>  to go revise            Tax       _____0.00
                                                     ============
     Method of Payment _____              TOTAL_____$0.00


  Press <HELP> for information on shipping costs. <TAB> after entry.
```

Figure 8-8: Windows in JAM

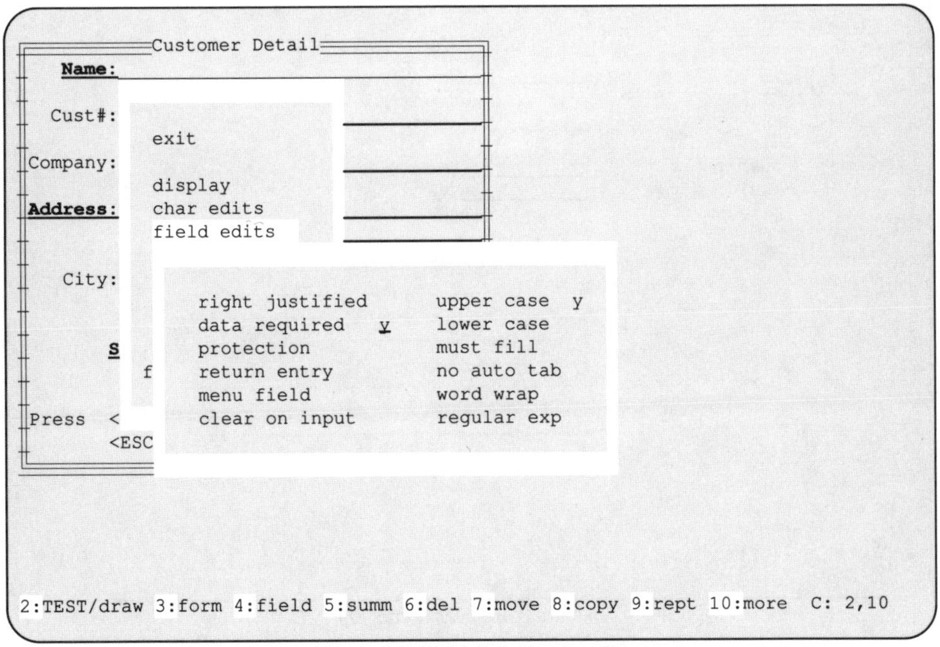

```
            Customer Detail
     Name:

   Cust#:      exit

  Company:     display
               char edits
  Address:     field edits


    City:          right justified      upper case  y
                   data required   y    lower case
       S           protection           must fill
            f      return entry         no auto tab
                   menu field           word wrap
  Press  <         clear on input       regular exp
         <ESC


  2:TEST/draw 3:form 4:field 5:summ 6:del 7:move 8:copy 9:rept 10:more  C: 2,10
```

Figure 8-9: Field Definition in JAM

JPL is also the language used for interaction with the database via JAM/DBi. You store each trigger in a separate file and specify that file name in the field definition, window definition, or form definition. Remember that you will need separate SQL for inserting, deleting, updating, and retrieving data from the database. Thus, it is common to have several individual files for each window or form. As the number of interactive forms programs increases in your application, this proliferation of files becomes difficult to manage.

JAM maintains its own dictionary of field definitions. Figure 8-10 illustrates some of the components of this dictionary. Since its primary focus is forms development, the dictionary keeps information about display characteristics, validation criteria, and other form related information. You can define fields in this dictionary using either the screen shown in Figure 8-10 or while developing your form. Remember, however, that these fields are screen fields — they need not have any correspondence to the database tables or columns. Matching these field definitions to the database column definitions is up to you. There is no tool, at present, to synchronize the two data definitions.

Separation of JAM dictionary from the database can be both a boon and a bane. It means that you can design your screens, windows, and forms to suit your user needs. Users do not need to worry about understanding database structures, in an indirect way by understanding blocks and navigating them. However, it also means that your form design may make it very awkward to manipulate the database meaningfully.

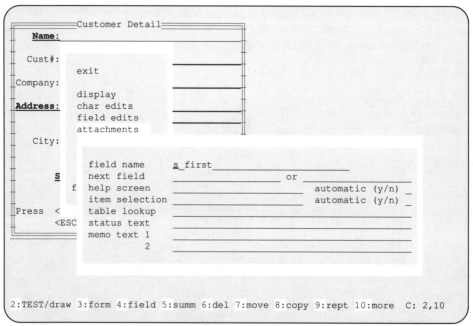

Figure 8-10: JAM Dictionary

I highly recommend that screen designers pay close attention to the underlying database structures. Otherwise, you will find yourself haphazardly altering database structures to suit screen displays. A well-designed database will support the logical displays on screens — if they do not, then, your data models have missed some important business rules.

JAM provides few tools to set project standards and then to enforce them. Its flexibility in building windows can cause inconsistent look and feel between screens developed by different designers. You will have to set your project standards for each common component, such as yes/no prompt windows and so on. JAM interface is function key-driven similar to the SQL*Forms interface. So consistent use of these keys in the user interface is very important.

Another development management issue is how to keep the JAM dictionary synchronized with the database definitions for fields stored in Oracle. Trivial discrepancies can affect the performance of database access; for example, a numeric column retrieved using a character constant causes Oracle to stop using the index, resulting in slow database access. You will need close controls to ensure that such discrepancies do not affect your judgment of both of these excellent products.

JAM's strength is in its prototyping facilities and windowing interface. It is a compact product which performs well in most of its local functions. It is small enough to allow you to build a significant number of screens even on a MS-DOS machine with its 640K memory limit. Its capability of switching between development and test mode allows you to build forms quickly. The resulting user interface is as flashy as you would care to make it.

8.6 ACCELL/SQL Alternatives

ACCELL/SQL is a forms development facility from Unify Corporation. Originally developed for this company's proprietary database management system, this package also interfaces to other DBMS back ends. We briefly review it here because it is one of the few third-party development tools which provides a comprehensive, integrated development facility.

ACCELL/SQL provides a windows based, function key-driven user interface. On MS-DOS PCs, it runs under Microsoft Windows environment. Thus, it supports the use of mouse. Unify Corp also plans to support X-Windows under UNIX with Open Look and Motif flavors soon. With such support, ACCELL provides a very nice interface, allowing you to develop intuitive applications.

The MS-DOS version is particularly interesting since it allows cooperative processing. Your form definitions could continue to live on the Oracle server machine, but execute on your PC workstation. With the proliferation of PCs on users' desks, this option allows you to make use of CPU horsepower at the user's desk.

ACCELL screens are in two parts: a form layout and a file defining the processing for that form. Unlike SQL*Forms or JAM, all triggers for a particular screen are in a single file.

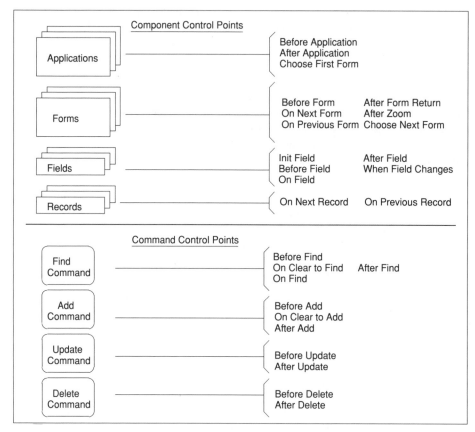

Figure 8-11: ACCELL/SQL Trigger Points

Thus, you can use a text editor to modify them. Figure 8-11 illustrates the points at which you can attach triggers. Notice that ACCELL supports the *post change* concept without requiring you to write extra code to compare field values.

The ACCELL procedural language is rich, with built-in concepts of pick-lists implemented with a single *zoom* statement. You can tie screens together with this zoom facility. Other ways of composing your applications from screens is in sequential order, or programmatically in the ACCELL language. Another unusual feature is that ACCELL pre-compiles the SQL statements in the procedural code that you write. Thus, it reduces the overhead of runtime parsing.

ACCELL/SQL for Oracle does not require its own dictionary, unlike JAM. It passes your SQL statements directly to Oracle. It provides a generation time option to bind screen variables to database variables. It does, however, use shared memory — which means you need to devote much more real memory to shared segments between this product and Oracle. The early releases of this product for Version 6 Oracle used DBA views compatible with Version 5. So make sure you install these views prior to installing this product.

It also assumes Version 5 locking and simulates it in its own lock implementation. Thus, it assumes that Oracle will lock the entire table while writing changes to the database. This assumption, of course, is incorrect for Version 6 with transaction processing option. Until future releases correct it, you may find this product falls short of expected high performance if you use this combination.

Some of the unusual features of ACCELL include its locking of forms which are currently being modified by someone. So two programmers cannot modify a form at the same time. None of the other fourth-generation tools discussed in this book provide such a facility. This features means fewer headaches in a team development environment. In addition under UNIX, its *makeamake* facility builds rules to compile only those parts of the application that changed. This facility, together with the UNIX source code control system (SCCS) provides project source management like few other forms development packages on the market today.

It is a shame that Unify Corporation uses copy protection schemes for this product. It makes installation rather cumbersome. However, the product has the potential to become a good alternative to SQL*Forms. It development environment features make it stand well above other fourth-generation environments which interface to Oracle.

8.7 Development Management Issues

In the wave of featuritis, many fourth-generation development environments have ignored this issue. SQL*Forms provides you with, at best, primitive debugging facilities. JAM completely sidesteps the issue, while ACCELL/SQL provides only source management facilities. Testing is very important with SQL*Forms, since it does not check the trigger statements for correctness until runtime. Misspelled column names can thus escape your notice until too late. So avoid embarrassed red faces — test every possible path through your triggers. Perhaps, product vendors will realize that debugging tools will improve programmer productivity even more than high-level languages. After all, programmers spend more time testing and debugging than writing the code in the first place.

SQL*Forms can be slow if you write long, complex triggers. Triggers are normally executed as soon as possible. Thus, multistep triggers on fields will slow the movement of the cursor between fields. If possible, avoid such triggers. Alter your design, and user expectations so that you can test complex conditions at the end of a block rather than after every field. Remember that Version 2.3 style trigger code causes much unnecessary database access, another reason for slowness. Wherever possible, use macros which are executed locally. As a last resort, you may try the FORMS ACCELERATOR from SQL Solutions, Inc., a third-party vendor. This utility claims to speed forms developed with SQL*Forms.

SQL*Forms definitions live in the SQL*Forms tables in the database, as well as in the *.inp* and *.frm* files. If you practice source code control using the *.inp* files, be sure to load the form definition from these every time. Keeping the form definition in the database tables is tempting, because you can then use reporting tools to print them. However, then you will find it difficult to track who made what changes to a form. SQL*Forms prevents two users from updating the same form due to Oracle's locking facilities, albeit the message you see is the generic *ORA-00054 resource busy and acquire with NOWAIT specified.*

Programs developed with SQL*Forms are fairly portable. The only difficulties relate to the use of graphics characters on different terminals. If you use boxes in your screen layout, chances are you will need to load your form definition back into the database, and regenerate the form for a different terminal type. If you plan to support multiple terminal types, I suggest you avoid using these graphics characters. Terminal control sequence definitions are contained in a CRT file. You can generate new CRT files using utilities supplied with Oracle. To run SQL*Forms temporarily on a different terminal type, specify the *-c* option together with the new CRT file name.

9

Report Programs

The major part of applications, after interactive screen programs, is reporting. In fact, we generally retrieve data more often than enter it. When developing applications for users who are used to another, older, system, you have to take into account that they are likely to demand printed reports for everything. You may have put a screen on each of their desks which makes their typical queries much simpler via interactive forms. But getting them used to querying on the screen takes time—you are changing their culture! Your best bet is identify the purposes for which they currently use printed reports and then make sure you supply all of that data on the screen. A sneaky trick is to get one of the brighter (or newer) members of user staff to be your champion for the new way working. It's surprising how quickly procedures change when you rouse the competitive spirit.

In the meantime, you still have to develop tedious reports, many of which are rather simplistic. Listings of all clients sorted by the names, or grouped by some column, is not exactly stimulating. This is where a good fourth-generation report writer proves its mettle.

Rather than reiterate the product manuals, I will describe how to develop the types of reports we discussed in the design phase. I find that you learn the uses of reporting tools more easily in this manner. You will have to extrapolate from my examples to suit your particular reporting requirements. This chapter is not a tutorial in how to drive a product keystroke by keystroke. In this chapter, we cover the following topics

- An overview of the tools available for generating reports from an Oracle database. We will examine the types of reports each tool is best suited for.

- Some of the performance considerations when writing SQL statements. Regardless of which tools you use, you write SQL to access data from the database.

- Report formatting techniques for SQL*Plus, SQL*Report Writer, and a third-party report writer, SQR. Annotated example code for each of these products illustrate the concepts.

- A brief review of facilities offered by SQL*Report (RPT). Our focus is primarily newer products than this precursor to SQL*Report Writer.

9.1 Tools for Reporting

A report is really just data from the database formatted to look pretty. The SQL language allows us to retrieve data: a query language standard with Oracle DBMS. However, standard SQL has few formatting facilities. We cannot, for example, specify page headers. Oracle's implementation adds report formatting facilities to SQL; hence its name SQL*Plus. SQL*Plus includes page formatting, limited control break processing, and column formatting facilities. With these facilities, you can make even quick and dirty reports look good.

SQL*Plus is particularly suited to writing **tabular reports**, which we discussed in the design phase. Such reports are a large proportion of typical data processing reports. Typically, you are limited to a single SQL statement per report. Some of these statements become quite complex, especially when you join tables and use subqueries. So you are not limited to data from a single table in a SQL*Plus report. In fact, with certain types of data, you can also produce a **matrix report**, though such reports stretch the abilities of the formatting facilities of SQL*Plus.

The SQL *select* statement is the primary means of retrieving data from an Oracle database. We used some of the simpler statements in an earlier chapter for developing forms. In this chapter, we use more complex facilities of SQL, including table *joins*, *Union* operator, *Decode* function, dummy columns, and so on. Many of these functions are standard and are extensively covered by textbooks on SQL such as those listed in the bibliography. I annotate the examples in this chapter extensively to clarify the clauses of each SQL statement.

In addition to SQL*Plus, Oracle provides the SQL*Report product, which is known to Oracle fans as RPT. To avoid confusion with Oracle's newer product, SQL*Report-Writer, we will refer to it as RPT. This product allows procedural processing of the rows retrieved from a SQL statement. Its basic operational concept is to process all the data one row at a time, writing it to an intermediate file interspersed with formatting commands. These formatting commands are somewhat similar to those found in text processors like runoff on VMS and nroff on UNIX. The formatting companion utility, RPF, generates the final output from this intermediate file.

RPT works by dividing the page into tables made up of columns, as you would need for tabular reports. The default table is the full width of the page. Each column can be a different size within one table. You can define several tables, each with different column layout. Formatting a report then consists of initializing the required table, placing data items in appropriate columns, and closing the table. You can, of course, nest tables within other tables. By the way, I have come across a few typesetting packages which work on similar principles, especially for typesetting columnar information like telephone directories. (Note: I do not mean to imply that RPT has any pretensions at typesetting facilities).

RPT is an interpretive language. In fact, it executes many operations by using SQL on an Oracle dummy table, *system.dual*. The resulting database accesses tend to make it slow. RPT provides a few primitive arithmetic commands, such as add A to B and store result in C. So, when you use its rather primitive *reverse-polish* style arithmetic operations, expect your scripts to run slower than without them. There are third-party products which claim to convert RPT code into C for performance improvement. For expressions involving more complex arithmetic, I would resort to SQL rather than multiple RPT statements. A single SQL statement, in such cases, is much more efficient than several RPT statements, each performing a single operation. This technique is an obvious conclusion when you realize that each statement performing one operation translates into one SQL statement, behind the scenes.

The newer SQL*ReportWriter product implements a completely different method. I expect that it will replace SQL*Report (RPT) for reporting activities. RPT may still be used in procedural batch processing until PL/SQL becomes widely available.

SQL*ReportWriter implements a visual interface to defining reports. It is still a utility for developers — I think it is too complicated for end users. It is based on Oracle's new style of utilities with ring menus and simulated windows. The primary command menu allows you access to matrices of details for each aspect of a report, such as group control breaks, field formatting, summary definitions, trim text, and so on. Making effective use of these facilities requires you to change your perspective on what a report is made up of. The key concepts you need are the following:

- A report is made up of pages, starting with a title page, then report pages, and ending with a report trailer page. Title and trailer pages are very useful for you to identify who the report is for and whether the report ended successfully.

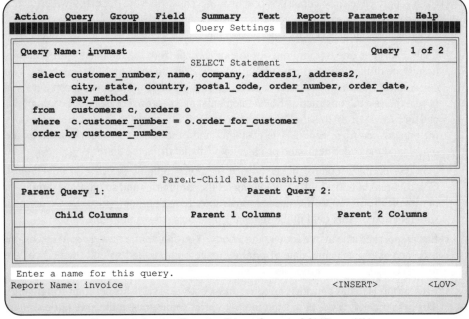

Figure 9-1: Invoice Report—Parent Query in SQL*ReportWriter

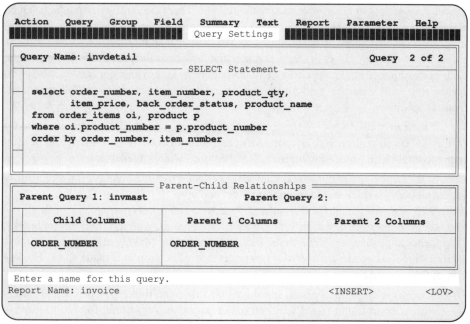

Figure 9-2: Invoice Report—Child Query in SQL*ReportWriter

- Each report page may consist of one or more panels if your report is wider than a physical page. For example, you can print a report which is as wide as two pieces of paper pasted together side by side — each piece of paper corresponds to a panel.

- Each report has one or more queries to extract data from the database. Query definition is one of the options on the primary menu. Each query is an SQL statement. You can connect queries into master detail relationships or into a matrix report. You will need expertise in constructing SQL statements, one potential reason for keeping your end users away from this tool. Figures 9-1 and 9-2 illustrate the two queries necessary for our *invoice form report*. The customer and order data (invmast) is liked as the *parent* and the order items and product data (invdetail) is the *child*.

- You can define a control break on one or more columns selected in your query. Control breaks are useful for calculating totals, summaries and so on. For example, in our invoice form report, we need an order total based on item_price. So we define a sum function on this field in the *summary* option as shown in Figure 9-3.

- Each report has a header, a footer, and a body. You can define these to contain custom text such as report name, date of printing, page number, and so on. The body of the report consists of each group and detail lines.

- Each group also has a header, a footer, and a body. Use this header to print summary data before detail lines, or use the footer to print summaries at the end. For example, print the count of customers in a state using a group header before a detail name list.

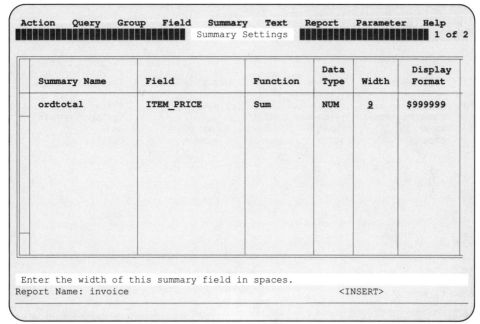

Summary Settings   1 of 2

Summary Name	Field	Function	Data Type	Width	Display Format
ordtotal	ITEM_PRICE	Sum	NUM	9	$999999

Enter the width of this summary field in spaces.
Report Name: invoice   <INSERT>

Figure 9-3: Invoice Report—Summary Definition Screen in SQL*Report Writer

- The body of the report is the detail data — each row that you extract in the query. This body differs by the type of report you want. For a tabular report, it consists of columns corresponding to those extracted from the database. For an embedded data report, you can write your own wording to make up a form letter with customer names inserted at the appropriate places. In our invoice report example, we intend to use preprinted forms and hence there are no headings in this part of the report definition. In Section 9.6, we illustrate a form letter example.

SQL*Report Writer presents each of these components to you as a table of options. For example, it presents a list of fields as shown in Figure 9-4. The columns to the right are different formatting options available to you. Unfortunately, you cannot see the effect of each change, unless you execute the report after each one. I would highly recommend frequent execution of your report — to make sure your changes have a desired effect. Remember that you can execute the current report definition at any time by simply choosing *execute* option from the *action* menu. You need not leave any definition screen.

The order of primary menus is fairly significant. Its left-to-right orientation is the typical sequence for developing a report. Check the report output after each change as you proceed with each option, left-to-right in the menus. For example, start by defining the queries for the report, one at a time, testing the output after each one. Then move on to specifying groups, and get them correct before moving on to columns, and so on. Correcting earlier items such as queries after changing later items such as field definitions causes many discrepancies — recovering from them is a nontrivial task.

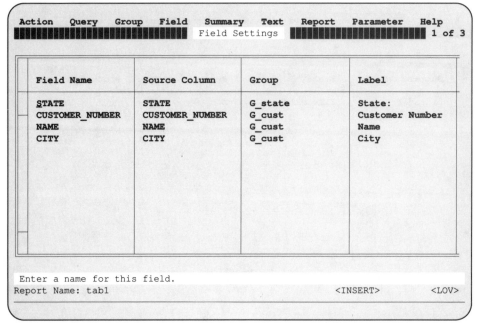

Figure 9-4: Invoice Report—Field Definition Screen in SQL*Report Writer

From this description, it should be obvious that you cannot simply sit down at SQL*Report Writer and start developing a report. You need some idea of the layout of your report before you start. Identify the style of your report: a tabular, matrix, preprinted form, or embedded data — the styles we discussed in our earlier chapters on design.

Don't expect great productivity improvements from SQL*Report Writer. I found its performance disappointing, even with a fast 386-based PC workhorse all to myself. The initial version of the product, Version 1.0, spent most of its time in database access. Putting in an expensive fast disk on my machine helped a lot. Version 1.1 is supposedly faster. On multiuser machines, remember that you share resources with many other users. Hence, you get a smaller piece of the disk access action.

There are several third-party tools for report writing, in addition to the Oracle's tools. Typically, these tools work with Oracle as well as other well-known database management systems. In this chapter, we will look at Easy SQR and SQR products offered by SQ Software, Inc. ESQR offers a visual, interactive report definition interface. It comes the closest, in my estimation, to removing the need for knowing the SQL language when defining reports. It presents lists of tables and columns for you to pick when defining your select statements, specifying joins between tables, and for defining sort order of output. Behind the scenes, it composes a SQL statement for accessing the Oracle database.

SQR, its mature counterpart, is a more traditional report-generation language. Its facilities compared to RPT and speed of execution are the reason for its popularity. ESQR can also generate SQR code, so you can use it to generate a starter template.

9.2 Performance Considerations

The main consideration for making your report run faster is the wording of your SQL statement with respect to the table indexes. From our overview of the tools in Section 9.1, it should be obvious that you cannot get away from SQL in any of the tools, except perhaps ESQR. So project managers should establish some procedures for reviewing the SQL statements used in each of the performance-critical programs. Although performance is typically less critical in reports, make sure they can complete in the time period for overnight runs. Poorly written reports become resource hogs — slowing down other processing on the same machine.

Here are some tips to keep in mind when writing SQL statements:

- Make sure there is an index on each column used in a join. The index may include other columns from the table, provided that the join column is the first in index sequence.

- At least one of the join columns should have a unique index. This rule is natural if you join along a relationship in the entity-relationship diagram. One of the columns in the join will be a unique identifier (primary key) for its table.

- If you have Version 6 Oracle, try the *Explain* facility to determine the order in which it will execute statement clauses. The SQL optimizer has very definite rules for ordering the execution, with no knowledge of the size of your tables. Shuffling conditions in the *where* clause around, such that the most restrictive clause is last, can improve execution time significantly.

- Keep the use of *system.dual* to a minimum. Remember that each reference to this table is a database access. In a distributed processing environment, such an access can slow response significantly, unless a local *system.dual* table is available. Keep in mind that some tools make hidden references to tables, such as performing arithmetic operations in RPT.

- Reduce the use of subqueries in SQL — try joins whenever possible. Oracle's SQL optimizer is tuned for joins, especially when adequate indexes exist. Try your own experiments to see how much of a speed difference there is between subqueries and joins when the tables contain several thousand rows.

- Avoid single table accesses with programmatic joins, unless you have small tables and use memory array facilities, such as SQR provides. The SQL optimizer typically works much faster than any other programming tricks.

Let me illustrate the side effects of poorly written queries. One of my consulting clients was convinced that accessing flat files from a program was much faster than using Oracle. So adamant were they that they were prepared to write off their $250,000 investment in Oracle software. Close examination revealed pages and pages of code scanning Oracle tables one record at a time. They were using the tables as flat files! This programmer was merely substituting SQL statements for record read and performing all matches in the program. A slight rewrite of the code, to use SQL facilities not only reduced the code to about one page, but ran quite a bit faster than the C program that worked against the same data in flat files. Such mishaps are common among programmers who have little prior experience with set-oriented query languages and even less training.

9.3 Tabular Reports

Let us consider a simple report: a list of customers by state. This report involves only the customer table. We would like to start a new page for each new state, and the state name should be printed once at the top of the page. Figure 9-5 shows an annotated SQL*Plus script to produce this report. This type of report is really a remnant of the days of batch systems, where we primarily worked from paper reports. It might be useful for dividing customer calls between many sales staff. With an online lookup, such as is possible with a SQL*Forms program, we probably do not need this report.

SQL*Plus is a good tool to develop such simple reports. Its reporting capabilities are ideal for making a quick and dirty report look sufficiently pretty to satisfy most users. However, it is not flexible enough if you try to make the report format exactly as you wanted. It only provides limited formatting capabilities.

We could use such simple tabular reports for more complex business functions. For example, consider a report showing sales by product, useful for finding our biggest sellers. We can find sales information in the *order items* table. So we could use the following select statement:

```
select product_number, sum(item_price)
from order_items
group by product_number
order by product_number
```

The *sum* function allows us total item values. The *group by* clause ensures that the totals will be for each product number. Obviously, a product name would be more useful to the recipient of this report than product numbers. So we need to use the product numbers in the order items table to find their corresponding product names from the product table. The SQL *join* operation is intended for associating the order items table to the product table. (This, at last, is the practical use of the relationships we drew in entity-relationship diagrams!) The final annotated report is shown in Figure 9-6.

There is no limit on the number of tables you can join in a single SQL statement. However, how fast it executes depends on the wording of the statement. Remember the earlier hints on optimizing statements.

So writing reports in SQL*Plus is not difficult, if you know the structure of the database. I would hesitate to offer this utility to a nontechnical user for ad hoc reporting, at least without extensive training. There are other reasons for my hesitation. I suffer from memory failures — I cannot remember the exact spelling for column and table names. I imagine this is not an uncommon failing. Digging around for dictionary printouts causes a severe decline in my productivity. Using the *describe table* statement interactively is frustrating because I need to switch back and forth between the editor and interactive SQL*Plus.

Note that these annotations should be really comments in the script.

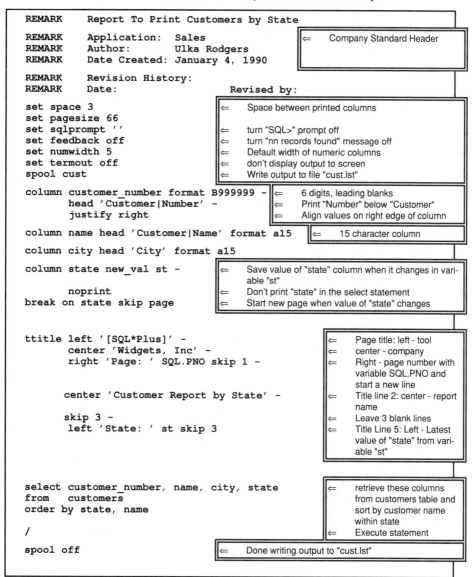

Figure 9-5: SQL*Plus Simple Tabular Report

I like tools which show me lists of tables and columns for me to pick from. Oracle's SQL*Report Writer offers pick-lists for many report writing tasks — not, unfortunately, for writing SQL statements. Easy SQR, from SQ Software, offers a visual way of defining joins. Figure 9-7 shows the screen presented by Easy SQR for defining a join between

```
REMARK      Report To Print Sales by Product
REMARK      Application:  Sales
REMARK      Author:       Ulka Rodgers
REMARK      Date Created: January 4, 1990
REMARK      Revision History:
REMARK      Date:                  Revised by:
REMARK      Description:
REMARK
REMARK      Tables: customer
REMARK

set space 3
set pagesize 66
set sqlprompt ''
set feedback off
set numwidth 5
set termout off
spool salesum

column product_number format 0999999 -    ⇐    6 digits, leading zeros

      head 'Product|Number' justify right
column name head 'Product|Name' format a15

column sales head 'Sales' -          ⇐   Alias for sum(item_price) column assigned in
                                          the select statement
      format $99,999,999.99          ⇐   Leading Dollar Sign, comma separated value
                                          up to 99 million
break on report skip 2               ⇐   At the end of report print 2 blank lines
compute sum of sales on report       ⇐   Grand total of sales at the end of report

ttitle left '[SQL*Plus]' center 'Widgets, Inc' -
   right 'Page: ' SQL.PNO skip 1 -
   center 'Sales by Product' skip 3

select order_items.product_number,      ⇐   Explicitly state the table for
                                            ambiguous columns
   products.product_name,               ⇐   Table name here is good practice
   sum(order_items.item_price) sales    ⇐   Total over item_price, call this
                                            column "sales" for this statement
from   order_items, products            ⇐   Tables to used in select
where  order_items.product_number =     ⇐   Join based on common column -
          products.product_number           product_number:
                                            only take rows with matching
                                            product numbers
group by order_items.product_number,    ⇐   To get totals for each product
          products.product_name
order by product_name
/

spool off                            ⇐   Done writing output to "salesum.lst"
```

Figure 9-6: SQL*Plus Complex Tabular Report

Products and *Order Items* tables. Easy SQR does not have some of the facilities of SQL*ReportWriter such as matrix reports discussed later. However, its interactive report writing interface makes development of simpler reports a lot easier.

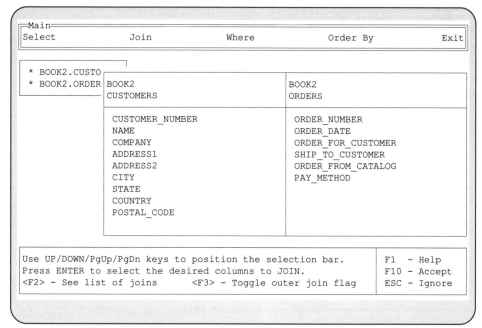

Figure 9-7: ESQR Join Definition Screen

If you have a lot of simple reports, it is worthwhile investing in a tool such as ESQR, just to have it generate the SQR scripts for you.

9.4 Form Reports

Form reports typically use preprinted forms which come in any number of flavors from checks or customer invoices through to year-end payroll tax forms. The tricky part with these reports is the need to align your printing exactly to spaces provided in the pre-printed form. Misalignment of the check amount leaves you open to potential fraud. On a less severe case, you lose credibility with your customers when they can't read your misaligned invoices.

Unfortunately, few DBMS tools provide you with the necessary tools to try alignments repeatedly until you get it right. Instead you must depend on the print spooling facilities of your operating system. On multiuser systems with remote or shared printers this scheme makes sense. On single-user machines such as MS-DOS, there is no such spooling facility.

An alternative trick is to create a table which contains a small number of dummy rows, say five or six. The format of this table should match the data for your preprinted form. You could then print these dummy rows repeatedly until your form alignment on the printer is satisfactory. Then, print the report with real data perfectly aligned. In each test print you would only waste a few pages of preprinted forms. If your preprinted forms have a consistent layout, you could use the same alignment test for several different forms.

SQL*Plus has very limited facilities to change the layout of reports. For example, you cannot specify that you would like the customer name printed starting in column 15, except perhaps by concatenating the customer name to a literal of 15 spaces. However, such machinations remove the quick report development benefits of SQL*Plus. Instead, you need to use a real procedural report generator, like SQR, or in desperation, even the anti-quated RPT.

Building form reports in SQL*Report Writer is not very easy. It is more suited to reports where you can make up the layout to fit its mold. Layouts dictated by an outside force such as a preprinted form means you do more up front work to translate into SQL*Report Writer's development style.

Figures 9-8 illustrates the SQL*ReportWriter screen where you might edit the layout of the report fields. Unfortunately, there are no column counter or ruler displays for easily locating a field position. You will have to guess at the approximate location and test the printout several times.

Remember to use this part after you have verified that the report content is correct. Changing the report content later, that is, the calculations and columns in the report, means that you will have to redo some of the layouts. Figures 9-1 through 9-3 illustrated the queries and total definitions for this same report.

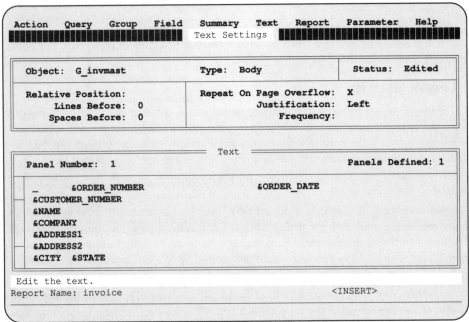

Figure 9-8: Invoice Report—Text Layout Screen in SQL*Report Writer

```
!   Report to Print invoices on preprinted forms
!   Application:    Sales
!   Author:         Ulka Rodgers
!   Date Created:   February 12, 1990
!   Revision History:
!   Description:
!
!   Tables: Customers, Orders, Order_items, Product
begin-setup                        ⇐    Page is 40 lines, 80 columns
   page-size 40 80
end-setup
begin-report                       ⇐    beginning of report initializa-
   do startup                           tion
   do invoice                      ⇐    print them
end-report
begin-procedure startup            ⇐    Once at beginning of report only
   move 0 to #inv_total

end-procedure

begin-procedure invoice            ⇐    print invoice header, then call
                                        get_ord_items to print lines
                                        and total
begin-select                       ⇐    Database access starts here.
order_number     (4,15,9)          ⇐    Short-hand print statement:
order_date       (4,32,9)               line 4, column 15, length 9
customer_number  (5,2,9)                digits

name             (6,2,32)

company          (+1,2,32)              ⇐    +1 for next line

address1            (+1,2,52)
address2            (+1,2,52)
city             (10,2,20)
state            (10,23,20)
country          (11,2, 20)
postal_code      (11,25,10)

   do get_ord_items                ⇐    Loop once for each row, and print order
                                        lines
   new-page                        ⇐    ready for next invoice

from orders o, customers c
where o.order_for_customer = c.customer_number
end-select

end-procedure                      ⇐end invoice procedure
```

Figure 9-9: Invoice Report (Part 1)——in SQR

```
!
!    Procedure: get_ord_items
!
!    Called once per order to print order details
!    Note: We assume that all order items fit on one page!
!          In real life, you will need to check & print
!          multiple pages for each invoice.
!
begin-procedure get_ord_items

move 0 to #total          ⇐    initialize variables for each invoice
position (14,1)

begin-select
!   test and handling for multiple pages should go here.

item_number      (+1,  2,  9)        ⇐   +1 specifies next line
product_name        (0, 11, 30)      ⇐   0 means same line.

product_qty    (0, 43,  9)
item_price     (0, 53,  9)
back_order_status   (0, 63,  2)

    add &item_price to #total        ⇐   once for each order_items row in
                                          this order to get invoice total

from order_items oi, product p
where oi.product_number = p.product_number

and   oi.order_number = &order_number    ⇐    most restrictive clause
order by item_number                          is last for speed
end-select

    print #total (31, 53,  9) edit        ⇐    format and print
$,$$$,$$9.99                                   end-of-invoice total

end-procedure                  ⇐   end get_ord_items
```

Figure 9-9: Invoice Report (Part 2)——in SQR

SQR has facilities for more precise placement. Figure 9-9 illustrates the same pre-printed form invoice report written in SQR. Notice that there are two standard procedures in this report. The initialization procedure, *begin-setup*, is executed once at the beginning of the report. The report procedure, *begin-report*, is where the meat of the report is. From this procedure, we called two of our own procedures, *startup* and *invoice*. There are other standard procedures such as *begin-heading* for setting page headers, *begin-footing* for page footers, and *begin-document* for page layout including trim text. These were not necessary for our preprinted forms report.

In this report, we retrieve from the database using the invoice procedure and the get_ord_items procedure. The *select* statement enclosed within the *begin-select* and *end-select* clauses is actually a loop. The statements to be executed in the loop start immediately after specifying which columns we want to select and complete as we specify the *from* clause for the *select* statement.

In this report, we call the *get_ord_items* procedure once for each invoice printed. We select only those order items that relate to the particular order using the order number in the *where* clause. Clearly, the best indexing scheme for these retrievals is a unique index on the *order_number* column in the *orders* table and a concatenated index on *order_number* and *item_number* columns in the *order_items* table. CASE*Dictionary's default index design utility will suggest indexes that are close to the optimum. However, it will recommend the concatenation of *order_items* and *product_number* columns for the order items table. You may have to add in the *item_number* column to its recommended index on *order_items*.

9.5 Matrix Reports

These reports look like a spreadsheet printout. They are very common in financial and management reporting. In our example Widgets sales system, we need a report of customer buying patterns by state. Rather than analyzing the patterns for individual products, we use product categories. Thus, the report consists of product categories as columns across the top, states as rows, and each cell in the matrix shows the number of items sold in this category. The output format for this report is shown in the chapter on application design.

This report could be developed in SQL*Plus, if you hard code the product category values into the SQL statement as shown below. Notice the use of the *decode* function — one of Oracle's extended facilities. This function matches its first argument (product_category) to its second argument (literal value of category). If these two values match, it returns the third argument, and if they don't match, it returns the fourth argument. You can repeat the second and third argument pairs with different values, which was not necessary in this example. It would be necessary if our report showed the combined sales for, say, appliances and tools.

```
select state,
    sum(decode (product_category, 1, product_qty, 0)) 'Appliance',
    sum(decode (product_category, 2, product_qty, 0)) 'Clothing',
    sum(decode (product_category, 3, product_qty, 0)) 'Tools'
    sum(product_qty)
from order_items oi, orders o, customer c, products p
where oi.order_number     = o.order_number
and    o.order_for_customer = c.customer_number
and    oi.product_number    = p.product_number
group by state, product_category
order by state
```

Imagine if we had to write this report for several dozen categories in SQL*Plus — the result would be an ugly SQL statement. Its performance would be dreadful as it churned its way through megabytes of sales data. Using SQL*Report Writer or the third-party SQR software is a good alternative.

In SQL*Report Writer we need to write three queries for such a report — one for listing states as rows from the states table, one for listing product categories across the page as columns, and one to calculate the value of each cell. Figure 9-10 shows the most complex of these three queries, the cell calculation query. This query is then linked as a child to the other two queries as shown in the *Parent-Child Relationships* section on the screen.

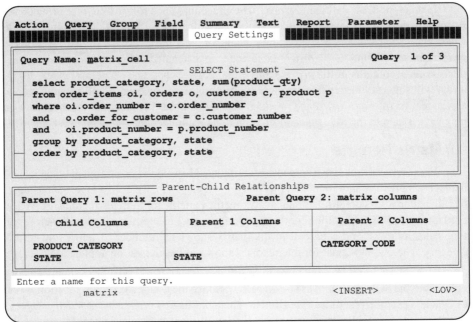

Figure 9-10: Sales Analysis Report—Cell Query Screen in SQL*Report Writer

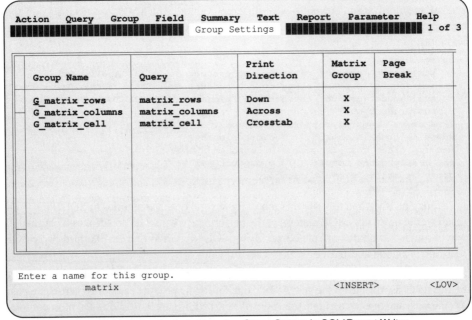

Figure 9-11: Sales Analysis Report—Group Screen in SQL*Report Writer

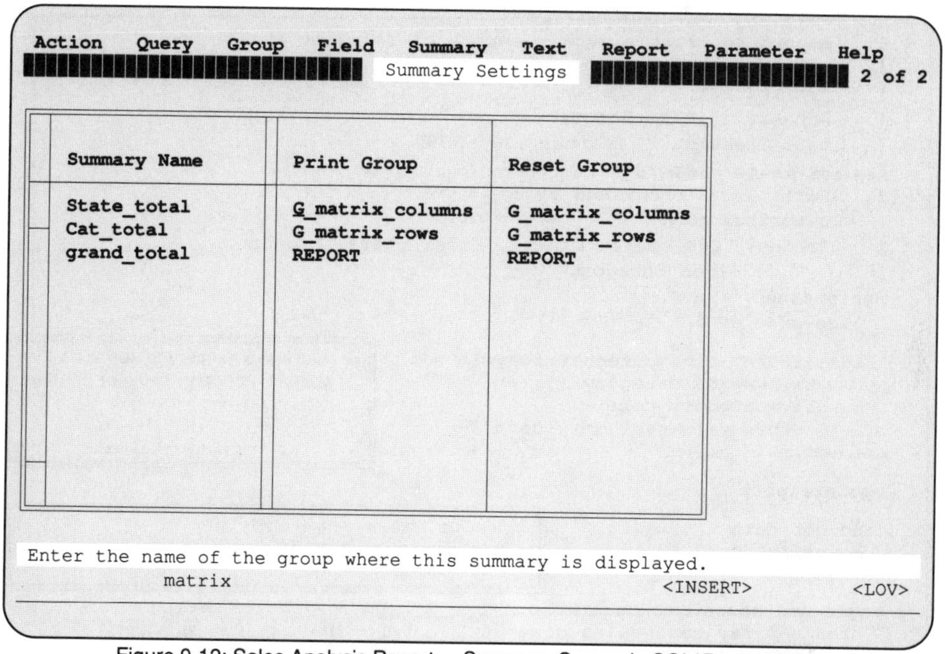

```
Action   Query   Group   Field   Summary   Text   Report   Parameter   Help
████████████████████████████    Summary Settings    ████████████████████████  2 of 2
```

Summary Name	Print Group	Reset Group
State_total	G_matrix_columns	G_matrix_columns
Cat_total	G_matrix_rows	G_matrix_rows
grand_total	REPORT	REPORT

```
Enter the name of the group where this summary is displayed.
        matrix                                    <INSERT>        <LOV>
```

Figure 9-12: Sales Analysis Report—Summary Screen in SQL*Report Writer

We have to describe the layout of the selected columns from each of these queries in the *Group* settings screen. Figure 9-11 illustrates these settings. By the way, don't forget to remove the field labels in the *Field* settings screen. Otherwise, your report layout will look like spaghetti. In addition, we would like totals for each category and each state. We use the *Summary* screen for this purpose — like in our invoice example. Figure 9-12 illustrates the summary settings for these totals. PC Oracle developers should watch out — SQL*Report Writer requires enormous amounts of expanded memory over and above Oracle itself. The repetitive prototyping cycle typical of my development style caused it to run out of memory while I was developing this report on a 4-megabyte PC. The work around is to exit from SQL*Report Writer every so often and restart it.

The same matrix report is illustrated below in SQR. This report illustrates some of the efficiency features of SQR, notably, in memory lookup arrays and storage array structures. Note, however, the undisguised resemblance to a third-generation language in the *print-data* procedure. Debugging this code would have been a lot easier if I had a decent debugging utility, which is unfortunately not available.

```
!     Report to Print a matrix report of Sales by State
!
!     Application:    Sales
!     Author:    Ulka Rodgers
!     Date Created:    February 12, 1990
!     Revision History:
!     Date:          Revised by:
!     Description:
!     Tables:  Customers, Orders, Order_items, Product,
!           Prod_category
begin-setup
  page-size 60 80

  load-lookup name=category rows=10 -        ⇐ load into a memory table values for
     table=prod_category -                      product category - used for printing
     key=category_code -
     return_value=category_desc
end-setup

begin-report

  do get_data                      ⇐ load up the array with analysis
  do print_data                    ⇐ print sales by product category
end-report

begin-procedure get_data                ⇐ load array for sales qty
  create-array name=sales size=70       ⇐ Maximum 70 states in matrix
     field=state:char -                 ⇐ Up to 10 product categories for each
     field=volume:number:10 -              state
     field=total:number                 ⇐ Total for each state
  move 1 to #j
  move 0 to #last_count

begin-select

state &ssst                       ⇐ Call it "&ssst" in this report
sum(product_qty) &qty             ⇐ "&qty" is an alias for sum(..)
product_category &prod_cat        ⇐ used to index into sales:volume array

  move &prod_cat to #pc                   ⇐ # = numeric var
  add 1 to #last_count
  if &ssst = $last_state                  ⇐ $=character var

     array-add &qty to sales(#j) volume(#pc)   ⇐ "volume" is the category
                                                 total in this state

  else

     move &ssst to $last_state            ⇐ Save new state in &ssst var
     add 1 to #pc                         ⇐ start a new entry in array
     put &ssst into sales(#j) state       ⇐ State name into array field

     array-add &qty to sales(#j) volume(#pc)
  end-if

  array-add &qty to sales(#j) total       ⇐ Keep running total for state
```

Figure 9-13: Matrix Report (Part 1) — in SQR

```
from order_items oi, orders o, customers c, product p

where   o.order_for_customer = c.customer_number        ⇐    Join tables to
and     oi.order_number = o.order_number                    get totals by state
and     oi.product_number = p.product_number               and category

group by state, product_category
order by state
end-select

end-procedure                                    ⇐       end procedure get-data

begin-procedure print_data

   move 1 to #j                           ⇐ category col counter
   move 15 to #col                        ⇐ col position for categories
   while #j < 4                           ⇐ print category values as heading

      lookup category #j $cat_name        ⇐    Lookup each category descrip-
      print $cat_name (5, #col, 15)            tion in the memory array and print it
      add 1 to #j                              across the page.
      add 15 to #col
   end-while

   move 1 to #s                           ⇐ state row counter
   move 1 to #j                           ⇐ category column counter
   move 7 to #line                        ⇐ print starting from line 7

   move 15 to #col

   while #s <= #last_count                ⇐    are we done yet?
      get $ssst from sales(#s) state      ⇐    print state name
      print $ssst (#line, 2, 15)
      move 1 to #j                        ⇐ for each product category print vol-
      while #j < 4                           umes for state

         get #qty from sales(#s) volume(#j)
         print #qty (#line,#col,5) edit 99999
         add 1 to #j
         add 15 to #col
      end-while

      get #tot from sales(#s) total       ⇐    Print total for state

      print #tot (#line,#col,5) edit 99999
      add 1 to #line
      add 1 to #s

      move 15 to #col                     ⇐       on to next state
   end-while
end-procedure
```

Figure 9-13: Matrix Report (Part 2)—in SQR

9.6 Embedded Data Reports

These reports have a lot of trim text, also called boilerplate text, with some data embedded into the text. A classic example of such a report is a letter for bulk mailing. Embedding data into such a letter is a similar concept to mail-merge in most word processing programs. Word processors, however, rarely interface with your database to include data.

Figure 9-14 illustrates the text layout screen in SQL*Report Writer for a form letter. In this example, there are no calculated fields embedded in the text. However, using the techniques illustrated in Sections 9.1 and 9.4, we could include calculated values just as easily. For example, we could generate letters to employees showing their performance bonuses, payroll deductions and known tax status, and request corrections.

For reports such as this, you could also use ESQR or SQR products. They support a *document* procedure for defining boilerplate text and assigning locations for database variables. Then, your print statements use these locations rather than line and column positions for each database column. You can even embed printer control strings for font changes, and so on.

The difficulty with using report generators in this type of report is the quality of the output. Report generators, today, do not have publishing features such as font selection, embedding graphics into text, and so on. As I remarked in the earlier design chapter, letters which are obviously computer printed are passe, in today's age of desktop publishing.

These features become particularly important when you need to graph the data in your database and print it as part of your bulk mailing report. For example, you might want a graph showing the performance of a mutual fund over several years as part of the prospectus sent to customers. Your database contains the necessary performance data, but how to extract, graph, and include the result into a publishing quality document?

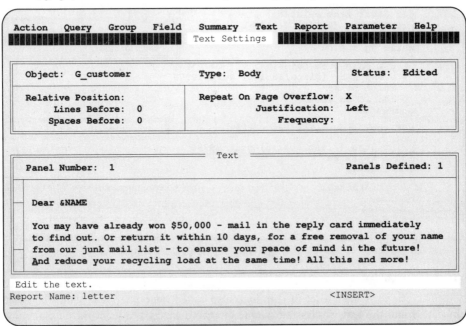

Figure 9-14: Letter Report—Text Layout Screen in SQL*Report Writer

The Oracle for Lotus 1-2-3 package might be one way to bring database data into a spreadsheet in order to graph it. As a separate manual step, you might include the graph in a desktop publishing package for final layout. This method is satisfactory, if you graph high-level trend data. More specifically, lower-level data changes too frequently for this technique to work effectively. Changes occurring since the last extraction into the spreadsheet make the data outdated. Keeping the data synchronized becomes a difficult task requiring expensive manual intervention.

Outdated data occasionally leads to amusing mistakes. For example, one of my past employers sent me enrollment forms for converting to a new pension investment plan when the company decided to change its pension plans. They delivered these forms to me via overnight courier delivery at some considerable expense. The funny part was that this happened three or four months after I had left. They had extracted my name from their database just before my last day in order to prepare a very nice personalized package. It had taken them nearly three months to produce the high-quality personalized package for mailing to an ex-employee!

9.7 Development Management Issues

Obviously, report generators do not come with built-in debugging facilities. Instead you have to use the old-fashioned method of putting in print statements to find out what's happening. Debugging nonprocedural interfaces such as SQL*Report Writer and ESQR is even more difficult. A change in one part of the definition can have unforeseen effects on other parts.

The solution is to test the output after each definition, at least until you gain familiarity with the way these products work. Test the output in SQL*Report Writer after you define the queries, after defining groups, after each field, and so on. Unfortunately, the product is rather slow to react, unless you have a moderately large machine with fast disks all to yourself. I found myself annoyed with its performance even on a 25-Mhz 386 with fast SCSI disk. The next release, Version 1.1, supposedly alleviates some of these performance issues. Until then, I recommend you practice perseverance or become an SQL*Report Writer expert so you won't need to test so often.

SQL*Report Writer needs each developer to have their own set of tables. The product supplies SQL scripts to add these tables and drop them for individual users. However, your development environment becomes much more complex to set up. The best way is to completely isolate each developer by giving each developer an Oracle user name and password and a complete set of tables. When developers complete their programming, they transfer developed reports to a different id for system test.

This scenario works well when you have a stable set of table definitions. If your table definitions change frequently, as I noticed in environments where little prior analysis and design is done, you will have to re create table definitions each time they change for each developer. The alternative method of using a single Oracle user name and password for all developers is almost as bad. You only have one set of table definitions to manage. But each person must share test data with all others. How could they set up and test extreme case handling and incorrect data handling when their data is constantly blown away by someone else testing their update/delete programs?

Source code management is even more difficult with this fourth-generation development utility. There is no source to manage! Rather you have some data stored in database tables where you cannot track what was changed, when, and who by. You could control the *generated* runtime report definitions. These definitions are in binary format, so make sure your source management package can manage binary files as well. With SQR, you still have traditional source code in a file, and it is therefore easy to incorporate into a source code management system.

Maintenance strategy on reports developed with fourth-generation utilities is rather simple — avoid it! It is usually faster to develop the report from scratch than to attempt to understand what another programmer did. Remember that there is no printed report definition (unless you consider *dumprep* output to be a report definition). Report definitions are completely nonprocedural with SQL*Report Writer. If you re-develop a report, remember that you will need to repeat all of the testing done on the original report. This last requirement makes a good case for you to develop automated regression testing for each report. The regression testing package should load data into tables which will cause each of the test cases to occur. Automating the execution of a report is relatively easy in most operating systems.

10

Interfaces for Batch Programs

In this chapter, we will discuss two ways of writing programs for batch mode processing of data: using PL/SQL and using Oracle's PRO*Oracle interfaces. We will use C as the example language, however, the same principles apply whether you use COBOL, Fortran, PL/I, or any such language. PL/SQL is available with some releases of Version 6 Oracle. It is a higher-level procedural language than C — incorporating SQL statements together with looping and other structured programming statements.

The third-generation languages supported for interface to Oracle differ based on your hardware and operating system. Pro*C is always available. Since Oracle itself is written in C — Pro*C is a necessity for porting some of the tools. Avoid using third-generation language interfaces if you can help it! Why? Because the resulting programs are even more difficult to debug and maintain than a fourth-generation program. There are some advantages to using a third-generation language. Programs requiring a large volume of data or calculations may run faster if written in a third-generation language using array processing facilities. Utilities like SQL*Forms, SQL*Plus, and SQL*Loader can take advantage of these array facilities.

This chapter covers the following topics:

- PL/SQL facilities for procedural programming and when they are useful. You can use PL/SQL for procedural programming as well as writing user exits in SQL*Forms Version 3.0.

- Oracle programmatic interfaces including the precompiler interface and the function call-based Oracle call interface (OCI).

- Dynamically constructing SQL calls to access the database. This facility allows you to access the database when columns, tables, or retrieval conditions are not known in advance.

10.1 Using PL/SQL

PL/SQL is an interpretive, procedural language that allows embedded SQL statements. It is closely integrated with Oracle. The interpreter environment is available with the RDBMS kernel or independently with tools such as SQL*Forms Version 3.0. You can also execute PL/SQL code using the SQL*Plus interactive interface and embed it in your third-generation language programs.

PL/SQL is a structured language. Its code is written in blocks enclosed within Begin and End statements. You can declare variables using the same data types provided by the RDBMS with a DECLARE statement. In fact, for PL/SQL variables matching database columns, you can specify *%Type* attribute to determine its data type dynamically at runtime. Then, any changes to the data type will automatically cause a change to the PL/SQL variable data type. No changes to your code will be necessary.

Our sample batch PL/SQL program creates a suggested price list, that is, a catalog and its items for liquidation. Widgets, Inc., will run this procedure in batch mode once a month as they compose their next catalog offerings. The suggested price list will include two types of products: products that had insufficient demand and products that were previously marked down. Insufficient demand is when total ordered quantity is less than half of the quantity remaining in stock. Markdown products are those where the price is less than unit cost plus the 20% profit margin. The first type of products will be marked down by half of their profit margin based on their lowest price. The second type of product will not be marked down further.

In addition, we need to ensure that a product which was previously marked down and still has insufficient shipment quantities is not marked down again. This is for illustration purposes only. In practice, Widgets, Inc., probably want to mark down such prices further — to get rid of stock and free up valuable warehouse space for other products. Figure 10-1 illustrates this program written in PL/SQL.

This PL/SQL program contains two sections: the DECLARE section, and the processing section enclosed within BEGIN and END statements. The DECLARE section contains a variable declaration for *catalog_no* and a cursor declaration for the SQL statement to retrieve products already in liquidation. We use this cursor to control a loop in the processing section.

The processing section starts by obtaining the next available catalog number from the sequence generator *cat_seq*. The *nextval* keyword generates the next value in the sequence. The sequence generator is a Version 6 facility. We created this sequence generator at database creation time with the statement

```
create sequence cat_seq increment by 1 start with 1;
```

The next processing step creates the new catalog entry in the catalog table. Details of the catalog are in the catalog_items table. Note that we could have used the sequence generator cat_seq with keyword *currval* rather than declaring and using the catalog_no variable.

```
Declare                                    ⇐  PL/SQL variable
  catalog_no number;
  cursor liq is                            ⇐  Cursor for row at
    select ci.product_number,                 a time processing
           min(unit_price_offer)
    from catalog_items Ci, stock s
    where min(ci.unit_price_offer) <
       (max(s.unit_cost) * 120 / 100)
    group by product_number;


Begin                                      ⇐ Assign catalog
  select cat_seq.nextval into catalog_no      number with
  from dual;                                   the sequence
                                              generator
                                              "cat_seq"
  insert into catalog (catalog_number,     ⇐ Create new
     catalog_description)                      catalog
  values (catalog_no, 'Suggested Liquidation');

  insert into catalog_items (catalog_number,
             product_number, unit_price_offer)
  select catalog_no, p.product_number,
    max(s.unit_cost) +
    ((min(ci.unit_price_offer) - max(s.unit_cost))/2)
  from order_items oi, product p, stock s, catalog_items Ci
  where oi.product_number = p.product_number    ⇐   Join all tab-
  and   p.product_number  = ci.product_number       les —— see
  and p.product_number  = s.product_number          how complex
                                                     SQL can get!
  group by p.product_number                    ⇐  filter products
  having sum(oi.product_qty) <                     which have insuf-
         sum(s.qty_in_stock) / 2;                  ficient demand
```

Figure 10-1: Liquidation Catalog Generation in PL/SQL (Part 1)

The select statement retrieves all products which have insufficient demand and inserts them into the catalog_items table, together with the marked down value for each product. This statement illustrates the typical complexity of writing practical SQL statements. Such a statement is almost as difficult to maintain as a three-page program in a third-generation language.

We use a nested block enclosed within FOR ... LOOP and END LOOP statements to put in products already in liquidation. It loops once for each row returned by the select statement identified by the cursor *liq*. Notice that we implicitly declared a row variable, *prod*, in the FOR statement. This variable simply represents to current row.

```
/* now create rows for all products already in liquidation */

  for prod in liq loop                        ⇐   For each product

     insert into catalog_items (catalog_number,   ⇐   Try to
          product_number, unit_price_offer)            insert
     values (catalog_no, prod.product_number,
          prod.unit_price_offer);

     Exception                                ⇐   Duplicate value
        when DUP_VAL_ON_INDEX then                error: just update
          update catalog_items                      unit price

          set unit_price_offer = prod.unit_price_offer
          where ci.product_number = prod.product_number
          and   ci.catalog_number = catalog_no;
     end;
  end loop;
  commit;
end;
```

Figure 10-1: Liquidation Catalog Generation in PL/SQL (Part 2)

In this block, we use the exception handling facilities of PL/SQL. The philosophy is that most products which are already in liquidation probably do not make our normal 20% profit margin. So we try to insert liquidation products into catalog_items first. If the previous processing inserted a product, this insert will fail with a duplicate index value error. Note that Oracle will track these unique values only if there is a unique index on catalog_number and product_number columns of the catalog_items table. The duplicate value error is caught by the exception handler, specified in the EXCEPTION section.

In the EXCEPTION section, the DUP_VAL_ON_INDEX keyword indicates an error due to duplicate value. We update the offer price with the previous liquidation price to override the markdown calculated by the previous processing. Figure 10-2 illustrates the use of another keyword, %NOTFOUND, which is used with a *cursor* to detect the end of data. PL/SQL implements several such keywords to make your code more readable. You can also use the SQLCODE facility to find the error code when it occurs.

I needed a lot more words to explain what the program does than the program itself. So you can see that the language is fairly high level. This program could not be written in SQL easily. Even if we could, the result would be an ugly, complex statement which no one could understand later. The complex SQL statement for selecting and inserting products with insufficient demand is a suitable example. Figure 10-2 shows a more maintainable, but procedural, way of achieving the same result.

The PL/SQL interpreter can live with the RDBMS kernel or independently with tools such as SQL*Forms Version 3. Figure 10-3 illustrates the relationship among this interpreter, the kernel, and tools. There are several advantages to running PL/SQL interpreters with the kernel as well as tools.

```
Declare
  new_price number (9,2);
  product number(9);
  cost number(9,2);
  offer number(9,2);

  cursor nosell is                    ⇐   Get products with insuf-
     select oi.product_number,            ficient demand
        max(s.unit_cost)
     from order_items oi, stock s

     where oi.product_number = s.product_number
     group by oi.product_number
     having sum(oi.product_qty) < (sum(s.qty_in_stock)/2)
Begin
open nosell;
For prod in nosell loop
  Fetch nosell into product, cost;
  Exit when nosell%NOTFOUND;

  select min(ci.unit_price_offer)     ⇐   Find lowest offer
  into offer                              price for this prod-
  from catalog_items Ci                   uct, called once per
  where ci.product_number = product;      product
  new_price := cost+((offer-cost)/2);  ⇐  mark down half of the
                                          current margin

  insert into catalog_items (catalog_number, product_number,
       unit_price_offer)
     values (catalog_no, product, new_price);
End loop;
close nosell;
End;
```

Figure 10-2: Liquidation Catalog: Procedural Alternative

Used with a tool such as SQL*Forms Version 3, you can avoid those database accesses implied by retrievals on the dual table. For example, to add two screen fields and display the result into a third screen field, you would have used the following statement in a trigger:

```
select :scr_block.field1 + :scr_block.field2
into :scr_block.field3
from dual;
```

This trigger accesses the database table *dual*, which is quite unnecessary. With the pl/sql interpreter, you could use a simple assignment statement

```
scr_block.field3 := scr_block.field1 + scr_block.field2
```

to perform the same task without accessing any tables. Reducing table accesses can improve performance of your forms application.

You could replace multistep triggers in SQL*Forms with a PL/SQL block. Its procedural capabilities such as IF-THEN-ELSE and loop constructs allow you to develop faster

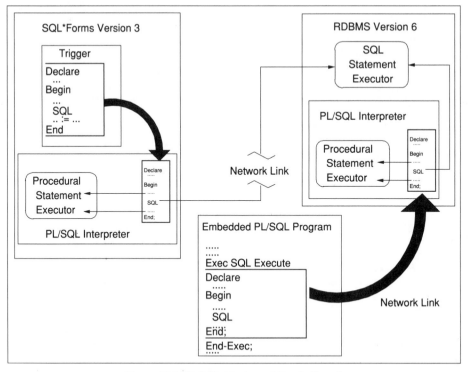

Figure 10-3: PL/SQL, Tools, and Oracle Kernel

than if you had to write Version 2.3-style triggers. The resulting code is much more readable than the equivalent multistep trigger. Thus, you can improve the maintainability of your forms application.

The PL/SQL interpreter resident with SQL*Forms handles as much of the code as it can, calling the kernel for processing SQL statements only. In a networked environment, this scheme reduces the network traffic by eliminating unnecessary calls to the dual table. However, the results of each SQL statement still cause network traffic. Be careful to avoid fetching unnecessary data over the network.

Using the PL/SQL interpreter resident with the kernel is one way to reduce data traffic over a network. You can execute blocks in the kernel resident interpreter. Thus, only the final result travels over the network. This scheme is suitable when your procedural code examines several data rows and displays the result of some calculation based on them to the user. You do not display individual rows, and there is no reason to transfer them to the workstation. Thus, executing the entire block on the database server machine will reduce unnecessary data traffic, albeit at the cost of increased CPU usage.

You can also execute PL/SQL from SQL*Plus. However, you really don't execute it interactively one statement at a time. You must input a complete PL/SQL block before executing it. You cannot use SQL*Plus extensions such as formatting commands within a PL/SQL block. However, you can mix formatting statements before and after a PL/SQL block. Remember also that commands such as BREAK ON and COMPUTE work on the result of a query. So you must retrieve the columns on which these commands operate. If you do not want these columns to be printed in the output, use the COLUMN .. NOPRINT command.

10.2 Embedded SQL Interface

The third-generation language interface to Oracle is a lower-level programmers tool than PL/SQL. This interface allows calls to the Oracle kernel from traditional languages such as C, Fortran, COBOL, and so on. It has been available since the early days of the Oracle RDBMS product, before fourth-generation utilities such as SQL*forms and PL/SQL were developed.

The initial interface consisted of a library of functions, the Oracle call interface (OCI). You could call these functions and link them into your programs. Within each call, you passed SQL statements which the kernel processed. You had little control over which access path Oracle chose when executing your query. This interface, therefore, provided independence from changes in table and index structures. It was also fairly portable. You can still use this interface with Oracle, although it is quite archaic.

The embedded SQL precompiler interface replaced this function call interface. In this interface, you embed SQL statements into your programs. The precompiler converts embedded SQL statements into calls to the Oracle kernel. You can, then, compile the resulting code just like any other program in that language on your operating system. Thus, the precompiler converts embedded statements into OCI calls.

Each executable SQL statement starts with the keywords EXEC SQL, which trigger the precompiler conversion. You can use any SQL statement in your program. For example, The sample program in Figure 10-4 retrieves the next available catalog number into a C variable called cat_num. Program variables are also called host variables. The INTO clause here is an extension to SQL similar to that in SQL*Forms and PL/SQL.

You need to indicate to the precompiler which program variables you intend to use in SQL statements. This is done by enclosing the declaration of your variables between the EXEC SQL BEGIN DECLARE and EXEC SQL END DECLARE statements. The precompiler *remembers* the individual addresses of these variables for substituion wherever you refer to them in an embedded statement. You must declare such variables prior to using them in an embedded statement. Look at the example program shown in Figure 10-4.

Oracle cannot handle recordlike *structures* which languages such as C and COBOL offer. So, use simple variables for those associated with a SQL statement. In C, this restriction means no *structures*, while in COBOL, you must use 01-level field definitions. Record definitions in COBOL cannot be used.

```
/*  Program:   liquidate.pc
 *  Author:    Paul Rodgers
 *  Date:      March 9, 1990
 *  Purpose:   Compose this months liquidation catalog
 *  Revision History:
 */

    #include <stdio.h>                         ⇐   Unix Header Files
    #include <string.h>
    #include <memory.h>

    #define  SQL_NOTFOUND    1403              ⇐   Constants: Code for no
                                                   more data

    char *sys_date();                          ⇐   Forward Declaration: a local function
                                                   that returns pointer to a string containing
                                                   current date

    EXEC SQL BEGIN DECLARE SECTION;            ⇐   PRO*C Variables:

    varchar userid[32];                        ⇐   users oracle id
    varchar passwd[32];                        ⇐   users oracle password
    int cat_no;                                ⇐   new catalog # to create
    int prod_no;                               ⇐   product number
    float cost_price;                          ⇐   unit cost for a product
    float cur_price;                           ⇐   price from current catalogs
    float new_price;                           ⇐   price in new catalog
    char sql_buff[1024];                       ⇐   dynamic SQL statement

    EXEC SQL END DECLARE SECTION;

    #include "/usr/oracle6/c/lib/sqlca.h"      ⇐   Pro*c Header file: must be
                                                   AFTER Declare section

/* ------------------------------------------------------------- MAIN*/
main(argc, argv)
int argc;
char *argv[];
{
    char *uid, *pwd;                           ⇐   Pointers to userid & passwd
    int  sql_status;                           ⇐   copy of sqlcode exit status
    char *sptr;                                ⇐   pointer into sql_buff
    char cat_name[1024];                       ⇐   buffer for new catalog name
```

Figure 10-4(a): PRO*C Program for Liquidation Catalog Generation

When declaring program variables for use within SQL statements, you must make sure that their data type in the language is suitable for the data type in the Oracle database. Mismatched data types cause incorrect data conversion and difficult to find bugs in your program. Oracle has some data types, such as Date, which have no corresponding types in third-generation languages. For example, in the C language, the Oracle Date data type corresponds to a character string. A Number data type, on the other hand, can be either a C *int, short, long, float, double,* or a character string depending on the length of the number.

```
  if (argc != 2)                    ⇐    Parse the command line for oracle slash
  {                                       separated username and password

    printf ("%s: Please supply username and password.\n", argv[0]);
    printf ("\tUsage: %s userid/passwd\n", argv[0]);
    exit(-1);
  };
  uid = strtok(argv[1], "/");
  pwd = strtok(NULL, "/");
  strcpy(userid.arr, uid);
  strcpy(passwd.arr, pwd);
  userid.len = strlen(userid.arr);
  passwd.len = strlen(passwd.arr);

  userid.arr[userid.len] = 0;       ⇐    Add null terminators, for normal
    passwd.arr[passwd.len] = 0;          C functions!

  EXEC SQL WHENEVER SQLERROR GOTO exit_label;   ⇐   Let Pro*C detect SQL
    EXEC SQL WHENEVER NOT FOUND CONTINUE;            errors, we'll check for
                                                     NOTFOUND explicitly
  EXEC SQL CONNECT :userid                     ⇐    Log on to Oracle,
    IDENTIFIED BY :passwd;                          error takes us to exit_la-
                                                    bel.

  printf ("%s: Successfully connected to Oracle.\n", argv[0]);
/* ------------------------------------------- CATALOG LOOKUP
*                 Example of Execute Immediate
*   Compose and execute statement to add a new catalog master
*/
  EXEC SQL SELECT cat_seq.nextval              ⇐    Next catalog
          INTO :cat_no FROM DUAL;                   number
  sprintf (cat_name,"Suggested Liquidation for %s",  ⇐   Catalog Name
          sys_date());


  memset (sql_buff, ' ', 1024);     ⇐    Preset array to spaces, Pro*C does
                                         not stop at null terminator
  sptr = sql_buff;                  ⇐    Compose statement in string variable

  sptr += sprintf(sptr,"INSERT INTO catalog ");
  sptr += sprintf(sptr,"(catalog_number, catalog_description) ");

  sptr += sprintf(sptr,"values (%d, '%s') ",   ⇐   Use single quotes
                  cat_no, cat_name);               around character data,
                                                   otherwise we get MISSING
                                                   COMMA error.
  *sptr = 0;                                   ⇐   Trailing null
  EXEC SQL EXECUTE IMMEDIATE :sql_buff;        ⇐   Execute immediate
                                                   since statement is used
                                                   only once.

  printf ("%s: new catalog %d created\n", argv[0], cat_no);
```

Figure 10-4(b): PRO*C Program for Liquidation Catalog Generation

```
/* ------------------------------------------- INSUFFICIENT DEMAND
 *                    Example of Prepare and Execute Using
 *      Compose and prepare statement to insert products
 *      with insufficient demand into catalog_items table,
 *      used within loop for obtaining products with insufficient demand.
 */

       memset (sql_buff, ' ', 1024);              ⇐    Reset statement buffer to spaces
          sptr = sql_buff;                              before reuse.

       sptr += sprintf(sptr,"INSERT INTO catalog_items ");
       sptr += sprintf(sptr,
          "(catalog_number, product_number, unit_price_offer)");

       sptr += sprintf(sptr,                      ⇐    Notice place-
          "VALUES (:cat_no, :prod_no, :cost_price)");   holder names
          *sptr = 0;                                    are same as
          EXEC SQL PREPARE cat_insert FROM :sql_buff;   variables to
                                                        avoid confu-
                                                        sion

       memset (sql_buff, ' ', 1024);              ⇐    SQL for finding the lowest price
          sptr = sql_buff;                              to date for a given product

       sptr += sprintf(sptr,"SELECT min(ci.unit_price_offer) ");
       sptr += sprintf(sptr,"INTO :cur_price  ");
       sptr += sprintf(sptr,"FROM catalog_items Ci ");
       sptr += sprintf(sptr,"WHERE ci.product_number = :prod_no ");
       *sptr = 0;
       EXEC SQL PREPARE price_lookup FROM :sql_buff;

       EXEC SQL DECLARE Nosell CURSOR FOR         ⇐    Cursor for
          SELECT   oi.product_number, max(s.unit_cost)   retrieving
          FROM     order_items oi, stock s               products with
          WHERE    oi.product_number = s.product_number  insufficient
          GROUP BY oi.product_number                     demand. Now
          HAVING   sum(oi.product_qty) <                 we're ready to
                   (sum(s.qty_in_stock)/2) ;             process.
       EXEC SQL OPEN Nosell;
```

Figure 10-4(c): PRO*C Program for Liquidation Catalog Generation

Remember that Oracle Version 6 can store up to 38 significant decimal digits which can be raised to the power of between -84 to 127. Oracle Version 5 can store up to 40 significant digits in a similar way.

Conversion from Oracle's data types to those of your programming languages raises some interesting portability issues. For example, in C, which is one the most portable languages, has different implementations of the data types *int, short,* and *long* on different hardware. Thus, a program using an int to hold a nine-digit value may collapse with a *core-dump* when ported to a machine where *int* is implemented as 2 bytes. This kind of hardware dependence makes a third-generation language less portable than PL/SQL. PL/SQL uses the same data types as Oracle. So there is no conversion of data.

```
      do                                    ⇐   Start loop, fetching one product
        {                                       with insufficient demand at a
            EXEC SQL FETCH Nosell               time
            INTO :prod_no, :cost_price;
        if (sqlca.sqlcode != 0 )            ⇐   Must be NOTFOUND error, so
            {                                   break out of while loop. Other
                break;                          errors go to exit_label!
            }
        EXEC SQL EXECUTE price_lookup       ⇐   Lookup minimum price to-date
            USING :cur_price, :prod_no;         for this product
        if (sqlca.sqlcode != 0 )            ⇐   Error indicates loss of DB integ-
            {                                   rity: continue to next product
                continue;
            }

        new_price = cost_price + (cur_price - cost_price) / 2;   ⇐New
                                                                   price

        EXEC SQL EXECUTE cat_insert         ⇐Insert item for this product with pre-
            USING :cat_no, :prod_no,         pared statement
                  :new_price;

        printf ("product %8d added at price %8.2f\n",
                prod_no, new_price);

        } while ( sqlca.sqlcode == 0 );     ⇐   End loop, close cursor
        EXEC SQL CLOSE Nosell;

/* --------------------------------------------------- EXIT SECTION */
exit_label:

    sql_status = sqlca.sqlcode;             ⇐   Save current SQL error
        if (sql_status == SQL_NOTFOUND)         code, NOTFOUND is taken as
            {                                   success since it means no
            sql_status = 0;                     more rows to retrieve
            }

    EXEC SQL WHENEVER SQLERROR CONTINUE;    ⇐   Reset error trap to
    EXEC SQL WHENEVER NOTFOUND CONTINUE;        avoid infinite loop!

    if (sql_status != 0 )                   ⇐   Got an error, output Oracle's mes-
        {                                       sage

      printf("\n%s: %s\n", argv[0], sqlca.sqlerrm.sqlerrmc);

      EXEC SQL ROLLBACK WORK RELEASE;       ⇐   Rollback changes, logoff
            exit (-1);                          from Oracle and exit with
        };                                      error status

    printf ("%s: Completed OK\n", argv[0]); ⇐   Drop through to success,
        EXEC SQL COMMIT WORK RELEASE;           logoff from Oracle and exit
        exit (0);                               with success status
    }
```

Figure 10-4(d): PRO*C Program for Liquidation Catalog Generation

```
char *sys_date()
  {
  static char *d = "APR-01-1990";
  return(d);
  }
```

⇐ **Dummy function, supposed to return today's date: Note static variable so we can safely return it without causing core dump!**

Figure 10-4(e): PRO*C Program for Liquidation Catalog Generation

You can make your program more portable by embedding blocks of PL/SQL code where data conversion may potentially cause portability problems. By embedding PL/SQL, you could also reduce network traffic as we discussed in the earlier section. Remember, however, that you cannot mix statements written in your programming language in PL/SQL blocks.

Don't think that I am making a mountain out of a molehill on the subject of reducing network traffic. Networks have a limited throughput capacity and speed. The speed of data transmission on an Ethernet is approximately equivalent to the speed of reading from a slow IBM PC hard disk. Overloading such a network has subtle effects on the response time for everyone using the network.

One of my clients asked me in panic, one day, why the Oracle server on their network refused connect requests at random. Earlier in the day, they had been working with nary a hitch. After much frantic investigation, a chance remark revealed the culprit. An application running on four Macintoshes was doing its daily download of data from the server to each of the Macs. Unfortunately, the 150 megabytes of data transmitted to each Mac concurrently was soaking the network capacity! The connect requests to the Oracle server were getting so many packet collisions that they would time out before the request packet reached the server.

10.3 Cursor Handling

SQL's set-oriented operation is appropriate when you want to retrieve data from one or more tables in the database. An SQL join will typically work faster than will similar code written in a procedural language, if it uses indexes. A program written in a programming language, on the other hand, must retrieve field data prior to attempting a join. When a join involves several tables, or the retrieval conditions are complex, you might choose to write procedural code. Procedural code, in such cases, may be slightly slower than equivalent SQL. But a well-written procedural program is much easier to understand and maintain.

For procedural handling of data, we need to convert from set-orientation to record-at-a-time orientation. Cursors are mechanisms for such conversion. A cursor is always associated with an SQL statement. It points to a row in the data resulting from executing the statement. You can think of it as pointing to the *current* record in a file containing the results of the SQL statement. Of course, there is no such physical file in Oracle, only a conceptual one.

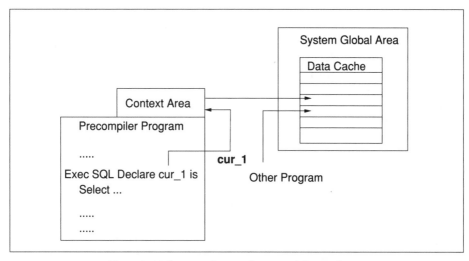

Figure 10-5: Cursors, Context Areas, and Cursor Cache

The cursor concept exists in all of the Oracle tools. However, you have explicit control in creating and using cursors in PL/SQL and the third-generation languages. In Figures 10-1, and 10-2 we saw examples of using cursor handling in PL/SQL. Figure 10-4 illustrates how we can use cursors in a third-generation programming language.

When you declare and open a cursor, Oracle allocates an area of memory in your program to hold information about it. This area is called a context area. It contains the SQL statement associated with the cursor, a parsed version of the statement, and addresses of appropriate program variables. Associated with this cursor are data buffers into which Oracle stores data retrieved by using the SQL statement. This association is illustrated in Figure 10-5. The maximum number of cursors in a program is therefore limited by two factors: the amount of memory available to the program, which is an operating system limit, and the number of open cursors allowed in the init.ora file.

Every SQL statement requires a cursor. When your program does not explicitly declare a cursor, Oracle creates an implicit cursor on your behalf. This is how SQL*Forms, SQL*Plus, and other utilities obtain implicit cursors. SQL*Forms obtains a cursor for each screen block, since these correspond to a table in the database. Hence, the infamous *Maximum cursors exceeded* error messages occurring in forms referring to a large number of tables. An SQL statement which returns a single row result does not require an explicit cursor. In our example program, the select statement for retrieving the next available catalog number results in exactly one row. Oracle assigns an implicit cursor to such a statement.

Statements which return multiple result rows in a third-generation language program must use an explicitly declared cursor. Then, you can fetch the results one row at a time and process them. Alternatively, you can use Oracle's *array processing* features to fetch several rows at a time. In this case, declare each program variable associated with the result as an array. Since C treats characters strings as arrays, you need two-dimensional arrays.

Your program will have to loop through the array and process individual rows in the array. So your code will be a little more complex than when you fetch one row at a time. Programs which use array processing reduce the number of accesses to the database, hence improving performance. Network traffic is in bursts rather than a steady stream of one row at a time. For interactive programs, short reads result in better user response times. In particular, batch reporting programs benefit from using arrays.

10.4 Dynamic SQL

So far, we only discussed embedded statements, which are constant. But how do we handle cases where they are not fixed but changed at runtime depending on user actions? For example, suppose a program composed the statement based on user input such as table names, column values, and so on. These are cases suitable for dynamically composed SQL statements in a third-generation program.

The simplest case is where the statement does not retrieve any data. An example is deleting rows from a user-named table based on a user-supplied condition. Other examples are creating or dropping tables, updating tables, changing access privileges for users on particular tables, and so on. In fact, you do not use any program variables with such statements. However, user input is essential before the statement is completely defined.

In the simplest case, you must first declare a string variable so that the precompiler knows its address. Then compose the statement including items supplied at runtime. The string variable contains the completed statement as a character string in your program. We could execute the statement from a program string variable with the EXEC SQL EXECUTE IMMEDIATE statement. Our sample program in Figure 10-4(b) illustrates this concept.

If you need to specify program variables in an SQL statement where you will place a new value each time the statement is executed, you need another technique. You must PREPARE the composed statement and then EXECUTE it. These are both embedded SQL statements prefixed with EXEC SQL keywords. The statement may contain a placeholder which the program replaces at runtime with a value in a program variable. The PREPARE statement allows you to specify which variable the placeholder should be replaced with. For example, consider a catalog purge program which deletes catalogs and catalog items older than a date specified at runtime. We compose the SQL statements for this purge in two string variables as follows:

```
items_stmt = "Delete from catalog_items
              where catalog_number in
                  (select catalog_number from catalog
                   where catalog_end_date < :pdate) "
cat_string = "Delete from catalog
              where catalog_end_date < :pdate"
```

Pdate in these statements is just a placeholder. You will obtain the date value by prompting the user into a program variable called *purge_date*. The purge_date variable replaces the placeholder pdate in the execute statements.

The corresponding prepare and execute statements are

```
EXEC SQL PREPARE items_stmt FROM :items_string;
EXEC SQL PREPARE cat_stmt FROM :cat_string;
EXEC SQL EXECUTE items_stmt USING :purge_date;
EXEC SQL EXECUTE cat_stmt USING :purge_date;
EXEC SQL COMMIT;
```

In this method, you only need to prepare the statement once. You can execute it multiple times in a session, each time with a different value in the program variable. The *commit* statement actually writes the changes to the database. Up to executing this statement, we could undo our deletes with *rollback* statement. We could have written our trivial example in SQL*Plus using its &variable (ampersand followed by a variable name) facility. In fact, SQL*Plus will do the same sequence of PREPARE and EXECUTE USING that we illustrated.

Both of the foregoing techniques work when you are manipulating data in the database without retrieving it. When retrieving data, you cannot know in advance whether the search conditions specified at runtime will retrieve exactly one row or more than one row. So you have to resort to using cursor-handling statements. Thus, you must DECLARE a cursor for the PREPAREd statement, OPEN it, and then FETCH rows one at a time. When the program finishes processing all rows, you can CLOSE the cursor. For example, prior to purging catalogs, you might want to review their descriptions and the number of printed copies remaining in stock.

The following SQL statements illustrate the sequence of retrieving:

```
cat_string = "SELECT catalog_number, catalog_desc, qty_in_stock from
            catalog where catalog_end_date < :pdate";
EXEC SQL PREPARE cat_stmt FROM :cat_string;
EXEC SQL DECLARE cat_cursor CURSOR FOR cat_stmt;
EXEC SQL OPEN cat_cursor USING :purge_date;
Start looping
    EXEC SQL FETCH cat_cursor INTO :cat_no, :desc, :qty;
    display catalog details to user...
Loop until no more rows
EXEC SQL CLOSE cat_cursor;
```

Remember that every program variable (prefixed by a : colon) used in this code must be declared within the Begin Declare and End Declare statements so the precompiler knows their addresses. The Prepare statement simply names the statement, *cat_stmt*, — the statement name is not a program variable. Similarly, *cat_cursor* is just a name for the cursor, so you can refer to it in the program, for example, in the open statement — it is not a program variable.

This technique is the most common form of dynamic SQL execution. You must use the cursor method with open, fetch, and close whenever you retrieve more than a single row. The cursor method is essential whether or not you use dynamic SQL to supply the program variable in an open statement with a using clause.

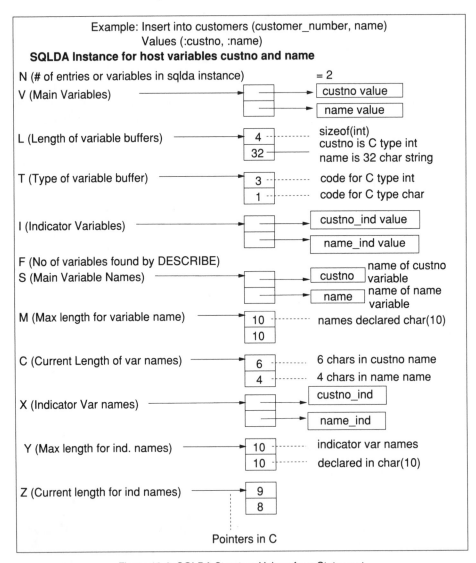

Figure 10-6: SQLDA Structure Values for a Statement

Occasionally, you may need to determine the select columns or tables at runtime. This need arises very rarely — typically only when you are building generic tools such as SQL*Forms developers utility or SQL*Plus. Some of my clients really believed they needed the fully dynamic SQL technique. In most cases, we found after a great deal of discussions that a little standardization in the way they used tables removed the perceived need. By the way, such a modification to their design also saved them several months of programming, because fully dynamic SQL development is not lightly undertaken.

Fully dynamic SQL is very complicated, and should not be attempted unless you have an in-house guru in structures and levels of indirect addressing in your high-level language. For example, in C, it is not sufficient to understand how to declare structures and reference their elements. You will also need to understand how to manipulate pointer to which these structure elements point — at least a double indirection as part of a structure. In addition, you must be able to cast pointers to variables of one type into a pointer of another type without losing track of the type of data you are really dealing with when you dereference the pointer.

Fully dynamic SQL requires the program to set up a structure defined in the SQL data area (SQLDA). In all other forms of dynamic SQL, Oracle allocates and populates this structure. Figure 10-6 illustrates the contents of this structure for the example statement

```
insert into customers (customer_number, name)
values (:custno, :name);
```

In order to populate the structure, the program needs to figure out the data types for each variable in the select list at runtime. Once the data type is known, the program must dynamically allocate memory space to hold the data and use the addresses and lengths of these variables to populate the SQLDA structure. Then, you need to use the DESCRIBE BIND VARIABLES statement with this structure to indicate to Oracle where it should look for the variables associated in the statement.

Writing fully dynamic SQL is not easy. In fact, I see little need for it in an application development environment. It is an essential utility, however, for developers of new tools to interface to Oracle. For example, someone building an integrated forms development or report development tool may need to use this technique. I would advise application developers to stay away from it, if they value their sanity, or delivery deadlines!

10.5 Development Management Issues

Each of the facilities discussed in this chapter is just like writing a program in any programming language. You must write the code in source code file with your favorite editor, compile it, and then test it.

Unfortunately, there are no debugging utilities to help your programming efforts. The PL/SQL facility is even more difficult since you have no idea of how far your program got before failing. You must resort to the primitive ways of interspersing print statements throughout your program to track its progress. I would suggest that you write your programs in small blocks and test each block individually. Then, pull all the blocks together to form your final PL/SQL program and test again.

Debugging utilities for your third-generation programming language are not going to help you either. Remember that the precompiler translates each embedded SQL statement into several OCI functions. The generated code resembles spaghetti more closely than your nicely structured code. Although the precompiler retains the original embedded statements as comments, trying to follow the logic of the generated code is not easy. Of course, the generated code is very consistent — for example, each select statement transforms into a similar set of calls. However, only a veteran of debugging precompiler code can see the similarities. In addition, some debugging tools, such *sdb* on UNIX, do not like working without access to source code for every function call. It is unlikely that most of us developers have source code for Oracle's function libraries.

Estimating the development effort for PRO*Oracle programs is very similar to any other third-generation programming effort. Take into account the debugging difficulties prior to estimating. So, although there will be fewer lines of code to write, debugging and testing will be rather more complex. Development with PL/SQL is easier since you do not have to worry about data-type conversions. In addition, it is a structured language which encourages you to write better code. However, don't try to use it like a third-generation language. Packed fields which require decoding, or bit manipulation, will only get you frustrated. Remember that Oracle is *not* a file manager where you can designate a field to be a composition of several values. Used as the relational database manager that it is, Oracle will make your development simpler and easier to maintain.

There are differences between the libraries provided by Oracle Version 5 and Version 6. In the best case, you will have to merely recompile your code when migrating from one version to the other. If you use UNIX facilities such as *make*, the product supplies files for *make* with the demo programs which will account for the different libraries. If, however, you use simple command files, you will have to change them when you migrate.

I advise you to set up a separate environment for Version 6 if you are migrating from Version 5. Although most of the internal differences between these versions are transparent to programmers, the only way to be sure is to test it. This means you will need to at least double the disk capacity needed for the software. Each version requires a significant amount of storage just for software. Then, worry about space for your test database under the new version.

11

Making Systems Perform

As I mentioned earlier, performance is built into the application from the design stage. Retrofitting applications for high performance is very difficult. So keep the techniques discussed here in the back of your mind as you write programs. These techniques apply regardless of the specific development tool. When building applications requiring fast performance, refer to them frequently. You will soon get into the habit of writing optimal database access code.

The first place to start for improving performance is your application. Review table design and physical implementation, indexes, and then the SQL code. Once you are certain that you have done all you can, then you can investigate other avenues of improvement. These avenues include changing the size of buffers in the shared memory area and changing the timing of background processes.

This chapter describes how Oracle processes application code. We will discuss tools for determining access paths and the rules which Oracle uses to determine them. You cannot ignore the impact of multiple users sharing the database. So, we examine the important contents of the shared system global area.

- How Oracle processes SQL statements. We will discuss the rules used to choose an access path, tools such as Explain for discovering this path, and what to do to alter Oracle's choices.

- Using SQL*DBA monitor facilities, we discuss ways of determining bottlenecks. Then, we examine ways of reducing these bottlenecks.

- In this process, we describe several important parameters from the init.ora file and their impact on Oracle's behavior. Some of these parameters affect the usage of shared memory. Others affect the behavior of background processes.

11.1 How Oracle Chooses Access Paths

When an application passes a SQL statement to the kernel for processing, the kernel parses it. Then, the SQL optimizer uses a set of rules to determine which available indexes it can use to execute the statement. Table 11-1 lists this set of rules. Both Version 5 and Version 6 optimizers use the same set of rules. Note that future releases of the optimizer may change the order of precedence of these rules, or the rules themselves. However, the explanation of how it applies these rules should still hold.

Rank	Where Clause Condition Type
1	ROWID = constant
2	Unique indexed column = constant
3	Entire unique concatenated index = constant
4	Entire cluster key = corresponding cluster key in another table in the same cluster
5	Entire cluster key = constant
6	Entire nonunique concatenated index = constant
7	Nonunique indexed column = constant
8	Entire concatenated index = lower bound
9	Most leading column in concatenated index specified
10	Unique indexed column BETWEEN low value AND high value, or Unique indexed column LIKE '...%' (bounded range)
11	Nonunique indexed column BETWEEN low value AND high value, or Nonunique indexed column LIKE '...%' (bounded range)
12	Unique indexed column or constant (unbounded range)
13	Nonunique indexed column or constant (unbounded range)
14	Sort/Merge (used on joins only)
15	MAX or MIN of single indexed column
16	ORDER BY entire index
17	Full table scan
18	Unindexed column = constant, or Column IS NULL, or Column LIKE '%...%'

Table 11-1: Ranked Rules for the SQL Optimizer

Indexes improve performance when you retrieve a small proportion of rows from a table, typically 25% or less. The purpose of an index is to reduce the number of key values compared before finding acceptable rows. An index contains only key values and pointers to data blocks. So more key values fit into one block than the number of data rows in a block. Thus, using an index for a small proportion of rows also reduces the amount of I/O necessary. The optimizer prefers unique indexes since it knows that a lookup for an exact match in a unique index yields exactly one row.

As a rule of thumb, when you retrieve a large proportion of rows from a table, a full table scan is faster. This is because the search discards fewer rows than it accepts, and Oracle must retrieve data for the accepted rows. The discarded rows probably share storage blocks with accepted rows. Thus, Oracle will need to do very little extra I/O to scan them and does not need to do any I/O to read the index.

An index on a small table increases the amount of I/O necessary for retrieving data. For example, if a table has 50 rows each containing an average of 100 bytes, the entire table fits in three Oracle blocks of 2 K bytes each. Based on your query, Oracle probably reads all of these three blocks anyway. If it uses an index, it reads at least one extra block to read and scan the index. Good examples of such tables are reference data tables which typically hold a code column and a column for the corresponding description. When estimating the number of blocks a table requires, use average sizes for character columns. Oracle stores character data as variable length without any trailing spaces. Remember that you need a unique index on a column, if you want to enforce unique values in that column. In such instances, use the index suppression techniques described below to force a full table scan on these small tables.

The optimizer parses from right to left, that is, from the end of the statement toward its beginning. It formulates the set of actions necessary to process the statement. It then uses the rules and their order of precedence to rank each action to decide the action to process first, then second action, and so on. You can help it to choose the most optimal access path by rewording your statement. It then constructs a tree structure of each action it must process to execute the statement. You can find this tree structure using the Version 6 utility, Explain. Since Version 5 and Version 6 optimizers use the same rules, you could use this utility to optimize statements for a Version 5 application — if you have access to a Version 6 database for running explain.

11.1.1 Unearthing the Optimizer's Plan

The Explain utility consists of a new SQL statement and a table, usually called *plan_table*, which contains the execution plan. Create this table before using the explain statement. Oracle supplies the creation script for this table in a file called *xplainpl.sql*. Table 11-2 describes the columns in this table. The syntax for the explain statement is

```
Explain plan [ set statement_id = '<your constant>' ]
[ into <plan_table_name> ]
for
<statement for which you need the execution plan>
```

Column	Format	Description
Statement_id	Char(30)	Optional identifier.
Timestamp	date	Date and time when statement analyzed.
Remarks	Char(80)	Your comments, optional.
Operation	Char(30)	Action to perform at this node of the tree.
Options	Char(30)	Amplification of the action, such as type of index scan, etc.
Object_node	Char(30)	The name of the network database node that owns the object.
Object_Owner	Char(30)	The user name that owns the object.
Object_Name	Char(30)	Name of table, view, index etc.
Object_Type	Char(30)	Amplification of object, such as Unique for indexes.
Object_Instance	Number	A number identifying the sequence of the object in the *from* clause, assigned from left to right.
Search_Columns	Number	The number of leading columns used when searching an index. Useful in conjunction with a concatenated index.
Id	Number	A unique number assigned to this action in the tree. (Corresponds to a preorder traversal.)
Parent_id	Number	Id of this node's parent action. For a root node, this column is null.
Position	Number	Order of this child within its parent.
Other	Long	Other useful information about the source, if any. For example, the select statement to a remote node in a distributed query, etc.

Table 11-2: Plan Table Columns

Explain stores output for all statements in the same table, so assign a statement id for each statement to differentiate between them. The default name for the table is *plan_table*, but you may create it under another name. If you choose another name, you must specify the *into* clause listing the table name.

You can use normal SQL statements to retrieve the execution plan from the plan table. Figure 11-1 illustrates a simple SQL*Plus report that I find useful. Notice that this report only retrieves columns that are of particular interest. Alternatively, you could use Oracle's *Connect by ... Start with* extensions to SQL to print out the tree structure. You can draw a tree structure from the output of this report.

Oracle executes the statement starting from the bottom left of the tree, that is, the child with position 1 at the lowest-level. Thus, it executes the lowest level node first, then proceeds to its parent at the next higher level. To get the best performance, your aim is to reduce the number of rows it has to process as it moves higher in the tree.

The optimizer does not know how many rows exist in each of the tables or views. So it uses the order in which you list objects in the from clause, using the last object (the rightmost) as the starting point. Figure 11-2 illustrates the execution plan for a simple join between the tables, *customers* and *orders*, and the corresponding tree. Notice that the optimizer plans to do a full table scan on the *orders* table, that is, read every row in this table. The nested loops action means that for every row in the *orders* table, it will lookup the corresponding row in customers table. The index action states that it will use the unique index, *cust_idx_1*, for the lookup.

```
Remark    Report to Print Access Path Plan Generated by Explain
Remark    Usage:
Remark      sqlplus user/password @printplan.sql 'statement-id'
Remark    Application:   Programmers Toolkit
Remark    Author:        Ulka Rodgers
Remark    Date Created:  February 15, 1990
Remark    Revision History:
Remark    Date:                    Revised by:
set verify off

column operation    format a15 head 'Action'      ⇐   Set display for-
column options      format a15 head 'Options'          mats such that
column object_name  format a15 head 'Object'           output fits on
column object_type  format a10 head 'Type'             one line, and
column id           format 999 head 'Id'               define headings
column parent_id    format 999 head 'Parent'
column position     format 999 head 'Order'

select operation,  options,  object_name,  object_type,
       id,  parent_id,  position
from    plan_table

where  statement_id = &1           ⇐   Ampersand variable allows
order by parent_id, position, id       specification of statement id
/                                      at runtime, either on command
exit                                   line or for SQL*Plus to prompt.
```

Figure 11-1: Report to Print Execution Plan

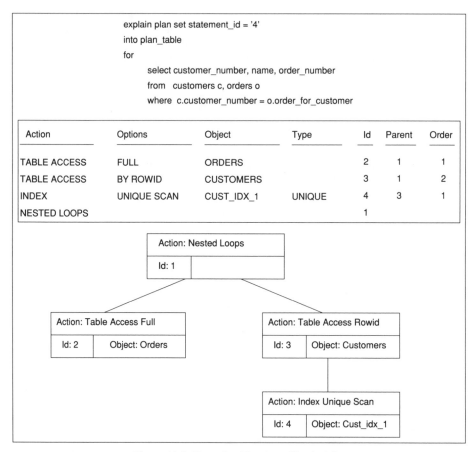

Figure 11-2: Execution Plan for a Simple Join

One of the first actions you should look for is an index action. This will indicate whether the optimizer is using any indexes. Then, decide whether the chosen index is the best one for the query, based on your knowledge of the data. In this example, there is a unique index on *customer_number* column of *customers* and a nonunique index on *order_for_customer* column of *orders*. The optimizer chose a full table scan on *orders* simply because we listed it last in the *from* clause. Suppose we knew that there are fewer rows in *customers* than *orders*, we could change the order of table names in the *from* clause to cause a full table scan on *customers* instead. Figure 11-3 illustrates the result of such rewording.

Another way of disabling the use of an index is to modify the indexed column in some way within the *where* clause condition. The optimizer will not use an index if you modify the corresponding column. Use a harmless function, such as NVL, to modify a column. On character columns, concatenate a space using the ‖ (vertical bars) symbol. On numeric columns, add a 0 (zero).

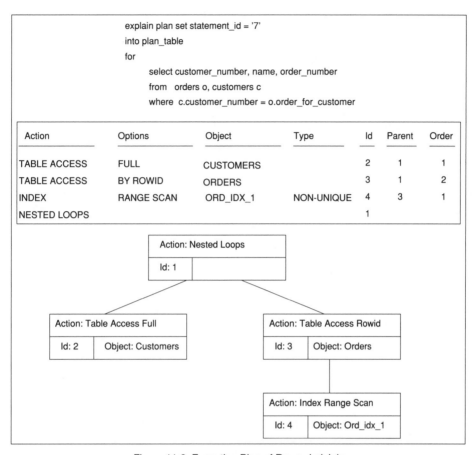

```
explain plan set statement_id = '7'
into plan_table
for
        select customer_number, name, order_number
        from   orders o, customers c
        where  c.customer_number = o.order_for_customer
```

Action	Options	Object	Type	Id	Parent	Order
TABLE ACCESS	FULL	CUSTOMERS		2	1	1
TABLE ACCESS	BY ROWID	ORDERS		3	1	2
INDEX	RANGE SCAN	ORD_IDX_1	NON-UNIQUE	4	3	1
NESTED LOOPS				1		

Figure 11-3: Execution Plan of Reworded Join

Conditions which test for IS NULL or IS NOT NULL suppress the use of an index. To enable the use of the index, replace the IS NOT NULL condition by a test against an unlikely low value. For example, to find all orders which have a *ship_to_customer* value — that is, *where ship_to_customer is not null*, use

```
where ship_to_customer > 0
```

As a general rule, any condition involving a *not equals* comparison suppresses the use of indexes. Oracle transforms inequality conditions involving a *not* such that it can use an index. For example, a *not >* (not greater than) comparison translates into <= (less than or equal to) comparison. Remember that you might inadvertently suppress an index using one of the foregoing techniques. A good habit is to review each statement as soon as you write it to remove all potential cases which may degrade response. Suppress indexes with caution and only after determining the need from Explain output. The next section suggests some rules of thumb for good and bad habits.

If the statement accesses only indexed columns from a table, and there are where conditions involving those columns, the optimizer resolves the query using only the index. In such cases, it does not read row data at all. Where the optimizer has a choice of indexes with no clear preference, it chooses unique indexes over nonunique ones. It can use a maximum of five indexes. After the maximum number of indexes, it will use row data for further filtering.

The order of conditions in the *where* clause also determine the order of executing actions. The optimal order depends on whether you use OR or AND logical operators. When you use ORs, the optimizer performs actions similar to a *union* — that is, one statement execution for the first clause and another for the second clause, filtering the result of the first clause. Thus, you should place the most restrictive condition first. When you use ANDs, place the most restrictive clause last. So that based on the optimizer's parse order, it will be executed first. A rule of thumb is: when using ANDs the most restrictive where clause should be last; when using ORs, place the most restrictive clause first.

Sometimes, Oracle creates a temporary segment to store intermediate results before performing the next action. Creation and cleanup of these segments is a time consuming process. For example, Oracle needs a temporary segment when you use a subquery with an IN operator to store the results of the subquery. You can avoid this overhead by using joins. Other cases requiring temporary segments are with Order by, Distinct, Group by, and any set operators like union, minus, and intersect. Joins where no indexed columns occur are also good candidates for requiring temporary segments. If the optimizer finds an index in the appropriate order, it will try to use it rather than using temporary segments. You can use explain output to determine whether it is planning to use this index.

11.2 Do's and Don'ts of SQL

Here is a list of the characteristics of virtuous SQL code. Use this list whenever writing SQL to ensure good performance. However, remember the previous discussion of the reasons for these items. They are only guidelines and not for blind faith.

1. Use joins in preference to subqueries.

2. Create indexes on join columns, except on small tables. Refer to our earlier discussion of what constitutes a small table.

3. Define unique indexes wherever applicable, and create the indexed column as NOT NULL.

4. List tables in a FROM clause in largest table to smallest table order.

5. State WHERE clause conditions using positive operators rather than using NOT.

6. Creating and dropping indexes is faster when processing large tables than unindexed accesses resulting in a full table scan of the large table. When processing bulk loads or updates, drop the index first to speed processing then re-create it on completion. The only exception is a unique index necessary to enforce unique values.

7. Use array processing to speed data retrieval. SQL*Plus implements the *set arraysize* option for this purpose.

The following list contains the seven sins of writing poor SQL. However, you may ignore them (at your peril) if fast performance is not important.

1. Don't use subqueries if you can avoid them. Try to use joins, or create tables for temporary use. Oracle's internal temporary segments have no indexes. If you create your own temporary table, you may create an index on it.

2. Don't allow NULLs in columns — use a zero or space, except where that has a meaning. Testing for nulls suppresses indexes resulting in poor performance.

3. Avoid using operators like OR, UNION, MINUS, and INTERSECT except when there is no other way. These cause processing similar to subqueries and tend to be slow.

4. Don't index small tables, as explained in the earlier section. A full table scan on such tables is faster than using an index.

5. Don't use a function on a column within a WHERE clause condition. These cause suppression of the index and may result in a slower full table scan.

6. If a condition applies at a row level, don't use the HAVING clause for it. Use the WHERE clause instead to filter out unwanted rows early.

7. Avoid reparsing of SQL statements that are executed repeatedly within one program. Utilities such as SQL*Forms and pre-compiler products provide settings that allow you to control reparsing.

11.3 How Oracle Manages Database Access

In this section, we examine how Oracle processes use the system global area (SGA) and the parameters used to control its use. These techniques affect the behavior of the entire system, so only DBAs should use them. Consider carefully the effect on all applications sharing the database before changing these parameters.

The SGA contains buffers (also called caches) shared between all users of a database. Parameters which control the sizes of these buffers are in the init.ora file. There is one init.ora file for each instance. The instance reads these parameters at database start-up time only. So, if you change any parameter in this file, you have to shutdown and start-up the database before they will take effect. There are init.ora parameters that control other aspects of running a database, such as names of database, control, and log files. Most of them are self-explanatory. We will concentrate on parameters which relate to performance improvement.

The SGA uses shared memory on most operating systems. When you increase the size of a cache in the SGA, the size of shared memory needed increases. On some systems, this may require reconfiguration of the operating system or relinking Oracle executables. In addition, make sure that you have sufficient *real* memory available to avoid swapping or paging which can negate effects of increasing buffer sizes.

Oracle Versions 6.0.27 and later also have several dynamic performance tables, which are owned by the *sys* user name. They are really virtual tables and occupy no space in the database. Their names typically have a prefix of V$. Some of the views on these tables are the basis of the SQL*DBA monitor facility discussed in the next section. Some of these tables contain performance statistics useful to us. In particular, we will examine V$ROW-CACHE, V$WAITSTAT, X$KCBRBH, and the X$KCBCBH tables during the discussion that follows. Note that not every column in virtual tables has values in every release — each new release of Version 6 appears to provide values in additional columns.

There are three main sets of caches in the SGA: dictionary, data, and redo. A user's back-end Oracle (shadow) process first searches these buffers for the required data. If found in the buffers, the shadow process uses that data. Otherwise, it retrieves the data from disk and allocates space in SGA buffers to hold it. So, all users share the data in the SGA caches.

The dictionary cache contains information from Oracle's database dictionary. For example, it contains database table and column information, user access security information, and so on. There is one init.ora parameter to control buffers for each type of information. Each dictionary cache-related parameter starts with a prefix DC_. For example, parameter DC_COLUMNS controls the size of the cache for column descriptions; DC_TABLES controls the size of the cache holding descriptions of tables, views, clusters, and so on.

A rule of thumb is that the size of these caches should be large enough to hold all of the information that your application accesses at one time. Two caches you can ignore both relate to constraints, which are not implemented in Oracle Version 6. You can use the Monitor Statistics User display to determine whether the cache is large enough. In addition, you can examine the SYS.V$ROWCACHE table to determine the effectiveness of the cache. We examine these in more detail in Section 11.5 Finding and Reducing I/O Bottlenecks.

This set of buffers hold application database data, index, cluster, and rollback (undo) information for transactions in progress. Buffers for rollback information are grouped logically as rollback segments. You can control their allocation size with appropriate storage parameters in the *Create Rollback Segment* statement. Each buffer is the same size as an Oracle block, typically 2K. These buffers account for the largest portion of the SGA.

The main purpose of these buffers is to reduce the amount of physical I/O necessary for servicing user requests. Thus, the rule of thumb is to define as many data buffers as you have memory to support. Increase the value of the init.ora parameter DB_BLOCK_BUFFERS. Be conscious, however, that at some point, increasing buffers will not improve performance. You can determine this point from the cache hit ratio statistics from the Monitor I/O display. In addition, you can use the X$KCBRBH table to determine the number of extra blocks to allocate for performance gains. The X$KCBCBH table statistics help in determining whether you could reduce the cache size without affecting performance. The V$WAITSTAT table helps you in determining whether user processes wait for a excessive number of times with the current buffer configuration.

11.3.3 Redo Log Cache

These buffers are a circular area from which the Log Writer (LGWR) process obtains redo log file entries. A user's Oracle shadow process writes into these buffers when committing a transaction. These buffers are the closest in nature to Version 5 before image buffers, except that they do not hold rollback information.

The important statistic to look for is the *redo log space wait* item in the Monitor Statistics Redo facility. If this item has a value of greater than zero, then you need to increase the buffer size using the init.ora parameter LOG_BUFFER.

Latches are locks of a short duration on resources in the SGA. Oracle uses these to control concurrent access to structures in the SGA. UNIX semaphores are the common mechanism for implementing latches. Some examples of SGA resources controlled with latches are cache buffers, redo buffers, sequences, and locks.

Suppose our Oracle shadow process wants to obtain some cache buffer space. It first obtains a latch on the cache buffers list. This list is organized in a least recently used *(lru)* order. The latch prevents other processes from changing the structure of this list, causing them to wait until our process releases the latch. Our process then determines which cache buffer blocks it can use, reorganizes the cache buffers list so that the chosen blocks are at the end of the list, and then releases the latch.

In the meantime, other Oracle processes may choose to wait for the latch held by our process. The length of wait time depends on Oracle's implementation for your operating system. When their wait time expires, they may choose to retry and the wait cycle begins again. Processes may choose to *time out* either at the first attempt to obtain a latch or after retrying several times.

11.3.5 Locks

Oracle utilities refer to locks as *enqueues*. These work in a similar manner to latches, except that they control concurrent access to database resources. Examples of resources requiring locks are database objects (TM), redo log buffers (RT), data dictionary objects (TD), temporary segments (TS), and transaction or an active process's row (TX). Oracle implements several types of locks:

- **Share:** More than one process may obtain this type of a lock on the same resource. You will frequently see them on dictionary objects, since while a process executes any SQL statement, Oracle prevents others from altering the structure of that object.

- **Exclusive:** Only one process may hold a lock of this type at a time on a resource. Such locks on dictionary objects mean the process is executing a DDL statement such as create, alter, drop, and so on. Seen on transaction resource, it means that row is exclusively available to that process.

- **Row Share:** This type of a lock is like a Share lock but on a row within a database object. Processes typically use these when accessing a table without the intention of updating the locked row.

- **Row Exclusive:** This type of a lock is similar to an Exclusive lock but on a row within a database object. Processes typically use these when updating, deleting or inserting a row.

- **Share Row Exclusive:** This type of a lock is a combination of a Share lock on the database object with a Row Exclusive lock on a specific row within it.

Oracle uses its own structures in the SGA to implement locking. Thus, a process trying to obtain a lock must first latch these structures before manipulating them. A process holds several latches and locks at a specific time. For example, a SQL*Forms application querying data from a single table may hold:

- A Share lock on the dictionary definition of the table (TD).

- A Row Exclusive lock on the database table.

- Several Row Share locks, one for each row already viewed on screen.

- A Row Exclusive lock on the row currently displayed on screen. It obtains this lock as soon as the user types into one of the fields starting an update transaction. Before the user types into a field, only a Row Share lock is held. Changing from one type of a lock to another is called *lock conversion*.

- A latch on the lock structure for a very short duration while it converts a Row Share lock to Row Exclusive lock.

11.4 Finding Bottlenecks

Oracle provides a *monitor* facility as part of the SQL*DBA utility for you to watch database activity. This utility groups types of activities logically allowing you to display one group at a time. It counts how often each type of activity in a group occurs through an interval specified by *cycle time* and displays them on your screen each interval. Table 11-3 describes activity groups. The continuous display and counting imposes quite an overhead on your system, so use it sparingly. Choose a longer cycle interval to reduce the impact of monitoring.

You can discover most of the bottlenecks causing performance degradation in your system using this utility. Use it as the next logical step after improving the application SQL statements. The counts displayed with this utility change depending on which programs are running. So the ideal time for using it is during peak activity when performance degradation is at its worst.

Make sure your users know each of the periods when you plan to monitor, particularly since they will notice an additional performance degradation during their busiest periods. Most of them will appreciate your attention to their needs and forgive the intrusions.

Discovering specific causes of performance degradation requires repeated monitoring sessions with lots of think time in between. The steps I use iteratively are

1. Formulate a hypothesis about the cause of degradation.

2. Determine which programs are active when degradation occurs.

3. Choose the best time period for monitoring based on when these programs run.

4. Determine which database activities to monitor to verify the hypothesis.

5. Guesstimate the count values you expect for these activities to verify your hypothesis, based on your knowledge of the active programs, and ***write them down beforehand!***

Group	Class	Description
File I/O		One row for each operating system file assigned to the database. Useful if you use multiple physical disks. If you know the physical disk on which each file resides, you can determine the load on that physical disk.
I/O		This displays a histogram of logical and physical reads and writes performed by each active process. This display helps determine whether you need to increase buffer caches. You can choose a range of processes to limit your display.
Latch		Displays latches currently held for each SGA resource.
Lock		Displays locks currently held, type of lock, and the id of the resource on which lock is held.
Process		Displays one row per active process. Each user may have more than one process listed here. Shadow processes for SQL*Net may not have corresponding system process id.
Rollback		One row per rollback segment listing its size, actions, and I/O rates.
Statistics		Several screens displaying runtime statistics on rates of use per second and performance. These are divided into classes. You may choose to display a particular class or display all classes of statistics. In each case, values displayed are current, average, maximum, minimum, and cumulative total since screen display started.
Statistics	User	Activities performed by user processes, all or selected processes.
Statistics	Enqueue	Rates of locking activity, all or selected processes.
Statistics	Cache	Activity on cache buffers, all or selected processes.
Statistics	Redo	Activity on redo buffers, all or selected processes.
Table		Lists tables currently accessed and which Oracle process is using each table.
User		Summary information about a process together with the most recently executed SQL statement.

Table 11-3: Monitor Display Groups

6. Select the activity groups from the monitor facility and which processes they apply to.

7. Monitor these displays for a period comparing actual count values to those you expected. Turn the spool option on to log the actual values in a file so that you can examine them at your leisure.

8. Determine which init.ora parameters you need to modify to improve performance. Some causes of degradation may require other work such as redefining tables with appropriate storage parameters.

9. Estimate the new values and apply them to your database. Remember that you have to shutdown and restart your database for the new values of the init.ora parameters to take effect.

10. Monitor displays again at the appropriate time to verify the effects of the change.

Tuning performance is very much an art even though my steps imply an engineering approach. The art is in deciding which count values to consider too high, that is, indicating a cause of performance degradation. So expect to spend some time just monitoring together with the relationships described here before forming a hypothesis. Don't be discouraged when some of your hypothesis do not bear out. Just form another hypothesis and try again. Expect to get radically wrong results on your first try.

If users of a specific program experience sluggish performance, choose to monitor those processes initially. However, you may need to monitor others to determine if their activities affect the program under consideration. We discuss the circumstances for including other processes in Section 11.6 Finding and Reducing Multiuser Contention.

In the following sections, we examine two areas which encompass the commonly occurring causes of performance degradation, I/O and multiuser contention. Beyond these, you need expert help since the tuning you might perform has complex interdependencies. The primary area to attack is I/O. It accounts for most of the performance degradation.

In each area, we discuss possible causes, how to verify if they are the culprits, and what to do to reduce their effect on performance. We show some sample monitor displays so you know what the screen looks like. Producing appropriate count values in these examples is very difficult, so don't pay much attention to the actual counts in these examples.

11.5 Finding and Reducing I/O Bottlenecks

I/O occurs due to several different activities:

- User's shadow (Oracle) processes retrieving data from disk into the SGA.
- Oracle calling itself *(recursive calls)* to service a request by a user's shadow process.
- DBWR (database writer) writing data from the SGA to disk.
- LGWR (Redo Log Writer) writing redo buffers from the SGA into the redo log files on disk.

```
                      ORACLE Statistics Monitor        Mon Aug 20  09:04:26
_
       ORACLE PID: 6     Session #: 1    User Name: ULKA
Statistic Name             CUR        AVG        MAX        MIN        TOT
--------------------    --------   --------   --------   --------   --------
logons                         1       null       null       null          1
current logons                 1       null       null       null          1
cumulative opened cu          19       null       null       null         19
current open cursors           2       null       null       null          2
user commits                0.00       0.00       0.00       0.00          0
user rollbacks              0.00       0.00       0.00       0.00          0
user calls                  0.00       0.00       0.00       0.00          0
recursive calls             0.00       0.00       0.00       0.00          0
messages sent               0.00       0.00       0.00       0.00          0
messages received           0.00       0.00       0.00       0.00          0
background timeouts         0.00       0.00       0.00       0.00          0




ALT-F10  HELP  | VT-100    |  FDX  |  9600 E71  |  LOG CLOSED  |  PRT OFF  | CR  |  CR
```

Figure 11-4: SQL*DBA Monitor Statistics User Display

The first two activities are interrelated. A recursive call may be to retrieve dictionary information into the SGA, or to allocate additional extents for a table if an insert or update is in progress. Use the Monitor Statistics User display to discover whether too many recursive calls are occurring. Figure 11-4 illustrates this display. The values shown for recursive calls on this display are rates per second.

Immediately after database start-up, the rate for recursive calls will be high while Oracle fills the empty dictionary caches. After users have been active for a little time, the rate should reduce. Ideally the rate should be zero as shown in Figure 11-4. Since there are two possible reasons for high rates of recursive calls, you need further investigation.

11.5.1 Investigating Dictionary Cache I/O

The SYS.V$ROWCACHE virtual table reflects data dictionary activity since database start-up. It has one row for each dictionary cache, listing the total number of requests for dictionary information (GETS), the number of requests that were not satisfied from the cache (GETMISSES), the number of entries in that cache (COUNT), and the number of entries that are used (USAGE).

If Count and Usage values are equal, look at the Getmisses value. A high value in Getmisses indicates recursive calls for retrieving dictionary information. You should minimize these calls by increasing the size of the corresponding dictionary cache. The Parameter column of the V$ROWCACHE table lists the init.ora parameter corresponding to the cache.

If Usage value is significantly less than Count, then you may be wasting SGA memory space that is useful for other caches. Decrease the corresponding init.ora parameter. Aim for Count values a little greater than Usage values.

11.5.2 Investigating I/O Due to Fragmentation

If recursive call rates are still high after this tuning, their cause is probably dynamic allocation of additional extents for tables. Your database may be fragmented or chained; that is, your tables are made up of a lot of extents which result in noncontiguous sets of blocks. Oracle reads each contiguous set in a single multiblock read. A single read is much more efficient than several reads, one for each extent.

If you discover fragmentation, reorganize your tables using *storage* parameters as described in Chapter 6. Aim for a single extent to hold all data for a table, thus obtaining contiguous blocks. The reorganization takes effect when you export tables, drop them, re-create them with new storage parameters, and then import back table data.

11.5.3 Investigating Buffer Cache I/O

Use the Monitor I/O display for this purpose. Check the hit ratio to determine the proportion of reads where the data was found in the SGA cache buffers. The maximum possible value is 1 which indicates that data was already in the SGA for every read. A highly tuned system will have hit ratios of 0.8 or higher. Lower values indicate that you could improve performance.

There are several possibilities for the cause of low cache-hit ratios. The program may be performing unnecessary I/O or there are insufficient number of data cache buffers. Another, less likely, reason may be that DBWR is not cleaning out cache buffers fast enough.

11.5.4 Investigating Unnecessary I/O

From the Monitor I/O display you can determine which process performs the I/O. Use the Monitor Process display to discover which program causes it. Also, use the Monitor User display to discover the most recent SQL statement that caused it. This procedure is difficult because more than one SQL statement from the program may be the culprit. Repeat the monitor displays several times to find the culprits. Use the Explain facility to determine if you can improve these statements.

11.5.5 Finding the Optimal Increase to Data Cache

After exploring the above avenues of improvement, consider increasing the data cache buffer size. You can confirm the need with the values for *free buffer inspected, free buffer requested, free buffer scans,* and *free buffer waits* activities in the Monitor Statistics Cache display. If you see high rates-per-second values in FREE BUFFER SCANS and FREE BUFFER WAITS activities, then there are insufficient buffers. If *free buffer inspected* rates are high also, you may have DBWR problems.

By increasing the init.ora parameter DB_BLOCK_BUFFERS, you increase the size of the data cache. Rather than guessing how much to increase it by, use the X$KCBRBH virtual table. You have to enable the collection of these statistics by setting the init.ora parameter DB_BLOCK_LRU_EXTENDED_STATISTICS to a little more than the number of additional cache buffers you might consider. The number of additional buffers you may consider depends on whether you have sufficient *real* memory available. For example, to consider an additional 100 buffers, set DB_BLOCK_LRU_EXTENDED_STATISTICS to 120. This will result in 120 rows in the X$KCBRBH table, one row for each additional buffer.

The X$KCBRBH table contains two columns: *Indx*, which indicates the potential number, less 1, of additional cache buffers, and *Count*, which indicates the number of additional hits you would obtain. For example, the lowest value in the *Indx* column is 0, the next lowest value is 1, and so on. The best way is to consider incremental cache buffers in groups, say 50 buffers at a time. In this case, use the following SQL statement to group data into 50 buffer ranges

```
Select    (50*Trunc(Indx/50)+1) || ' to ' ||
          50*(Trunc(Indx/50)+1) Range,
          sum(count) Expected_Hits
From      sys.X$KCBRBH
Group by  Trunc(Indx/50)
```

The *Range* column in the result indicates the maximum number of buffers you might add to get the number of hits in the *Expected Hits* column. Choose the number of buffers which provide the optimal trade-off between available memory and cache hit ratios.

Don't forget to use the operating system analysis tools to see if swapping or paging occurs. If so, then, you need even more memory to bring swapping under control first. Then, you might use this procedure to find out how much more memory you need to buy.

11.5.6 Distributing Disk I/O

Once you have reduced disk I/O as much as possible, consider further gains by using multiple physical disks. This may allow I/O in parallel, if your operating system provides such facilities. If you distribute your database so that parts of it reside on different disks, parallel I/O reduces the overall time required to read and write to disks. We discussed methods for distributing the database across disks in Chapter 6.

To determine the proportion of I/O to each disk, use the Monitor File I/O display. The important activities are rates per second for *read* and *write requests* and the *batch size blocks per write*. If these disks contain files used by non-Oracle applications, use the operating system facilities to determine I/O distribution.

To balance Oracle I/O between disks, you can store tables accessed together on separate disks, store tables and their indexes on separate disks, and store redo log files and database files on separate disks. If heavy concurrent access is necessary to any one large table, divide it over one or more disks. To do such *striping*, you need several files, distributed across disks. Assign all files to one tablespace which will hold the table to be striped. When creating the table, make sure the storage parameters specify extent sizes which are a little smaller than file sizes. Remember to reserve the entire tablespace for this table.

11.5.7 Investigating DBWR Efficiency

DBWR is the only process that writes to the physical database files and thus imposes a significant overhead whenever it works. Maintaining optimal DBWR efficiency is a fine balance between the frequency of waking it and the number of buffers it writes each time.

DBWR batches several blocks into a single write whenever possible to reduce I/O. It wakes up periodically to clean out the data cache, attempting to maintain an optimal number of free data cache buffers. Each time it wakes, DBWR writes out twice the number of buffers specified in the init.ora parameter, DB_BLOCK_WRITE_BATCH.

A user's shadow Oracle process, which cannot find a free data cache buffer, may wake DBWR to do its job. Frequent signals from the shadow process to DBWR result in high values for activities *free buffer waits* and *dbwr free needed* on the Monitor Statistics Cache display. You should increase the data cache size, if you can, before paying attention to these values. Check the value of the init.ora parameter DB_BLOCK_MAX_SCAN_CNT to ensure that it is set to the default value for your operating system.

While searching the free buffer list, if the shadow process finds a certain proportion of modified blocks, it wakes DBWR to write buffers to disk. This proportion is one half of the value of the init.ora parameter DB_BLOCK_WRITE_BATCH. To reduce the frequency of waking DBWR, increase the value of this parameter. However, increasing this value is only beneficial if your operating system provides the ability to write blocks to different disks in parallel or to write adjacent blocks in a single I/O.

DBWR also wakes up whenever a checkpoint occurs requiring DBWR and LGWR to synchronize database and redo log files. A checkpoint occurs whenever LGWR switches to a new redo log file, and each time LOG_CHECKPOINT_INTERVAL number of blocks are written to the redo log file. The *dbwr checkpoints* activity on Monitor Statistics Cache shows the number of checkpoints since database start-up. You can increase the value in LOG_CHECKPOINT_INTERVAL to reduce checkpoint frequency. However, each checkpoint will then cause a larger number of buffers for DBWR to write. Also, recovering from the last checkpoint will take longer to complete.

11.5.8 Investigating LGWR Efficiency

LGWR's effect on performance is an issue only in applications with high transaction rates. Use the Monitor Statistics Redo display to verify the value of the *redo log space wait* activity. A nonzero value for this activity indicates that processes wait for space in the buffer. In this case, increase the value of the init.ora parameter LOG_BUFFER which specifies buffer space in bytes.

11.6 Finding and Reducing Multiuser Contention

Multiuser contention occurs when more than one user's shadow Oracle process access a resource at the same time. Latches control the sharing of resources in the SGA and locks (enqueues) control sharing of database resources. The most important of these two is locks. Applications usually control the type of locks necessary in their code.

On multiple CPU systems, more than one process can access some resources in the SGA at the same time. On such systems, Oracle allows multiple latches for these resources. Such resources include redo copy latches and free lists for data cache buffers.

11.6.1 Data Cache Buffers Contention

Contention for cache occurs when processes try to obtain either data or rollback buffers. Oracle uses rollback buffers to hold changed data for rollback and read consistency purposes. Use the Monitor Statistics Cache display to determine whether your systems suffers contention for these buffers. The important activities are *consistent gets*, *db block gets*, and *buffer busy waits*. The ratio of *buffer busy waits* to the sum of the other two indicates the proportion of requests that had to wait. If this ratio is more than 10% or 15%, then you need to determine whether most of the contention is for rollback buffers or for data buffers.

The V$WAITSTAT virtual table contains information on the *class* of blocks requested and contention since database start-up. We are interested in *undo segment, undo block,* and *data block* classes. The *operation* of interest is *buffer busy waits*. Other operations and classes do not help us in this tuning. The best way to retrieve information from this table is using the following query

```
Select   class, sum(count) Total_Waits
From     sys.V$Waitstat
Where    operation = 'buffer busy waits'
and      class in ('undo segment header',
                   'undo block', 'data block')
Group by class;
```

Large values in the *Total_Waits* column for undo segment header or undo block indicates that you have insufficient rollback segment buffers. In this case, add more rollback segment buffers using the Create Rollback Segment statement. A general rule of thumb is 4 rollback segments for each set of 16 concurrent transactions. Remember that concurrent users may not be performing concurrent transactions, but is a good starting point for your estimate.

Large values in the *Total_Waits* column for data block class indicates insufficient free lists for data blocks. There is one free list per table containing a list of blocks which have sufficient free space for inserting new rows. This type of contention is likely if several processes are inserting rows into the same table concurrently. Each process must access a free list for that table. Contention indicates that there are fewer free lists than processes trying to insert. Use the Monitor Table display to help determine which tables need extra free lists.

The init.ora parameter FREE_LIST_PROC specifies the number of free lists to maintain for each table. The ideal value for this parameter is the number of concurrent processes requiring access to the same table with a maximum value of 32. For the new values of init.ora parameters to take effect you must shutdown and restart the database. This parameter only affects tables created since changing its value. So, to affect existing tables, you will need to recreate them.

11.6.2 Latch Contention

Use the Monitor Latch display to determine which latches, if any, may be the cause of performance degradation. Although this display shows several different types of latches, you can control only a few. On most single CPU systems, you may not have the choice of controlling any. Also, Oracle uses operating system facilities, such as semaphores on UNIX, to implement latches. So increasing their number may require reconfiguring your operating system.

Typically, if the *timeouts* value for a latch is more than 10% or 15% of the *total* value, your system is suffering because of latch contention. Here are some of the latch contentions that you can reduce:

Redo Allocation Latch Contention

Most processes obtain the Redo Allocation Latch and immediately copy the redo entries into the SGA. There is only one latch of this type. The init.ora parameter LOG_SMALL_ENTRY_MAX_SIZE controls the maximum redo entry size for which a process can copy immediately. Redo entry sizes larger than this must obtain a Log Copy Latch — they can only obtain redo log buffer on the Allocation Latch.

Redo Copy Latch Contention

Single CPU systems have only one Redo Copy Latch, multiple CPU systems can have one Redo Copy Latch per CPU. The init.ora parameter LOG_SIMULTANEOUS_COPIES defines the number of Redo Copy Latches on multiple CPU systems. You may define up to twice the number of such latches as there are CPUs with beneficial effects.

Another method, for multiple CPU systems, is to force prebuilding of more log entries prior to processes requesting the latch. This method reduces the length of time a process holds a latch by reducing the number of redo entry pieces to copy into the SGA. The init.ora parameter LOG_ENTRY_PREBUILD_THRESHOLD defines the maximum size of redo entries which may be pre-built. Increasing this value causes more redo entries to be prebuilt. However, this will increase the memory requirements for each process.

11.7 Development Management Issues

The good and bad habits for SQL should be pinned on every Oracle programmer's wall. Although they should follow these habits whenever they write SQL, I find that most programmers do not initially. So code reviews for the performance critical portions of applications are essential. In addition, you need to follow them for the rest of the programs as well — in a multiuser environment. As we saw in this chapter, a poorly written program can affect well-written programs by causing contention or unnecessary I/O.

DBAs and application programmers must work closely together when investigating performance issues. Ideally, both types of staff work on the project together, even have offices close to each other. If both groups know enough about Oracle's internal structures and the application, they can combine their ideas. In practice, I find these groups in separate corporate reporting hierarchies. Such environments require a formal staff assignment to the project. DBA and programming staff are often spread over a wide area. This may be a reason why initial programming overlooks performance issues. During system testing, or worse, even later, you have to initiate a performance retrofitting project. You can avoid such a belated reactive approach by including an experienced DBA from the start of the project.

Oracle provides many choices for improving performance. However, the principal gains in my experience come from good table design, well-written SQL, use of indexes, and increasing data cache buffers. Ultimately, the more *real* memory you can devote to the SGA, the better Oracle programs perform.

Part 4

Distributed Systems with Oracle

Networks have proliferated in the last few years. Initially, they simply allowed terminals to access central machines. More recently, networks connect multiple machines to each other. Software is just now catching up to these advances in hardware technology. While techniques for structured analysis and design for such implementations are still in their infancy.

In this part, we examine some of the potential ways to implement database applications in a networked environment. Our focus is still on Oracle. So our discussions will limit possibilities to the current limitations of Oracle. We will examine the facilities provided by Oracle's networking tools. In addition, we will briefly review how these facilities also allow some third-party products to access Oracle.

MIS staff should pay close attention to the discussion in this part. Here, at last, you will find ways of integrating those PCs on your users' desks. What's more, such integration will be beneficial to both parties, even if it increases administrative headaches.

12

Building Distributed Systems

There are many flavors of distributed systems. You can distribute the processes across several machines, or distribute the database, or both. Each option is fraught with its own issues. The overriding consideration in all such architectures is the bandwidth of the network used to connect the pieces. Although the processing capabilities of machines have doubled manyfold, as has storage capacity, network speeds are far behind in their speed and throughput. This disparity is even more noticeable in long distance, wide area networks.

In this chapter, we examine configurations that are possible with today's technology. Then, with these configurations in mind, we will discuss the differences in building applications from those in a central machine environment. The topics we cover are

- Network traffic issues and some possible configurations to make network traffic manageable. These configurations include local area networks as well as wide area networks. Dial-up connections are a special case of a wide area network with very slow speeds.

- What is a client-server architecture and how Oracle tools fit into it. I prefer to call this a cooperative processing architecture for reasons explained during the discussion. We examine ways to build applications to take appropriate advantage of local workstations and server machines.

- Distributing data over multiple machines. We examine some of the drawbacks of this configuration, with attempts to reduce their effect. Primarily, we will discuss some of the techniques I have found effective.

- Differences in application behavior due to different character sets. These issues are important when you mix EBCDIC character set with ASCII, and even more so when you mix languages. Version 6 offers some tools for handling national languages which apply to each installation of Oracle.

12.1 Network Issues

There are many types of networks and even more ways to combine them. I do not intend to discuss the theory underlying each of these types, or the hardware bridges and routers necessary to combine them. I merely introduce their properties as they apply to our discussion. Details of networks are vital to communications administrators, but of little importance to developers of Oracle-based applications. Figure 12-1 illustrates my high-level view of the components of a network system as it relates to Oracle products. This diagram bears almost no resemblance to OSI layers which depict network interaction at a much more detailed level.

The hardware connection level, the network type, and the network software are closely tied together. For example, to use Ethernet on an AT&T 3B machine, you must buy the add-on cards for the machine and the software from AT&T, though you may use cabling materials from your cable installer. In the PC world, there is a little more flexibility as vendors support each other's hardware cards.

The protocol on your network depends heavily on your choice of software. For example, vendors like DEC have their own protocol, DECnet, which runs on Ethernet, though you could also run TCP/IP on Ethernet. Whether the different protocols will coexist on a single wire depends on the software. Some ethernet software implementations will not coexist. Among Ethernet protocols, TCP/IP is a widely used standard.

In addition to the interdependencies between hardware, protocols, and network software, you have to worry about SQL*Net support for the your choice. Since there are many implementations of network protocols, Oracle can support only a few. Be very careful in checking the hardware and software supported by Oracle's SQL*Net for your hardware platforms.

When configuring networks, keep in mind that you can connect different types of networks to each other via hardware or software packages. There are many hardware boxes for connecting two networks, called gateways, bridges, routers, and combinations of these. The differences between their operation is too much detail for our purposes here. So, I will use the name *bridge* interchangeably for all of them.

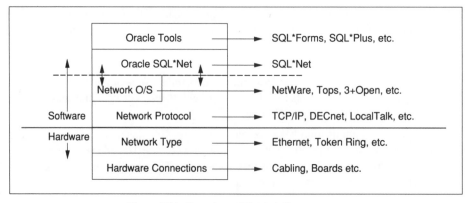

Figure 12-1: Overview of Network Components

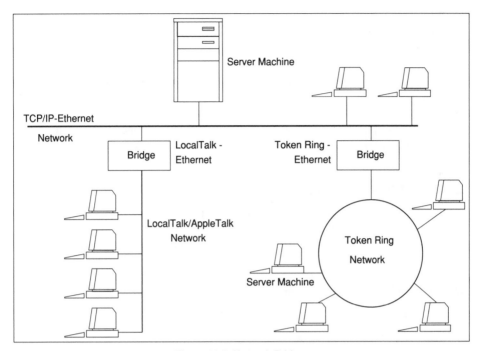

Figure 12-2: Network Bridges

Figure 12-2 illustrates a configuration of three different types of networks bridged together. These bridges convert data packets on the network from one protocol to another. They can also determine whether a network packet needs to be passed to the other network or if the packet is for a node on the local network. Thus, some bridges can filter packets such that they convert and pass through only those destined for the other side of the bridge.

Each type of network has its own throughput and capacity limits. For example, a standard IBM token ring network can theoretically work at 4 megabits per second while Ethernet can theoretically work at 10 megabits per second. Realize, however, that these figures include the overhead for each packet added by the network management software. Each packet must contain information about where it originated, where its destination is, and error checking data. Thus, the maximum actual data throughput on the network is typically about 75% of the network bandwidth.

Beware of judging network throughput based on such theoretical figures. In practice, the number of nodes on the network and the traffic volume determines the actual speed. An Ethernet with a large number of nodes and high volume of network traffic will reduce throughput to 50% of network capacity in most cases.

The typical services provided by networking software, such as Novell's Netware and DECnet, are the ability to share files stored on a server, printers, and other devices. The machines that support such services have multitasking operating systems. In some cases, the operating system is multiuser as well, for example, DEC VAX/VMS, or UNIX operating systems. MS-DOS, unfortunately, is a single-user, single-tasking operating system. For this reason, vendors such as Novell, Banyan, and 3Com supply their own multitasking operating systems for supporting network servers on PCs.

Remember that an Oracle database is *not* a set of shared files. It requires a multitasking operating system to act as a database server. We describe the Oracle server architecture in the next section. So, on Novell and 3Com networks, Oracle servers must run on a machine separate from the network server. Banyan is based on the UNIX operating system which is multiuser. So, on Banyan networks and other multiuser operating systems, Oracle server can run on the same machine as the network server.

12.2 What Is a Client-Server Architecture?

Each DBMS vendor uses this buzzword to mean different things. Some use it to describe a division between front-end interface process and the back-end database access processes. Others use it to describe how to execute the front-end interface tools on a workstation with the database running on a server machine. Some vendors mean a single process for the back-end database access while others mean multiple back-end processes. Figure 12-3 illustrates the two common process architectures for DBMSs.

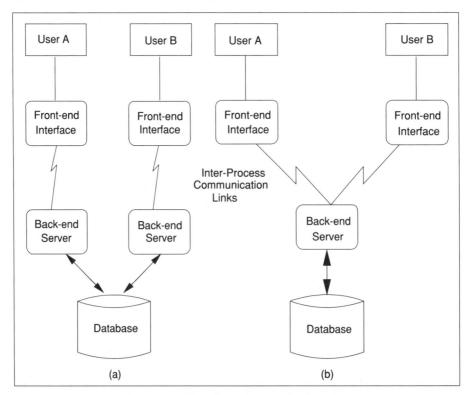

Figure 12-3: Client-Server Process Architectures

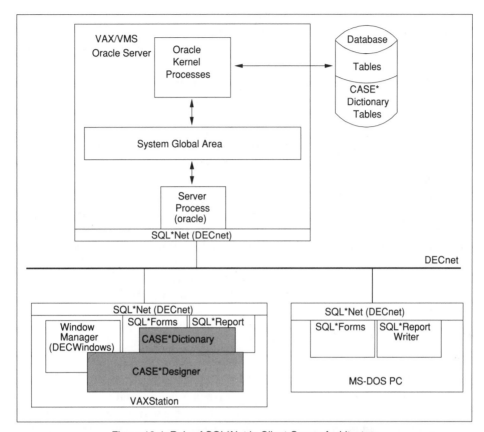

Figure 12-4: Role of SQL*Net in Client-Server Architecture

Oracle uses the process architecture described in Figure 12-3(a). The key to using this architecture in a networked database server environment is the link between the front-end and the back-end interfaces. Oracle's SQL*Net product replaces the interprocess communication links. Figure 12-4 illustrates how SQL*Net allows this link to be connected over a network.

SQL*Net has a component program on each machine which accesses Oracle over the network. These programs implement a high-level protocol for communicating between Oracle database servers and user interface tools. They connect a user's process to the Oracle server process on the database server machine. Note that many third-party products also support a SQL*Net connection from their front-end interface tools.

SQL*Net comes in many flavors, one for each network type. Figure 12-4 illustrates the DECnet flavor. Other flavors include TCP/IP, asynchronous, and 3270. This list will expand as Oracle supports other network types. The flavor necessary for a machine depends on which protocol that machine uses. There is little dependency on the protocol used by the database server machine, except in the hardware connections. For example, your workstation may be on a token-ring network, while the database server machine is on a TCP/IP network. A bridge between the two networks must convert protocols. You would use SQL*Net token-ring on the workstation, and SQL*Net TCP/IP on the server machine.

SQL*Net Asynchronous is an unusual product, different from the networking flavors. It allows you to execute programs in a distributed fashion just like the others, however, it works over a dial-up public telephone line or an RS232 direct connection. This could be a poor man's alternative for cheap networking. Realize, however, that the performance of your programs, with this flavor, depends entirely on the speed and the quality of the telephone connection. Using a 2400-baud dial-up modem will be many orders of magnitude slower than a 10-megabit network.

SQL*Net supports specific hardware and software combinations. For example, under the XENIX operating system on a PC, SQL*Net might support only the EXCELAN Ethernet card. Although other vendors also make Ethernet cards, they might not be supported. Oracle valiantly attempts to add support for as many hardware and software combinations as possible. However, the sheer number of vendors makes it almost impossible to support everything. So be very careful when choosing the combinations of hardware and software you use. Make sure that SQL*Net supports that combination prior to any major purchases.

12.3 Client-Server Applications

In this section, we still deal with a single database running on a server machine. Distributing data raises many design and implementation issues, which we discuss later.

Application programs, such as SQL*Forms applications, specify how to connect to the Oracle database server over the network each time a user starts up the application. This specification is called the *database string*. The database string specifies which SQL*Net driver to use, the name of the network node which is the database server, and which database instance to connect to on that server. For example, to run SQL*Plus with a database string to connect using the TCP/IP driver to a network node called ACCT which runs the database with the Oracle SID (system id) HQ you might type

```
sqlplus user/password@T:ACCT:HQ
```

In this example, the driver T specifies TCP/IP. There are other drivers, one for each type of connection. In fact, even front-end interfaces running local to the database use a local driver such as P — a pipe driver under UNIX. This type of string is much too complicated for an average user. Your application must hide it, so that remote connection is transparent to the user. Use the *config.ora* file on the workstation to define remote connection strings for commonly used remote Oracle servers.

If you run a database locally on each workstation, as well as the shared server machine, you can create aliases or database links. Aliases are just one way of giving a meaningful name to the cryptic database string. Thus you might substitute the alias *accounting* for our example database string. If your environment is fairly stable, that is node names and addresses rarely change, then you could consider hard-coding the database string into your programs. In general, aliases or database links are preferable.

Applications in the client-server environment must address two key issues:

- Reducing network traffic
- Application portability to all workstations

Realize that a theoretical 10-megabit throughput is very slow compared to the throughput speeds of today's disks. The practical throughput from networks is only slightly faster than that of a floppy drive on a typical 386 PC. So, the less data transmitted over the network, the faster our response time will be. With an asynchronous dial-up interface, speed is even more important. Don't forget that one workstation using the network for a large-volume data transmission affects everyone else connected to that network. The network is, in every sense, a shared resource which you should avoid abusing.

Application developers need to become very conscious of every database interaction. Each interaction causes network traffic. Thus, scrutinize carefully each trigger in SQL*Forms which uses a *select ... from dual* to see if you could perform the same task locally. Although using DUAL is very convenient for the programmer, the statement must be transmitted over the network, processed by the Oracle kernel, and the result passed back to the workstation. This transmission back and forth results in a slower response than when using a local database. These network traffic issues were one of the driving forces behind SQL*Forms Version 3.0 with PL/SQL. The procedural capabilities of PL/SQL eliminate the need for unnecessary database access over the network.

An advantage of using PL/SQL at the database server end is that you can send the entire query once across the network and retrieve the end result. You do not need to retrieve intermediate results for further processing. This option is possible with tools such as SQL*Plus, PRO*C, and other programmatic interface products. Intermediate results in a multiple-step process can generate a significant volume of unnecessary network traffic. Performing most of the work on the database server machine does increase its load. So don't expect to support a large number of users on a 386 machine, even one with a high clock rate.

Data from lookup tables are culprits of unnecessary network traffic, since their values are included in almost every row retrieved. If this data changes only rarely, you should store them locally on the workstation. With SQL*Forms, this would mean that you will need a small database locally on each workstation. This can be an expensive option, since beefed up hardware configuration for workstations becomes necessary — just to run Oracle locally. Many third party products, such as SQR, offer in-memory arrays which are useful for local storage without requiring copies of Oracle for each workstation. Just load these arrays once at the start of your program and use them repeatedly throughout.

Another way to reduce network traffic is to use Oracle's array facilities. When retrieving a large number of rows, transmitting one row at a time results in a lot of network packets. Instead, obtaining a set of rows at a time reduces the volume of packets transmitted over the network. Remember, however, to only retrieve the columns needed. There is a limit on the maximum size of network packets. So retrieving an array of rows, where each row is quite large, will not reduce the volume.

Once you start thinking in terms of where the programs will execute, you need to become fussy about portability issues. SQL*Forms applications are fairly portable, except to the Macintosh environment. SQL*Forms is not available on the Macintosh. Use of graphics characters in forms layout, C user exits, and #HOST calls to the operating system can make your application almost impossible to port.

Watch for differences in Oracle versions supported for the workstation platforms. If all of your workstations are MS-DOS PCs, there is no problem. However, if your workstations are a mixed bag — SUNs, VAXStations, MS-DOS PCs — then you will probably have to use the oldest version, the one common on your platforms. Remember that newer versions of software can usually run programs developed with older versions, not vice versa. This also lead to *update lags* since you need to wait months after a new version *ships* before it is available on all of your platforms.

12.4 When to Distribute Data?

Although a central database has been the common way, more and more companies are looking for ways to use cheaper technology by distributing data. Centralized databases make database administration easier than distributed databases. However, such close control also fosters bureaucracy, which makes users' lives difficult. Central databases require large expensive machine simply to support the large number of users who need to access the data. Requirements for interactive access compounds the horsepower requirements.

Distributed databases allow you to use cheaper technology such as smaller machines on a network. Advances in hardware have greatly increased the horsepower and storage capabilities of such small machines. In addition, it opens doors to making some local autonomy possible. Users take ownership of their data and applications, since they are closely involved in its inception and maintenance.

The key to successful distributed systems is reducing the amount of access necessary to remote systems. A majority of the data required by a set of users should reside on their local machine. Occasional access to other, remote machines is possible with the network speeds available today. Remember that wide area networks are slower, and more expensive, than local area networks because of the distances involved.

The scenario in which distributed databases make most sense is when departments of a company are geographically distributed. Typically, in such cases, business responsibilities are also distributed to allow local decision making. Headquarters provides guidance on policy issues, one of which could be data requirements. Figure 12-5 illustrates a schematic of this scenario.

Each department could have its own system, either a database server with a network of PC workstations or a single machine with dumb terminals. Networks are a local area network, with a bridge to a wide area network to connect to the central headquarters

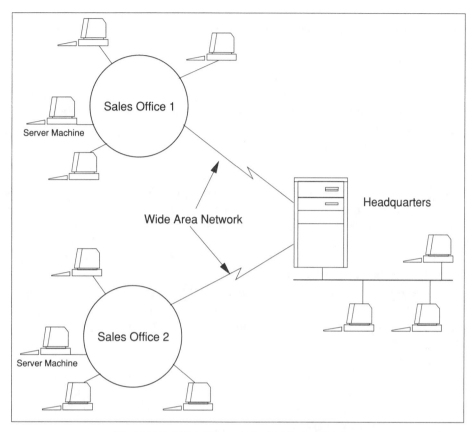

Figure 12-5: A Good Scenario for Distributed Database

machine. Most of the data necessary to the department resides on the local system. Occasionally, access to the central database may be necessary to obtain data supplied by other departments or locations.

The central database, on the other hand, needs access to data from each of the departmental databases. Typically, this data is only required in a summary form. Nitty-gritty details are of little interest to corporate headquarters. In fact, up-to-the-minute information is unnecessary at the central location. So an old-fashioned *batch* daily upload can suffice.

Oracle provides some facilities for dividing your database on more than one machine. Both Version 5 and Version 6 allow queries which access data from multiple machines. However, neither of these versions allows updates which span multiple machines. You have to write such updates individually yourself and account for partial update failures. Thus, the programmer has to write hairy code to implement two-phase commit processing. Future versions of Oracle may add two-phase commit.

Distributed queries in Oracle use the database link facilities. A database link is a predefined access path to another database. You can create a database link while connected to one database using the following SQL*Plus command:

```
CREATE DATABASE LINK chicago
CONNECT TO user IDENTIFIED BY password USING database string;
```

This command is one of Oracle's extensions to the SQL language. Once you define this link, you can refer to any accessible table on the remote database by simply specifying the link name after the table name. For example, suppose one of our remote database tables is *product*; we can retrieve data from it with

```
SELECT * FROM PRODUCT@chicago;
```

A database link restricts your access according to the security privileges granted to the user and password specified in the create database link statement. A database link is only available to its creator user id. A DBA can make a database link available to all users by using the keyword PUBLIC in the Create statement. Public database links should typically use restricted user names on the remote database, to prevent undesirable updates. It is common to use a user name which has only select privilege. Otherwise, all of the careful security controls you place on each local database may be bypassed.

There are a few limits on such remote access. For example, you cannot retrieve a column with data type LONG (maximum size 64K) from the remote database. Remember that all of the results of your query on remote database tables get transmitted over the network. So be very careful in the types of queries you perform.

12.5 Database Design Issues

The basic design requirement for a good distributed database is that a large proportion of the database accesses should be to the local database. However, it is not always easy to partition our data in such a way. There are two elementary partitioning strategies, horizontal and vertical. Before we discuss these strategies in more detail, review the data models we developed in the earlier parts of this book. Assume that each entity is equivalent to a table, except for those that we decided to denormalize. The discussion of data partitioning uses these preliminary table definitions as the basis.

A horizontal partition is dividing a table into sets of rows based on some column in that table. Thus, we might divide the customer table into North American customers and European customers. The complete corporate view of customers is the union of the two sets. In the case of Widgets, Inc., this partitioning works quite well. After all, customers do not move between North America and Europe very frequently. Customer buying analysis, similarly, is likely to be continent specific. However, if Widgets, Inc., wanted statistics on buying patterns across continents, it would have to consolidate the data at the corporate level. Since this process is infrequent, say, once every six months, copying all of that data from the local to corporate level is reasonable.

A vertical partition divides a table by its columns. For example, the catalog items table might contain pricing for both North America and Europe in separate columns. (This table is worth denormalizing since we are not likely to open new warehouse locations frequently.) We could partition the table into the parts for North American prices and parts for European prices. We have to duplicate some of the columns, such as catalog number and product number. Again, once we create a catalog — that is, printed and mailed it to our customers — we really cannot change it! So catalog number and product number are static, and data duplication is okay. A similar vertical partition of the customer table, however, would require frequent joins between the local and remote tables.

Lookup tables, as we noted in an earlier section, are good candidates for storing in the local database. However, lookup tables do change, albeit not very frequently. At Widgets, Inc., some of these tables will contain information spefic to the continent anyway. For example, a lookup table for state codes in North America could be country codes in the European system. We are not particularly worried about such tables of local significance. Other tables, such as the product table, are more critical.

We could use Oracle's auditing facilities to track updates and insertions into such critical tables. This is a sneaky trick. Oracle's auditing facilities can be set to record only specific types of access. Their real purpose is to track who is attempting to violate security or doing suspicious work. However, we are not interested in who made the change, only the fact that a row in a critical table changed. We would use the following statement to track changes to the product table:

```
AUDIT INSERT, UPDATE ON product WHENEVER SUCCESSFUL;
```

Don't forget to turn auditing on in the init.ora parameter a AUDIT_TRAIL. We only care about successful attempts to change this table. If the user rolls back a change, the table does not change. Then, we could set up a batch process, say, nightly, to query the AUDIT_TRAIL table to discover whether the table changed, and take appropriate actions to update all databases which locally store this table. Since we do not add many new products, or change existing ones very frequently, a nightly batch update should be sufficient.

Turning auditing on usually causes a significant overhead affecting the performance of the database. However, limited auditing such as above should impose very little overhead. I do not recommend general systemwide auditing due to the performance and disk overheads. It does offer a nice solution for tracking changes to replicated data in the case of distributed databases.

Notice that all of my suggestions for distributed database use infrequent access to the remote database. Your analysis for distributed systems should aim for a similar setup. The advantage is that you are not dependent on the remote system being up all the time. If you suffer communications difficulties, which are not uncommon, each local database can continue operation autonomously. Remember that Oracle provides only a local database dictionary. It does not replicate dictionary information or provide transaction updates and recovery across the distributed databases. So, if the remote system goes down due to some mishap, our setup does not cause the entire company to grind to a standstill.

12.6 Implementation Rules of Thumb

Here are some rules which I have collected over time. They will guide you when developing distributed access systems. Remember that these rules are based on today's technology. As network bandwidth and speed increases, you will have to adjust the figures appropriately.

- Calculate transaction size using the formula explained in Chapter 5. Divide it by network bandwidth to get an answer for the number of bytes per second, then double this result to allow for the request to be transmitted. Add an overhead of 2–3 seconds for the database server turnaround. This is the minimum response time you can expect on your network.

    For example, assume a 2400-baud dial-up connection with SQL*Net Async. This means our network bandwidth is aproximately 200 bytes per second. Assuming our transaction size is 1000 bytes, we take 5 seconds to transport it (1000 / 200 = 5). Double it and add 3 seconds for an estimated speed of 13 seconds — a slow response time by any standards!

- From the above calculation, figure out an optimum transaction size that will result in an acceptable response time. Use the *arraysize* tuning facility for SQL*Forms, SQL*Plus, and PRO*programs, to reduce the number of bytes retrieved at one time. Thus, the actual transaction size may be larger, but users will see more frequent displays of data retrieved. So the perceived response time will be much more acceptable. In cases such as the above 2400-baud connection, I have often reduced the *arraysize* to retrieve one row at a time, resulting in a sluggish but reasonable response time.

- Wide area networks are slower than local area networks. Even at the speed of light on fiber optic connections, expect an extra 1- to 2-second delays just for transport. So don't even think of systems operating at subsecond response times in such scenarios.

12.7 Heterogeneous Environments

I categorize heterogeneous environments into three types, to make this discussion easier.

- Different hardware and operating systems all running the Oracle database management system and tools. This environment is where Oracle is at its best. Oracle runs on almost every hardware platform and operating system. Programs developed in its fourth-generation tools are highly portable between these environments. The only exceptions are when one platform is a block-mode terminal environment, such as IBM MVS, rather than asynchronous terminal environment, such as VAX/VMS or UNIX. The behavior of SQL*Forms applications changes between these environments. Programs written in third-generation languages, or user exits, are very vulnerable to porting difficulties. Beware of different version of each product on each of the platforms. The large range of platforms supported by Oracle means that there is a significant time lag between new versions becoming available and their port to each platform.

- Different database packages and tools on one hardware platform. In this environment, you may have some applications written in FMS using RMS files as well as Oracle-based applications on a VAX VMS platform. Another example is DB2 on IBM machines. Oracle is making some progress in supporting such environments. The SQL*Connect series of products allow Oracle tools to use DB2 as the database on IBM MVS systems. A flavor of SQL*Connect is also available for accessing RMS files on VAX VMS systems. Oracle will probably add more products in the future.

- Different national languages, regardless of hardware or software platforms. As we develop multinational applications, handling multiple languages becomes an essential requirement. Even though programming is always done in English based-languages, the end user should see screens, reports, and data in the appropriate language. What's more, they ought to see error messages in their language of choice as well. Version 6 offers national language support for European languages using 1-byte character sets.

The major problem with national language support is that each hardware manufacturer defines its own character set codes. These codes, which are just numeric values to the computer, overlap between manufacturers, and sometimes even between two separate character sets from the same vendor. So Version 6 offers the ability for you to choose the language and character set for the RDBMS. This choice requires that you define certain init.ora parameters.

Based on your language and character set choice, Oracle uses a set of message files containing all messages to the user that the DBMS might display. There is a message file for the kernel and one each for each of the utilities such as SQL*Forms. Note that this choice applies to the entire system. So you will have to use terminals which all generate the same character set. This generally means that you must buy all of your terminals from one manufacturer. Terminals which each generate a different character set cannot be mixed in one instance of an Oracle database.

You can set the language individually for each user of a utility. For example, one of your users might use forms developed in French while another uses forms developed in German on the same database. Obviously, each one's terminal must support the appropriate language. They will each see forms interaction messages in their chosen language, although all RDBMS messages will be in the installation language. So, if the language specified in init.ora is French, the user working in German will see all ORA-nnnn messages in French. Realize, however, that Oracle kernel will treat the data they enter as one character set.

The implications of national language support are far reaching. A normal numeric sort, such as used for ASCII character sorting is insufficient. In fact, it will produce incorrect ordering of results. Version 6 also allows you to specify sorting in the national language, via a parameter in the init.ora file. An Oracle internal date converted to character format will yield day and month names in the language of choice. There are two new functions added to the repertoire of SQL functions.

CONVERT: This function allows you to convert character data from one source language to another destination language character set. This function merely converts a character from one character set representation to another. It does not convert the language itself.

REPLACE: This function allows you to define a replacement character for a particular character in the specified string. This function is useful to handle cases where a character set does not include a code representing the appropriate uppercase or lowercase equivalent of the character. For example, if the accented e (é) in French does not have the uppercase equivalent in your character set, you could specify a replacement by the normal uppercase E as an acceptable alternative.

Both of these functions must be used in your application. The replacements and conversions do not occur on a permanent basis in the database.

Note that comparisons for < (less than) or > (greater than) on character strings are still done using their numeric values. So such comparisons may yield unexpected results. I recommend that you avoid inequality comparisons on characters strings entirely. Use the LIKE predicate or equality comparisons wherever possible. Remember that similar unexpected results occur between two machines using ASCII and EBCDIC character sets, respectively.

In all of these cases, handling cultural differences is left up to the designer. For example, salutations are not uncommon in the United Kingdom. A prefix of *Sir* to the name John Smith results in unexpected ordering. You will have to separate such prefixes and suffixes into separate columns. The problem yields amusing results in non-European languages. For example, Arabic names are often prefixed by EL as an honorific. If some names have this prefix and others don't, the ordered results are again unexpected.

Such differences between data are critical in a distributed database environment. Queries involving remote tables containing data in a different character set can completely mess up your query results. Remember that sorting done on your current North American character-set based database will yield completely different results from the same sort performed on the remote French character-based database. Be prepared to make users understand these limitations, but first, take the time to understand them yourself.

12.8 Administration Issues

Central database administration in a distributed database environment is quite a nightmare. Oracle facilities in Version 6 allow you to monitor a running database remotely. Most operating systems with networking support allow you log into the remote machine over the network. However, these facilities assume that the system is up and running. What can you do if the remote system crashes or the communications link is down? How can you perform a backup which requires mounting a tape?

There are many operating system specific tools to administer machines on a local area network. However, few administrative tools exist for wide area network management. Resign yourself to maintaining some technical experts at each geographic location of a distributed database. You can then support these support personnel from a central pool of experts. The remote staff can also perform simple development tasks such as custom reports for local use.

12.9 Development Management Issues

The key benefit to users of distributed database systems is the local control it makes possible. You can sweeten the deal by allowing some customization of the application at a local level. After all, if the data design remains constant, your central consolidation processes will continue to run.

Don't be afraid that this will lead to the chaotic setup we are used to today — where every department chooses its own tools and builds its own database design. If you focus on controlling the data design, you can allow local variations in presenting that data without compromising business objectives. This is where enterprisewide models support your work. Remember to set standards for naming conventions — otherwise you will create communications barriers between technical staff in different locations.

If all applications, with or without local variations, are developed by a central pool of resources, you will need strict source management controls. Be sure to enforce formal application release procedures, so you have master copies of all programs actually in production. Ad hoc methods of program enhancements and release, common in a central database environment, if used in a distributed environment spell disaster.

Application portability is more critical in a distributed environment since you can no longer assume a single hardware and operating system platform. The beauty of a distributed environment is that you can use the best option for hardware and operating system available for the site. So pay particular attention to enhancing portability of all designs.

There are several advantages to managing the implementation of a distributed system. Instead of getting all of your users trained and ready for the new system before cutover, you can phase your cutover by each location. You could even persuade one site to become a beta test site. If you can publicize the importance of such pilot testing throughout the company, they will be proud to be part of the effort, despite all the ensuing difficulties. Thus, you will be able to test your software in a production environment without risking a major companywide disaster.

You can schedule user training one site at a time. Be sure to allow sufficient *oops* recovery time between the scheduled training and implementation at each site. Expect a few mishaps at each location — *oops* recovery time gives you a chance to handle them before your next deadline. The responsiveness you can show with such planning is sure to win user support. Winning their support is important if they are to assume ownership and commit themselves to making it successful.

Appendix

Recommended Standards

When using Oracle products, setting some standards and conventions in your organization will save you a lot of heartache. There are many significant benefits of standards:

- New staff can come up to speed quickly since they won't nee explanation of every nitty-gritty detail.
- Improved communication via the use of well-defined terminology. When you say pick-list, another person will not visualize a pop-up window if your standards do not define it to be so.
- Better use of CASE tools — they are only as good as your use of them. If you use cryptic naming with no explanations, your staff will have difficulty no matter how good the CASE tool is.

1. Naming Conventions

Object	Convention
Entity	The name used most commonly in business, singular noun. Use synonyms to relate all other business names. Define alias as a two- or three-character string so that foreign key column names derived by CASE*Dictionary will be short but still indicate the source entity.
Attribute	The name used most commonly in business.
Function Label	Hierarchical labeling with each level separated by a period, for example, level 1 function label is *1*, level 2 function labels are *1.1, 1.2, 1.3* etc.
Function	The name most representative of the activity. Use active verbs such as *Accept, Distribute, Ship,* etc. Keep function descriptions short — typically less than 10 words. Avoid ambiguous names such as *process*.

Object	Convention
Process Label	Same as Function label.
Process	Same as Function.
Data Store Label	Sequential numbering prefixed with the letter *D*. Sequence is top to bottom, left to right starting from the top-level data flow diagram, for example, *D1, D2, D3,* etc.
Data Store	Use the name most representative of the data in the store, a business term where possible, for example, *Product Stock, Customer List,* etc.
Data Flow Name	Representative of the data in the flow. Use the business name where possible, for example, *Customer Order, Return Authorization,* etc. Keep it short — typically less than five words.
Module Name	Noun form of the function or process represented. For example, *accept customer order* process becomes *Order_Entry* module. Keep module names short, as they may become file names for forms, reports, PRO* programs, etc.
Application Name	Representative of a logical group of activities — typically performed by one department or user group within a department.
Table Name	Same name as the entity it represents, except use plural, for example, *Products* as the table representing the entity *Product*. When denormalizing two or more entities into a single table, use each of their names separated by an underscore.
Column Name	Same name as the attribute it represents, prefixed by a two- or three-character prefix. The prefix allows you to easily identify which table the column belongs in. Where a foreign key column name is derived from the relationship, CASE*Dictionary uses the entity alias in the derived column name.

Object	Convention
Database File Name	dbs<SID>.dbf in V6, dbs<SID>.dbs in V5. Keep the filename to a maximum of eight characters and file extension to three characters for portability.
Redo Log File Name	log<SID><nn>.log. nn is a number indicating the sequence of the file within the set of Redo Log files. Same rules as Database File Name for portability.
Before Image File Name	In V5 only, bi<SID>.dbs. Same rules as Database File Name for portability.
Control File Name	In V6 only, cntrl<SID><nn>.dbf, where nn indicates the copy of the control file. Thus, when you have 3 copies of the control file, the file names will have 1, 2, and 3 as the values for nn. Same rules as Database File Name for portability.
Init Parameter File Name	init<SID>.ora in both V5 and V6. Same rules as Database File Name for portability.
Form Name	Same name as the module it represents. Keep form name to a maximum of eight characters for portability.
Form Block Name	Same name as the base table for the block.
Form Field Name	Same name as the column of the table it represents, if any.
Report Name	Same name as the module it represents. Keep form name to a maximum of eight characters for portability. File extension will be *.rpt* for SQL*Report programs, and *.rep* for SQL*Report Writer.

2. Form Concepts

Object	Convention
Terminology	A *form* is a single SQL*Forms program. It has a unique name. A *screen* is a single page in a form. It defines the information displayed at one time on a terminal or monitor. Screens are numbered sequentially (page numbers in SQL*Forms. The page number is displayed on each screen.
Screen Layout	Each screen has the form title (module name) displayed on the first line, together with the page number. This convention allows users to indicate precisely which screen they are using when a asking for support. The screen displayed on initial entry to the program is called the *main* screen. It must display at least the key information for that activity. All other screens must contain a control block at the top with key information copied from the main screen. Examples of key information are *customer number, customer name, order number,* etc. This convention allows users to eaily identify which master row thay are working on. A screen may display more than one block. Each such block must have a box drawn around it.
Form Keys	Disable all unused keys at form level.
Pick-List	In SQL*Forms 2.3, use the fake-windows method to display a pick list. In SQL*Forms 3.0, use the pop-up list of values. Always defined on the key *List-of-values*.

Object	Convention
Master-Detail	Two tables whose entities have a one-to-many relationship between them. Each table is one block in SQL*Forms. The master block displays one row at a time and the detail block displays multiple rows, if screen size makes it possible. Blocks must be coordinated for query. They may also be coordinated for insert and delete if the relationship is mandatory on both ends. Pressing the *next-field* key on the last field of the master block should move cursor to the detail block.

3. Report Concepts

Object	Convention
Report First Page	Must include company name, Oracle user name, date and time of report, and report name to identify who ran the report.
Report Last Page	Must include the words *Report <Report Name> Complete* to indicate that report completed successfully.
Page Header	Each page must list the report name on the left, company name and report title as two lines in the center, and the page number on the right. The report date and time must appear under the page number on the right.
Page Footer	Each page must list the words *<Company Name> Confidential* as the footer.

Bibliography

ANSI Database Language SQL (X3.135—1986).

Bisland, Ralph B. Jr., *Database Management Developing Application Systems Using Oracle*, Englewood Cliffs, NJ: Prentice Hall, 1989. An academic approach to learning relational database theory and practice with examples based on Oracle tools. The extensive coverage of SQL for novices is one of the best I have seen. Although this book refers to UFI, the Oracle Version 4 precursor to SQL*Plus, all of these facilities still exist.

British Computer Society, *The Computer Journal: Special Issue Databases*, Vol. 31, No. 2 (April 1988). Current research papers on database languages, expert systems, and object-oriented and distributed databases.

Chen, P. P., "The Entity-Relationship Model: Toward a Unified View of Data," *ACM Transactions on Database Systems*, 1976.

Codd, E. F., "A Relational Model of Data for Large Shared Data Banks," *CACM* 13, No. 6 (June 1970). Reprinted in CACM 26, No. 1 (January 1983). The first proposed ideas of the relational model.

Codd, E. F., "Extending the Relational Database Model to Capture More Meaning," *ACM Transactions on Database Systems*, December 1979. Extended relational model called RM/T.

Codd, E. F., "Relational Database: A Practical Foundation for Productivity," *CACM* 25, No. 2 (February 1982). Paper presented by Codd on the occasion of his receiving the 1981 ACM Turing Award.

Cronin, Daniel J., *Mastering Oracle*. Indianapolis, IN: Hayden Books, 1989. Good coverage of the development process after the analysis is complete. This book is a little light on Oracle's CASE products and their use in real life. It has extensive coverage of the programming tools, SQL*Plus, SQL*Forms, and SQL*Report Writer with worked examples. Its tutorial style makes it difficult to locate specific coding examples.

Date, C. J., *An Introduction to Database Systems*, Vol. II, Reading, MA: Addison-Wesley, 1984. Advanced topics in database theory; very heavy reading for professionals.

Date, C. J., *A Guide to DB2* Reading, MA: Addison-Wesley, 1985. Good coverage of IBM's DB2 product.

Date, C. J., *An Introduction to Database Systems* Vol. I, 4th Ed., Reading, MA: Addison-Wesley, 1986. Standard textbook on database theory, rather heavy for professional reading.

Gane, Chris, *Computer Aided Software Engineering: The Methodologies, the Products, the Future*. New York: Rapid Systems Development 1988

Gane, Chris, and Trish Sarson, *Structured Systems Analysis: Tools & Techniques* (Improved System Technologies, 1980). Saint Louis: McDonnell-Douglas Corporation, 1981–1985.

Hursch, Jack L., and Carolyn J. Hursch, *Working with Oracle Version 6.0*. Blue Ridge Summit, PA: Windcrest Books, 1989. A rehash of the Oracle manuals, with a few examples. Better used as a reference manual after you understand which utility to use and how it actually works. I would not recommended it for beginners.

Inmon, W. H., *Oracle Building High Performance On-Line Systems*. QED Information Sciences, 1989.

ISO-ANSI, Working Draft of Database Language SQL2, June 1988.

Kent, W., "A Simple Guide to Five Normal Forms in Relational Database Theory," *CACM* 26, No. 2 (February 1983).

Martin, James, *Recommended Diagramming Standards for Analysts and Programmers: A Basis for Automation*. Englewood Cliffs, NJ: Prentice Hall, 1987.

Rodgers, Ulka, *UNIX Database Management Systems*. Englewood Cliffs, NJ: Prentice Hall, 1990.

Sobell, Mark G., *A Practical Guide to UNIX System V*. Benjamin/Cummings, 1985.

Yourdon, Edward, *Modern Structured Analysis,* Englewood Cliffs, NJ: Prentice Hall, 1989. The authoritative book on Yourdon's structured methodology; includes additional material on real-time systems, prototyping, and data modeling which did not exist the older publications such as the Gane and Sarson book.

Index